Paolo Cangelosi is renowned in the world of martial arts and is the founder of one of the most prestigious martial arts academies in the world.

Nathalie Tocci is a student of Kung Fu.
She is also the director of the Institute of International Affairs, honorary professor of the University of Tubingen, Special Advisor to the High Representative of the EU, and an independent advisor to energy company Eni.

MY PATH
TO BECOMING

Paolo Cangelosi

MY PATH TO BECOMING

with Nathalie Tocci

Europa
editions

Europa Editions
1 Penn Plaza, Suite 6282
New York, N.Y. 10019
www.europaeditions.com
info@europaeditions.com

Library of Congress Cataloging in Publication Data is available
ISBN 978-1-60945-713-6

Cangelosi, Paolo
My Path to Becoming

Book design by Emanuele Ragnisco
www.mekkanografici.com

Cover photo: *Sifu* Paolo Cangelosi

Prepress by Grafica Punto Print – Rome

Printed in Italy

CONTENTS

"Give a man a fish, feed him for a day.
Teach a man to fish, feed him for a lifetime"
—CHUANG TZU, Taoist philosopher
369 AD–286 AD

MY PATH TO BECOMING

Preface

I was going through the most difficult period of my life. It was the first time I was forced to slow down, to allow space and time to expand within me.

It was a period when all the activity in my life was reduced to nothing. Gone were my weekly trips across countries and continents. Gone was rushing from meetings to media appearances. Gone were the conferences and constant buzz of my networked life. My mind had been too tyrannical to allow me to stop, so my body was wise enough to do it instead. I had no choice but to listen.

That period is now a haze, a time outside time in which the days blended into nights, with no real difference between the two. I groped in the dark. And I found an anchor.

I had practiced martial arts since I was a teenager and joined *Sifu* Paolo Cangelosi's school in 2003, when I returned to Italy after ten years abroad. Kung Fu had long been a part of my life, but it meant something different back then. It was my secret garden, a safe space where I could unplug and didn't have to prove myself to anyone, where I could simply enjoy myself.

But during my difficult period, my Kung Fu practice took on a whole different meaning. It was no longer a gated space in which I could recharge my batteries, which became depleted in the chaos of my professional life. My practice grew from just a secluded garden to something that touched every part of my life and became a way for me to get in touch with my center and really hear myself. My daily morning practice in the park became the anchor of my days.

I had always admired *Sifu* Paolo Cangelosi and was enchanted by his charisma, passion, and the depth of his teachings. I relished the opportunity to learn from him when he came to Rome, or when I travelled to Genoa for the occasional private lesson in the *kwoon*. But in that period, I realized how grateful I was to him. Thanks to him, I had acquired my small treasure, which came to my rescue in my hour of need. On a black lava beach in Lanzarote, on a warm New Year's Day, I understood how precious that treasure was.

It was right after that holiday in Spain that I began to feel a bit better. I still had a long way to go, but I could see the light at the end of the tunnel. Suddenly, I felt the urge to write. I love writing. Since I was a child, I have always felt that it was only through writing that I could fully dissect what I really thought and felt. Writing is a major part of my professional life. I've written dozens of books and articles over the last twenty years. Without a shadow of a doubt, writing is the most enjoyable part of my job and the reason I love it so much.

I felt an urge to write, but this time not about international politics. My energy was slowly beginning to flow again, but I felt no desire to use it to go back to where I had come from. I was, am, and probably always will be passionate about Europe and international relations, but it was not the time for that. I felt a strong desire to pay homage to the experience I had just been through, and to the person and the method that helped me slowly find my way through the most complex situation of my life. I wanted to write about Kung Fu, about my *sifu*, and about Paolo Cangelosi's Kung Fu. Like the other students at his school, I had heard various anecdotes about his life, but I didn't have an intellectual interest in cobbling together the pieces of his adventurous jigsaw puzzle. What I felt was an instinct, as he would put it. I felt it was the right thing to do, and didn't give much thought to its purpose or consequences.

I didn't know how he would react. We had known each other for fifteen years, but we only saw one another occasionally, and usually with many other students. I knew we had a connection, but it's one thing to connect and quite another to allow someone into the depths of your life. When I blurted it out, he smiled. He didn't say yes or no, but reassured me that he would give it some thought. But I knew right away that it would work out.

It did. The next time we saw each other, we plunged into the concept of the book. Yes, it would be a biography, chronologically recounting the major ups and downs of his life. But it would be more than that, too. By unpacking the characteristics, qualities, and conditions by which a boy became a Kung Fu grand master, I intended for the book to trace a broader path to becoming. It was his path, but it could be someone else's, too. In fact, in many ways, it was my path as well.

Hewing closely to my instincts, I began writing the book in the first person singular. I was drawn to subjective experience over objective facts, and it was the power of the exchange between us that was so appealing to me. He could have rebuffed me outright, preferring to keep me at the safe and objective distance of a third person singular. But neither he nor I feel comfortable with safe distances. He embraced the idea and fully let me in. And so the magic began.

We shared the same passion but also the same methodical working style. I would travel up to Genoa once a month, but now, after our usual Kung Fu lessons, we would take a lunch break at our regular Chinese restaurant; after a good meal, a chat and a few drinks, we returned to the *kwoon* to begin our work. He talked and I took notes, prodding him now and then for more details. The hours flew by and we always had to rush to the airport at the last minute for me to catch the last flight home. In the weeks that followed, I would write a draft chapter in the evenings at home, on planes, business trips, during holidays, and in a few moments when I really should have been working. But I was changing: I had become far more gentle with myself. I was finding a new balance between my responsibilities towards others and those towards myself. After a few weeks I would send him the draft chapter, and at my next visit we would review and revise it together. After exactly one year, the full draft was ready.

Writing this book has been a profoundly cathartic experience. For the first time, I've written not just with my head, explaining and dissecting facts and opinions, but with my heart, putting myself in *Sifu*'s shoes and asking myself how I, Nathalie, would have felt. In writing about *Sifu*'s emotions, I was writing about my own. Through the lens of his life, I better understood my own. Thanks to this book, I overcame my own personal crisis and became more resilient.

But this book has meant much more than I could have ever imagined. It sparked a friendship that has continued to blossom ever since.

I knew that I would always be *Sifu* Cangelosi's student.

Now I know that I will always be his friend.

Nathalie
Rome, May 2020

Chapter 1
Curiosity

When and why does a child become a martial artist? What are the seeds, lying dormant in the fertile soil of childhood, that one day choose to blossom into an ancient art?

The first and most important is curiosity.

The child, any child, is curious. Every moment is discovery. Every seemingly insignificant detail is experienced with marvel and surprise. As the child seeks to define the boundary that separates the self from the outer world, he is drawn instinctively towards challenge. From the infant who naturally moves towards the edge of her cot, to the toddler magnetically drawn to the electrical socket, the child, every child, seeks both the protection of a boundary, and to overcome it.

For the shyer and more introverted child, curiosity translates into a simple desire to explore the world. Drawn towards the grounded, earthly, and feminine *Yin* energy, she tests her limits through a more solitary journey along the liminal space between the self and the world. For the more extroverted child, who hews more to the explosive, outward and masculine *Yang* energy, challenging boundaries often translates into competition. Competition with others becomes a means of competing with oneself, of overcoming one's emotional limits, of opening up to the world inside and outside oneself.

This, plain and simple, is what drew me to the universe of martial arts.

Martial arts allow the child, the adolescent and eventually

the adult to give form and direction to his curiosity, his sense of challenge, to all the enthusiasm, joy, and hardship that comes with experiencing and overcoming emotional boundaries. Martial arts allow us to do this without the cumbersome weight of the social structures, educational models, and external conditionings imposed on us by adulthood. Martial arts enable us to retain the levity of childhood; martial arts are fun.

I was a curious child. I constantly sought challenges. And challenging myself often translated into competing with others. I used to transform every challenge into a game. I loved playing and inventing competitions and situations that put myself to the test; I did so by challenging the forces of nature—the wind, usually—as much as my peers. The passion that would burn inside me throughout my life found its first spark within my childhood curiosity. That fire would eventually give me the strength to explore and persevere in a life dedicated to martial arts.

My origins

I was always destined for martial arts in one way or another. I could have been born at any time and in any place, and my path would probably still have led me towards martial arts. Like any other form of art, a martial art is a vocation and a passion, in addition to being hard work. That vocation is simply innate in me, like a magnet that draws me towards the path.

But I wasn't born at just any time or in just any place. I was born in Genoa, Italy, to Lidia and Piero.

My mother, Lidia, was six when her family moved from Bologna to Genoa so my grandfather could take a job in the passport department of the police office there. It was 1937 and that same year she met Piero, my father. Piero, seven years her elder, had befriended her brother. As time went by, the two boys became inseparable. Always running after them was little Lidia. My mom was a real tomboy as a child. She was full of energy and followed the two boys everywhere, hiking up mountains, climbing lampposts, and getting into the kinds of fights that only the boys had. She occasionally played with her girlfriends, but preferred hanging out with her brother, and his friend, including Piero. To her, my dad meant adventure, and he was her hero. Piero taught Lidia to whistle, to play football and to defend herself. When she was ill, he was the only one from whom she would tolerate taking medicine.

Lidia and Piero spent her childhood and his adolescence together. Despite their age difference, they had a lot in common. They were both adventurous, brave, and independent. They were both profoundly curious individuals. Their curiosity towards themselves and the outside world has always resonated deeply with me.

Of course, there were differences between them, too, which also speak to who I am. My mom gradually developed a deeper, more spiritual side. Many years later, after my father's death, she began practicing Tai Chi with me. In those painful months of mourning, I used to lay my hands on her to transmit energy between us. There was no need to explain; I knew she understood. Only recently, in fact, she told me that during this period I used to show up to visit her precisely when she needed it most. She recounted to me how one afternoon, in one of her darkest moments, I rang the doorbell, walked upstairs and as I touched her, she felt that she was slowly being lifted, as if walking on clouds.

To have the sensibility to understand, accept, and appreciate what I was doing was unusual. My mother undoubtedly had it. My dad, on the other hand, died young, at 64. In his final years he revealed all his strength and resilience, qualities that I deeply admired in him and have tried to cultivate in myself. He remained steadfast till the very end. He stopped working as soon as he realized that he was inexplicably forgetting details. He dreaded the prospect of damaging his reputation at work, so he voluntarily resigned ahead of time. But he did so without making a fuss. So much so that it took years before we realized that his health troubles and his occasional memory loss weren't minor incidents, but the effect of a cancer that had spread from his lungs to his brain over the course of almost a decade.

But back to their youth. When my father turned 18, at the height of the Second World War, he was drafted into the army. He was posted with the marines in Taranto, in southern Italy. Lidia and Piero were apart for only a few years, but by the time they saw each other again, they had both changed significantly. On the front, my father had become a man, while my mother had blossomed into a young woman back at home. The playfulness and confidence of their childhood years were gone. In their place was the attraction between a man and woman rediscovering one another.

It took some time to evolve the relationship. Lidia and Piero struggled to let go of the fraternal love they'd had in the past. He courted her, and she him, but they kept their distance for several years. At times, she would drop by his house, ostensibly to visit his family. At other times, he would stop by hers, to see her brother. Finally, one evening, Piero summoned his courage and went to her house, this time without hiding that he was there for her. They got engaged when mom was 18 and dad was 25. Five years later, Lidia and Piero got married. Carlo, my brother, was born in 1956.

I was born on the 18th of October, 1960.

My mom recalls that, as a child, I was a force to be reckoned with. At ten months old, I somehow managed to climb up on the kitchen sink; when I was two, I scaled the chest of drawers in my parents' bedroom, intent on throwing myself onto the bed, or so I must have hoped. I was extremely lively, but oddly disciplined, too. Despite the trouble I got myself into, I was naturally well-behaved, especially in public. I rarely threw tantrums and when we went out for dinner, I behaved like a little prince at the restaurant.

When I was two, my father's job brought us to Casella, a small village in the Ligurian hinterland. It took me a while to acclimatize to village life, but I soon came to enjoy the opportunities that it presented. Up in the hills above Genoa, Casella had typical continental weather, hot in the summer and freezing cold in winter. Each season had its beauty. In summer, I played soccer and built wooden huts and tree-houses with my friends. In winter, we went sledding on the hills near home. Given the safety of life in the village and the protection I had from my older brother, I led an incredibly free life in Casella. Carlo and I got on well, in fact, and always defended one another both at home and outside. The village was like a big family and my parents always knew my whereabouts in some way or another. I lived surrounded by nature, and nature allowed me to explore my curiosity and attraction to challenge in ways that were spontaneous, instinctive, and free.

The outdoors appealed to me tremendously. School did not. I cried so much in preschool that eventually my mom decided to keep me at home. On my first day of elementary school, I tried to run away. When the neighbours saw, aghast, a six-year-old me climbing out of the bathroom window, they ran to tell my mother. She was just as dismayed, but probably not as surprised as they were. I slowly got used to school, but let's face it: it was never my forte.

How it all began

I was nine years old. One day, in fourth grade, the village priest came to class to announce the imminent opening of a martial arts class. I remember that day like yesterday. The priest explained that the course would be dynamic and action-oriented. I listened to him in awe. Up until then, soccer had been the only sport I'd played. I liked soccer, much as I liked all sports or games in which I could move and run around. But when the priest mentioned martial arts something awoke in me. I felt this would be different. I didn't think twice about it and immediately enrolled.

My family encouraged me. My mom was enthusiastic. She knew nothing about martial arts, but instinctively knew that it wasn't just any sport: there was something serious and even spiritual about it. She had a natural propensity towards spirituality and natural remedies and immediately liked the sound of an Eastern-influenced class. My father supported me, too. He was a strong and brave man with a penchant for adventure. At home, he used to tell stories of difficult situations that he and his friends had resolved by making use of martial techniques. I was fascinated by these stories. I didn't need much encouragement to enroll, but it helped to have my parents' approval. My mother and father fully supported my enthusiasm.

At the time, however, there was no knowledge whatsoever of Eastern martial arts. The little my dad knew was about Greco-Roman wrestling. Up until the Second World War, Europe had had almost no exposure to Asian martial disciplines. It was only in the late 1940s that Eastern martial arts started making their way to Europe, starting with the Japanese Judo, Jiu Jitsu, Karate, Kendo, and Aikido, and then the Korean Taekwondo. And thanks to Maoist China's closure in those years as well as the Cold War environment that was taking shape, it wasn't until two decades later that the Chinese martial art of Kung Fu, from which all Asian martial disciplines derive, came to be known in the West. At the height of the Cultural Revolution in China, from 1966 onwards, many traditional Kung Fu masters escaped the wrath of the regime and the Chinese art of Kung Fu started to appear in Europe.

Back in Casella, I began taking Jiu Jitsu classes with my first teacher, Nicolino Rosa. Rosa had been a student of Gino Bianchi, a marine who had spent many years in Japan during the Second World War. During that time, he had been exposed to Japanese martial arts, notably Judo and Jiu Jitsu. Upon his return, Bianchi opened a school, and Rosa, who was from Genoa, was among his first students. When Nicolino Rosa first offered his class in Casella, we didn't have a proper gym to practice in. We used to lay tatami mats on the church stage. There, I received my first *gi* and white belt; we did basic gymnastics and were taught our first techniques, notably break-falls. That same Jiu Jitsu school survives in Casella to this day. One of Rosa's students teaches not far from the church where it all began.

In 1970, when I finished elementary school, my family and I moved back to Genoa on account of my father's new job there. In town, I found a new Jiu Jitsu school and realized that there was a far greater choice of martial arts classes there than there had been in Casella. I went to lessons twice a week, but I also enjoyed practicing what I was learning outside of class with my friends, everything from break-falls and grappling to projections and basic hand and leg techniques. Of course, I still enjoyed the other activities of kids my age, playing soccer and sneaking into shops to steal candy. But martial arts were becoming a method for playful interaction with my friends and would remain so throughout my life. My parents were happy to see me so enthused. They instinctively appreciated the mix of discipline and fun that martial arts created for me. What had begun as a seed of curiosity and challenge was rapidly taking root in me and blossoming into a passion. Above all, it continued to be great fun.

A life-changing encounter

One day, my friend Marco told me that his uncle, who worked in a carpenter's shop downtown, had an Asian colleague, whom he had once seen practicing martial arts. He assumed he was Japanese, since Japan was the only country in Asia that people in Genoa were vaguely aware of in those days. As a result, he thought that the techniques he practiced were Karate. But these were only assumptions. In truth, we knew nothing about this man neither where he was from, nor what martial art he knew. We did know, though, that he didn't teach martial arts. He was a mere carpenter, who barely spoke any Italian at all. But he was Asian, and in my mind an Asian was a martial arts master by definition. In fact, he was a god-like figure, to be revered. I wanted to meet this mysterious Asian at all costs.

Marco and I insisted so much that his uncle finally surrendered and arranged a meeting with the Asian man at the carpenter's shop. I distinctly remember taking the bus to our appointment, not knowing what to expect. I did not and could not know how that day would change my life.

When we arrived, Marco's uncle explained in his broken English that we two kids were there because we were fascinated by martial arts. The man, understandably, didn't take us seriously. He simply saw two eager eleven-year-olds with a fleeting interest. He limited himself to showing us the martial salute—*Lai*—as well as one of the basic stances, the horseman stance—*Ma Bo*. I watched the mysterious man in awe as he moved with tremendous simplicity, grace and strength. I begged him to teach us what he had done. He playfully accepted and told us to return the following day when the shop closed. I accepted without hesitation. The man, taken aback by our eagerness, waved goodbye. I was left standing in bliss and admiration. The thought that this mysterious man would teach me even the most basic techniques meant the world to me.

That first meeting was followed by a second, and a third. I began going to the carpenter's shop every few days, turning up exactly on time at each appointment. There was no structure to his "lessons." He simply demonstrated to us whatever techniques and stances came to mind, without any logical sequence or apparent purpose. He showed us how the different sides of a hand—the palm, the back, the external, and the internal sides—could be used in different ways. He taught us how to mimic different animals through the shape of our hands, the movement of our legs and our stances, and showed us a couple of hand techniques. I think in those early days, he probably assumed that we would soon grow tired of these rendezvous. He must have thought that it was just a game to us and that it would be simply a matter of time before we lost interest and moved on to our next childhood obsession of the hour.

But day after day our meetings continued, for over a month. In those first weeks, I discovered that the man was not Japanese at all. He was Chinese. And the martial art he had been teaching us was not Karate. It was Kung Fu.

Kung Fu is a Chinese martial art, whose history is intertwined with legend and can be traced all the way back to the era of the Yellow Emperor (2697-2597 B.C), Huang Di, also known as the founder of Chinese civilization. Nowadays, we talk about Kung Fu as a single concept, but in reality the term reflects a vast array of abilities, disciplines, styles, and practices, which for centuries were known only by their different names. This is why, unlike other martial arts, the origins of Kung Fu cannot be limited to a single time, place, or person. Multitudes of people, environments, and historical periods have contributed to the evolution of this great art.

The origin of Kung Fu owes as much to the sabre-rattling

of armies as to the silence of monasteries, to the sweat of farmers as to the scientific research of doctors. Soldiers developed the use of weapons, particularly steel arms like swords and spears, to refine the art of war. Buddhist and Taoist monks endowed this art with spirituality, incorporating practices from meditation to reading sacred texts, from self-defense techniques used to protect their monasteries to physical exercises to keep their bodies healthy. Farmers designed methods for combat and transformed their tools into fearsome weapons to keep their families, cattle, and land safe from intruders, and developed exercises to temper their bodies, which had to endure great physical hardship. Then there were doctors, who created practices to prevent and cure illnesses by fostering balance between Yin and Yang energies. But there were also painters, poets, and musicians, who blended their art with the physical, philosophical, and spiritual dimensions of Kung Fu.

Over the centuries, Kung Fu developed across different regions, adapting to different geographies, histories, ethnicities, and cultures. In turn, it developed different styles and methods, which only the expert eye can trace back to the same essence. As the life's work of so many people, in so many places and over such a vast stretch of history, Kung Fu is a foundational element of Chinese civilization itself.

In its essence, Kung Fu means great ability obtained through hard work. Across the different environments in which it developed, one thing remains invariably true: no matter what our talent, luck, or riches may be, there is no way of obtaining a great ability for Kung Fu without hard work. The martial artist must put in the effort; his master will guide him along the way.

I could not have known all this back then, but I sensed one thing: in the mysterious Chinese man I had found my master, my key to this ancient art.

In the neighbourhood, everyone called him "China," or his

American name, Joe. He hardly spoke any Italian. Our communication was mainly based on signs, demonstrations, and emulations. It was the language of martial arts.

"China Joe's" assumptions about us turned out to be correct, in part. After about a month, my friend Marco lost interest and stopped showing up to our meetings. But Joe's assumptions about me had been completely wrong. Far from losing interest, my passion for martial arts had grown exponentially in those weeks. I was only eleven, but I already knew that I had found a treasure, a treasure that I yearned for with the deepest part of my being.

My secret treasure

I was determined to cherish the treasure I had found. I would protect it at all costs. I had a Kung Fu master, and a Chinese one at that. Above all, he was master to me and only me. I would do everything I could to keep it that way. I began instinctively protecting my newfound treasure by keeping it secret, hidden from the watchful gaze of my parents and my flighty friends. It was a mix of respect, jealousy, and, I must admit, selfishness that compelled me to guard my secret. It was an awareness, or perhaps my gut instinct, that told me that no one would truly understand just how important this was to me. To my family, martial arts boiled down to a few frivolous anecdotes told around the dinner table. To my friends, including those who practiced martial arts, my lessons with Joe wouldn't have meant much else beyond what they'd experienced in crowded gyms or our soccer games in the park. I instinctively felt that giving away my secret to those who could not understand its value would debase it: I wouldn't be showing it the respect that it deserved.

My encounters with Joe belonged to a league of their own.

They didn't have the playfulness and lightness of the other martial arts courses offered around town. Our lessons were intense. They were serious. My master rarely smiled. He never joked. As the days went by, the frequency and intensity of our meetings increased. Our lessons became stricter and more demanding with each passing day. No distraction whatsoever was permitted. Far from the playful demonstration and emulations of our first encounters, my master now led me through a complex and sophisticated Kung Fu training.

We moved from the carpenter's shop to a basement, and eventually to a larger warehouse, where he had set up a punching bag, and, most importantly, where there was enough space to move freely, including with weapons. First he would make me warm up through various gymnastic exercises, and then we'd move on to the technical part of the lesson. At times, he taught me the sequence of a form; at others he concentrated on the technical specificities hidden within each form. Other times still, he focused on exercises aimed at increasing my strength, explosiveness, and flexibility, while improving my breathing. Finally, on certain occasions we would concentrate on sparring. This is when I started learning that Kung Fu includes hundreds of different styles: internal and external, from the north and from the south of China. I began learning external styles such as Wing Chun, Tang Lang, and Shaolin (which he used to call Siu Lam), as well as internal styles such as Tai Chi. As time went by and I got practice under my belt, my master would insert new styles into our programme, as well as introduce me to dozens of different weapons used in Kung Fu.

His teaching method was simple. He demonstrated a sequence or technique five or six times. I imitated him during the lesson. After every lesson, I diligently practiced what he had taught me for hours. The following day, I showed him what I had mastered. When he was satisfied with my progress, he moved on to the next lesson. When he wasn't, I was sent home to practice some more, until my performance was satisfactory enough for me to advance. My pace was set by the determination, perseverance and ability that I demonstrated with my own training. The better I was, the faster the progress of our lessons would be. The more I gave to my Kung Fu, the more I would receive back from my master. During those first months, I found out that his real name, or, as I would discover later, one of his real names, was Fu Han Tong.

The regular encounters between a Chinese Kung Fu master and an eleven-year-old Genovese boy, during which the only means of communication was Kung Fu itself, were radically personal. To guard my secret, I found myself lying more and more to my family, telling my parents that I was meeting friends to play football or attending the various other martial arts classes I was enrolled in. I did so not only because I was determined to hide the Kung Fu treasure I had found, but also because the *vicoli*, the rundown alleys where we met, were no place for a boy my age.

My parents had no idea about Fu Han Tong. They knew that I practiced martial arts and was often out of the house as a result. But they didn't know that I wasn't in a gym filled with dozens of raucous kids my age. They didn't know that I spent most of my time alone in a warehouse with a Chinese master in the strict discipline of traditional Kung Fu. My mother and father never found out about my secret and never met Fu Han Tong. I gradually started talking about him much later, when I was 16, one year before my master left Italy. I know all this would be impossible today. It is unthinkable that my daughter, Mei, who is more or less the same age as I was back then, could spend countless hours alone with an adult stranger, for several years, without her mother and I having the faintest clue of where she was. But in the early 1970s it wasn't that unusual. In Genoa, young boys and girls played out in the street, and parents gave them the freedom to do so because there were neither the same risks nor, perhaps more precisely, was there an awareness of the dangers the street could present. In fact there were risks. Drugs, and in particular heroin, were spreading like wildfire in the mid-70s, reaching a climax in the 1980s. It was only after too many young deaths that the public became conscious of the problem.

The three years of middle school flew by. Through Kung Fu, the language in which we communicated, Fu Han Tong gradually led me into a wider world of Chinese culture. Through and beyond martial arts, he gradually introduced me to different facets of Chinese food, tradition, and behaviour. In those years, I learned how to eat with chopsticks, to say thank you by tapping my fingers on the table, to respect my elders and my peers. Most important of all, he taught me how to respect him. He was becoming my master, my *sifu*, in the fullest sense of the word.

With *Sifu* Fu Han Tong, I met the small Chinese community that had settled in Genoa. I remember the old Chinese couple who ran Bar Shanghai on Via Pré. We often stopped by for lunch before our lessons, sitting in a crammed corner at the rear of the café. There, the owners cooked for Fu Han Tong, and also for me. Another family owned a restaurant on Via Balbi—*Trattoria Hong Kong*—where we had dinner after our trainings. And then there was Mr. Liu, a friend with whom Fu Han Tong ran a side business, importing and selling Chinese statuettes and ceramics. Sometimes Fu Han Tong would go to Turin with his colleague Liu to handle affairs for their small business.

Fu Han Tong introduced me as his student to all his Chinese friends and acquaintances. In time, I discovered that he had several students scattered around the world, reflecting the nomadic lifestyle he had endured. He taught certain things to certain students, other things to others. I was his only student in Italy. Given the sheer amount of time we spent together every day for years, I am probably one, if not the only, of his students to whom he taught the most. In Genoa, even though he wasn't widely known as a Kung Fu master, everyone in the community knew and respected Fu Han Tong. One day, a Chinese man in the neighbourhood told me that Fu Han Tong had incredible powers, and that he could move people and objects without touching them. Back then, I didn't know what this meant nor how it could be possible. Only much later did I find out that the man was unknowingly referring to Chi Kung: the ability to feel and channel energy, to the point of generating movement without physical touch. I spent countless hours over the years trying to move small objects without touching them, with the pure force of my energy—*Chi.* When the Chinese man told me about Fu Han Tong's powers, I knew nothing about Chi Kung. But I was certain that it was true and, above all, that it was possible through Kung Fu. Fu Han Tong was my *sifu*, and in my eyes he was capable of the most amazing things. The thought of being his only student made me swell with pride.

In his special way, Fu Han Tong was a teacher of life as well. I was little more than a boy and had just begun to show a fleeting interest in girls when, one day, Fu Han Tong sat me down and said to me gravely: "Women are your enemy. Sex is your enemy." I had no idea what he meant at the time. I didn't know much about sex, nor why it should have been an enemy. In hindsight, what he meant was that sex, especially while young, could be an unnecessary distraction from the martial arts path I had embarked on. Fu Han Tong didn't mean that I should lead a celibate life. Quite the contrary. In fact, I had my first sexual experience, perhaps a bit early, precisely because it was arranged by Fu Han Tong. The *vicoli* were rife with prostitutes, girls and women, mainly from Italy's poorer, southern regions, who had migrated north in search of better fortunes. Fu Han Tong knew them all, and as a result they knew me as his faithful student. At that time, my only other "sexual" encounter had been when I was 11, when a girl caught me somewhat by surprise and kissed me, forcing her tongue into my mouth. Determined that I should confront the "enemy," Fu Han Tong took me to a prostitute friend of his. She was 45 or so, and Austrian. Without a word, he left me in her experienced hands. Unsurprisingly, my first real sexual experience, at 13 with a 45-year-old prostitute, was nondescript at best. She was kind and somewhat amused by me, but all in all, she looked fairly bored by the circumstances. Who knows how many times she had ended up in situations like that? I didn't like her much, and so I wasn't particularly excited either. Afterwards, I felt no urge to tell my friends about what had happened. A mix of embarrassment and shame kept me from sharing my experience with them. With a touch of sadness, several years later, I found myself struggling to empathize with their enthusiasm as they told me about their own first encounters with girls our age. My experience had left me feeling terribly empty instead.

In truth, there was nothing that distracted me from Kung Fu. I anxiously waited for the school bell to ring in order to rush off to my afternoons with Fu Han Tong. As time went by, my awareness of the treasure I had found grew in proportion to my determination to protect it and my difficulty in doing so. My life with *Sifu* Fu Han Tong made me feel different from my peers. Sometimes, that difference made me feel special. I felt that I neither was nor wanted to be like other children. Other times, it made me feel terribly lonely. I think this is why, as soon as I felt attracted to girls, I immediately looked to them as friends and confidantes. Beyond physical attraction, I felt that I would find more understanding, comfort, and trust in the opposite sex.

The closer I became with Fu Han Tong, the more the gap between my friends and I widened. Of course, I still occasionally played football and other games with kids in the neighbourhood. But over time I lost interest in their hobbies. Looking back, I see that pursuing my passion meant sacrificing a lot for a boy my age. I was at a crossroads. My relationship with Fu Han Tong was so intense and all-consuming that it was simply incompatible with my lifestyle of my peers. I had to choose, and I had no doubt what my decision would be, regardless of the consequences.

My secret became harder to keep by the day. In order to conceal my relationship with Fu Han Tong, I enrolled in several other martial arts courses. Given that I trained for hours every day, including at home, I had to justify to my family what was going on. Why didn't I ever go to the movies or play football with my friends? What was I doing locked up in my bedroom in the evenings? How on earth had I managed to smash my bedside lamp, chip my desk and break the legs of my chair? An explanation was in order. To provide one, I enrolled in Karate, Judo, and boxing lessons.

These lessons served another important purpose: they allowed me to remain connected to children my age. The beating heart of my passion for martial arts—my relationship and training with Fu Han Tong—remained a secret, casting me apart from my family and friends. But the other martial arts courses I attended allowed me to be socially connected. My skill with martial arts made me quite popular amongst my peers.

I did not, however, tell Fu Han Tong about the other courses I attended. I feared that he would not approve. But I did it nonetheless. My secret was now double.

My choice

At the dawn of my teens, I had already decided: Kung Fu would be my life's path. In the footsteps of my master, I wanted to become a *sifu* too. It was a decision that took root in me gradually. Much like my secret encounters with Fu Han Tong, it was a decision that I refused to share with anyone for a long while. Only with time did I begin talking about it with my friends.

In those years, when the first Bruce Lee films were making their way to Europe, Kung Fu went from being literally unknown to becoming the new cool thing. Suddenly, what some of my friends had considered an arcane and somewhat quirky passion of mine became widely popular. I remember friends and acquaintances imitating Bruce Lee's moves. Scores of kids enrolled in Kung Fu schools, which mysteriously started sprouting up all over like mushrooms.

On the one hand, all this annoyed me tremendously. A bunch of money-hungry impostors were declaring themselves "*sifu*," clumsily mixing different techniques from different martial arts and repackaging them as Kung Fu. In doing so, they paid no respect to what Kung Fu was all about. My own knowledge of Kung Fu was still very limited at that time. I was, however, starting to learn about the myriad different styles that made up this millenary art. I was getting a taste of the rich Chinese culture and tradition that produced Kung Fu. Above all, I was beginning to experience all the sacrifice, discipline and work—the "hard work," as the Chinese ideogram of Kung Fu literally translates—Kung Fu was about. This was what my lessons with Fu Han Tong were like. What I saw happening all around me didn't even occupy the same universe.

On the other hand, the martial arts boom in that period encouraged me to come out in the open about my practice. As many of my friends and acquaintances got swept up in the martial arts craze, I slowly began disclosing my secret: that for three years, I had been learning Kung Fu, beyond and outside of the various martial arts classes I attended. I was constantly asked to demonstrate what I knew. I slowly became aware of my ability, cultivated through hard work and, yes, through talent. I was a teenager, after all, and as my confidence grew, I increasingly enjoyed sharing my passion with others. I recall organizing small sparring matches between martial arts students from different schools like Karate, Judo, Jiu Jitsu, Savate, and boxing. We would gather in the entrance halls of large apartment complexes for our self-styled competitions. Unlike most kids, who went to their classes a couple of times a week, I trained for many hours every day. The difference was plain for all to see.

As middle school drew to a close, the contradictions between the semblance of a normal schoolboy's life and my Kung Fu life became more apparent. I gradually lost interest in school, and going to class felt like time taken away from my passion. Which is not to say that I wasn't academically curious. I was. I was fascinated by anatomy, and later medicine, traumatology as well as physics. But I was interested in anatomy so as to better understand martial techniques; in medicine, because Fu Han Tong had introduced me to the basics of traditional Chinese medicine; and in physics, to better understand the principles underlying joint locks. In short, my intellectual curiosity was always related to martial arts.

By the time I finished middle school, my parents, and especially my father, were seriously worried. They thought my passion for martial arts was an unhealthy obsession. When they saw me leave the house in my tracksuit with my sports bag over my shoulder, my dad would raise his eyebrow, with a "there he goes again" look on his face. My mother was more understanding, but she also worried about the turn things were taking. Both my parents started viewing martial arts as a dangerous distraction and ultimately an obstacle that could negatively affect my future. They thought my total and unconditional dedication to martial arts was dangerous and might prevent me from graduating from high school, finding a good job, and enjoying a comfortable life.

My brother Carlo shared my parents' concerns somewhat, but deep down he understood my choice. He would despair at the chipped or broken chairs, table, and lamps in the bedroom we shared, the victims of my training sessions at home. We argued about what posters should go up on our walls: would it be Jimi Hendrix or Bruce Lee? But Carlo also defended me to my parents. One afternoon, as I was leaving the house for a training session, my dad commented scornfully that I should be playing with my friends in the neighbourhood rather than obsessing over martial arts. As usual, I kept quiet. Arguing with my parents didn't get me anywhere and might expose my secret about Fu Han Tong. Bearing the brunt of their scorn was far preferable to me. Carlo instead jumped in in my defence, telling them they should be grateful that I spent my time on martial arts rather than hanging out with that lot downstairs. He knew well, like I did, that those kids in the street weren't innocent children playing ball. They were heroin addicts and hung out in the neigbourhood doing just that. Some survived. Others did not. But my parents, like most parents at the time, had no idea what was going on. They found out only years later, when I had already left home.

Plus, Carlo admired my perseverance and passion, and believed in the spirit of martial arts. I remember my brother becoming visibly annoyed once with my father's dismissive attitude towards it. He prodded me to demonstrate the power of *Chi* to my disbelieving parents. I refused. I had a natural aversion towards revealing the secrets of martial arts, particularly to those who were sceptical of it. I felt that anyone who shunned something so precious didn't deserve to really know it. But that afternoon Carlo insisted. He pleaded with me again and again, and finally I relented. I asked my father to stand about thirty centimetres away from the kitchen wall with one arm raised. As I looked at him standing there, with his hand raised and a funny expression on his face, I smiled. But Carlo was dead serious that day. So, I did it. Standing several metres away from him, I channelled my energy towards his raised arm, and, without touching him, I pushed my father straight into the wall. Carlo looked triumphantly at my gobsmacked parents. My mother told me years later that that was the first time she and dad began to understand that I was doing something special.

When I turned 14, my parents enrolled me in high school. I was at a crossroads. My school workload became heavier. I could either pursue Kung Fu or complete high school. But I had made my decision long ago; my destiny was already set in stone. I began skipping school, turning up at Fu Han Tong's on mornings, too. By then, Fu Han Tong had stopped working at the carpenter's shop and was focusing on his import business. During this period, I also started studying traditional Chinese medicine. Fu Han Tong had introduced me to the subject a few months before, but I was eager to learn more, so he introduced me to a doctor friend of his, Dr. Su Chang. I studied with Dr. Chang for two years and have continued studying on my own ever since. Fu Han Tong must have known that I was supposed to be in school in the mornings, but we never spoke about it. It was simply not what our relationship was about. Fu Han Tong didn't exactly encourage my morning training sessions and studies, but he didn't object to them, either. His teaching method remained the same all along: the more I gave to Kung Fu, the more he gave back to me.

Unsurprisingly, my teachers noted my frequent absences from school to my parents, precipitating a family crisis over the summer. My parents moved me from a technical high school to an apprenticeship institute. After four months, when I was just over 15, I dropped out. My father was deeply disappointed. My mother, while concerned, was less sanguine. She seemed to be more resigned to the fact I was cut out neither for school nor for the kind of job that school would have prepared me for. She was also more hopeful about my future. In her feeble defence of my case at home, she prodded my father: "Can you imagine Paolo in an office?" Both knew deep down that the answer was no. At the same time, they both insisted, understandably, that if I didn't want to study, I had to work. My dad began taking me to work with him. He used to work in a mould printing shop, making prototypes of different objects, including the first scuba diving masks in town. He was extremely good at it, an artist in his own right. I began doing many different chores for him and helping out as best I could. In the few free moments I had, I would find an empty corner and practice my Kung Fu. As soon as the workday was over, I ran to my lessons in the warehouse with Fu Han Tong, and then trained some more in the evenings once I got home.

It was exhausting. My dad's workshop was far from where we lived. We used to leave the house at dawn and spend eight hours at work. Then I would rush off to meet Fu Han Tong and train for another eight hours or so with him and at home. After four months of stretching myself to the limit, I had a physical breakdown. I was tired all the time and started feeling a numbing pain in my chest. My mother was alarmed and took me to a cardiologist for a check-up. My heart was perfectly healthy. In fact, my left ventricle was well-developed, as is typical among professional athletes. But my body was exhausted. To ease the load of my schedule, my parents decided that it was time for me to stop working with my father and start helping my uncle, a welder. For him, too, I worked as a handyman, but the work was less demanding physically. Most importantly, my uncle's shop was closer to home, and this meant saving two hours commuting every day. Of course, in the extra hours I gained, I didn't just rest—I trained.

But still tensions at home did not dissipate. My parents continued to view my passion with suspicion. Their attitude was close-minded and negative, even if perhaps they were proud of who I was and what I did deep down. Each time I won a martial arts competition or tournament, they wore worried expressions. My parents didn't really know what I was up to. They took no interest in the tournaments in which I competed. They were uninterested in the details surrounding my practice, but were nevertheless worried about my achievements. My victories fuelled their anxieties, as they viewed them as incentives for me to continue down a path they resisted, rather than as a sign that I had made the right choice. I recall returning home once from a Japanese *kata* and combat tournament. I held two trophies in my hands: I had won both competitions. Most teenagers would have rushed home to show off their accomplishments to their parents. The opposite was true for me. My first and only thought that afternoon was about where I could hide my two trophies in order to avoid a flare-up over supper. I tiptoed into the house and quickly hid the trophies under my bed. But my parents had seen me coming back from our balcony. They came into my bedroom as I was crawling under my bed, and my mother said sarcastically: "Now that Paolo's won these two awards, he'll never stop practicing martial arts. We're doomed!" Thankfully, at dinner that night, they did not scold me over my victory. But no one congratulated me, either.

Months passed and I struggled to settle into my new life. I now helped my uncle, the welder. I received a monthly salary of ninety-thousand Italian liras—approximately forty-five euros today. It was decent pay, and the working conditions weren't bad. But I was a boy, I had a passion, and I had chosen to pursue it, come what may. Spending long hours in a rough, working-class, all-adult environment wasn't the best place for me. My co-workers spent their paycheck on drinks and prostitutes; I dreamed about Kung Fu.

Earning a living from a passion

After four months, I decided it was time to leave the job at the factory. The time had come for me to pursue my dream fully and to live with all the consequences—good and bad—of the choice I had made. I was 15.

One of the first and most distressing consequences of this decision was the near breakdown of my relationship with my family. My parents were totally against it. I was at home a lot during that period, but I became somewhat of a stranger to them. I was determined to prove that I could get by following my passion. I was determined not to ask them for a cent. I would demonstrate to my family, to my friends, and above all to myself, that I could make it.

By then, many in town knew about my ability with and dedication to martial arts. In the many martial arts courses I had attended over the years, at tournaments, or simply in our group training sessions, my peers had often watched me practice, and I had occasionally taught them a thing or two. A few already took martial arts courses, while others did not. But they all seemed to admire what I did and were fascinated by martial arts, not least because of their popularity at the time. I infected them all with my enthusiasm.

In early 1975 I began teaching a group of friends at a discounted rate. Emulating my dad's discipline and work ethic, I was extremely well organized and rigorous from the start. I began with only a handful of students, most of whom were my friends. But I immediately structured my lessons, took roll call every day, and meticulously wrote down the details of each session to prepare for the next. I wanted it to be a success, and first and foremost I had to believe in it myself.

Claudio and his brother Cosimo were my first students. They came from a loud and lovely southern Italian family and were great fun. We lived on the same street and had grown up together: we shoplifted together and played ding-dong-ditch, giggling silently from a hiding spot as our victim opened the door and looked around bewildered. I had taught them the occasional martial technique, so when I started teaching, they were eager to follow me. I liked teaching and training with them, because it meant spending time with my best friends. My life was very different from other kids' my age, and while I never questioned my choice, I often felt lonely. Claudio and Cosimo meant company, and fun. We trained together up in the mountains near Genoa, went jogging in the rain, and relaxed downtown over a hearty bowl of spaghetti or at the movies. They brought lightness and laughter to my days; I drew them into my world. They were students at my school for three years, and participated in my first exhibitions. Eventually they left and went their own ways. Claudio became a baker and Cosimo, a mechanic. Claudio also went through a rough patch, but eventually came out the other side. It warmed my heart when, forty years later, he walked through the door of my *kwoon* in Salita delle Fieschine in Genova. At first I didn't recognize him, but as he came closer the memories came flooding back, engulfing me in emotion. In one hug, forty years dissolved into thin air. After several decades and many ups and downs, Claudio had decided to sign up for Tai Chi.

When I began teaching martial arts in 1975, I didn't start with Kung Fu, nor did I tell my students about Fu Han Tong. Kung Fu was my secret treasure, cultivated through my exclusive relationship with my master. Sharing it with others was unthinkable. It would have meant an unforgivable affront to my *sifu* and to the art he was patiently transmitting to me. It was one thing to share my knowledge about purely physical combat; but it was quite another to share an art, in this case, martial arts, and through it an understanding of *Chi*, the vital energy that animates the self and the universe around us.

Teaching martial arts without teaching Kung Fu was my way of squaring the circle. *Sifu* Fu Han Tong knew little about my life beyond our training sessions and convivial moments with the Genovese Chinese community. In fact, he knew nothing about my teaching, nor about the martial arts courses I had attended out of curiosity, as a means of socializing, and above all as a way to protect my secret Kung Fu garden. I wasn't fully comfortable with the fact that Fu Han Tong knew nothing about all this. But I figured that by not teaching Kung Fu, I was doing him and his martial arts no harm. I also felt that teaching something other than Kung Fu had become a vital necessity for me. It was the only way I had to pursue my passion, that life choice that Fu Han Tong himself had been so instrumental in bringing about.

My first lessons were either outdoors, in the mountains near home, or, when possible, in a friend's father's garage. When the car was out and bad weather forced us inside, my friends and I crammed into the small garage. There I would teach gymnastic exercises that prepared them for martial arts as well as basic self-defence techniques and Karate. My lessons were immediately popular. As my group of students grew, I began looking for a better location to host my class. The first place I found was a church that allowed me to teach every once in a while in their basement; there was a cycling club down there that had an extra room where they stored their equipment. Their manager rented the room to me three times a week. It was my first "fixed" location. My teaching commitments quickly increased, often eating into my own training time, which was now concentrated in the mornings and evenings. It was an intense schedule. But I felt I was earning a living doing what I believed in and what I was good at. The response from my first students confirmed my feelings. I felt fulfilled. I felt free. It was time to tell Fu Fan Tong about the life choice I had made.

I remember vividly the day I told Fu Han Tong that I had decided Kung Fu would be my life's path. I told him I wanted to become a *sifu*, just like him. I told him that I wanted to make a living through Kung Fu, by teaching martial arts and eventually opening my own school. He nodded knowingly, dissipating my worst fears. He reassured me that if I continued training the way I had in those first five years, I would become a *sifu.* Maybe he suspected that I had already started teaching. Maybe not. Either way, he knew that I was ready to take that step and encouraged me to do it. He knew the time would soon come for me to stand on my own two feet.

In that conversation, he also spoke to me about money. In a quintessentially eastern way, money meant a lot to Fu Han Tong. Kung Fu had value, and it was precious. Teaching Kung Fu therefore had to be paid. Teaching Kung Fu for free would have signalled to my students that the art was worthless. It would have been a grave disrespect towards Kung Fu, towards him, and towards all the masters that preceded him over the centuries, and to whom I should be forever grateful. At the same time, he warned me: the relationships I would make through Kung Fu would be a source of great disappointment and pain at times. Those disappointments could not be erased. But if the financial side of the equation was in order, I would carry one fewer resentment. As he put it to me that day, "What is in your pocket is yours." At the time, I simply registered what he was saying. But in the years that followed, I would often be reminded of his prescient words. Only after many disappointments did I start acting on his wise words. It was a meagre consolation, but whenever people would let me down, I'd at least be left with "money in my pocket," and a small justice would be served.

As I started earning my own money, it was only natural for me to start paying my own *sifu* for his teachings. As is customary in Chinese culture, I would bring him a bag of oranges along with a red sealed envelope containing the money. I didn't pay him a regular fee; I put whatever I could afford in an envelope from time to time.

Thankfully, my financial situation was improving steadily. After a few months of teaching, I was earning more than I had been when I worked with my father or my uncle. This began easing the situation at home, albeit very gradually, as my father in particular started to understand that my Kung Fu may not have been a financial dead end after all. Years later, my mother told me that, during that period, she and my dad once followed me to one of my classes. They didn't believe that I was earning money, and quite a lot of it in those days, by teaching martial arts, and wanted to see with their own eyes what I was up to. I was just a teenager to them, and they struggled to believe that I could be taken seriously as a teacher. The lesson had already started when they snuck in and approached the receptionist. Unaware of who they were, the receptionist told them that there was an incredible teacher at work in the class next door. He was little more than a boy, but his seriousness and charisma kept the entire class enthralled. It was nothing like the noisy sports classes they were used to there: the discipline of this class was ironclad, and it was only a young kid who managed it all. The receptionist invited my parents take a look, which they did. They were stunned by what they saw: most of the students were twice my size and age, but there was total silence and concentration.

Most important of all, I was enjoying myself. What had been born out of curiosity and a desire for challenge, and later blossomed into a passion, was now becoming a profession, too. I felt accomplished. I was happy. In that period, I started receiving my first invitations to martial arts exhibitions, including somewhat big ones. I recall my first exhibitions in Lavagna and Chiavari. I had been practicing Kung Fu for several years, but I was still only a sixteen-year-old boy. Nevertheless, I didn't feel intimidated. I knew that I was being invited to perform among adults, alongside martial arts masters who had been training for decades. But I was confident in myself, and confident in what I was teaching to my students. I performed at the exhibitions either alone or with some of my best students as sparring partners. The responses to my exhibitions were enthusiastic. The exhibitions and the word of mouth that followed generated great publicity. Soon after, I was invited to teach Karate in a martial arts academy in Lavagna that already taught Judo and Aikido courses. My schedule filled up. I taught in Genoa and Lavagna, and spent the rest of my time training alone and with Fu Han Tong. It was intense, but I was deeply satisfied.

Roots and rebellion

One morning, Fu Han Tong told me he was going back to China. The time had come for him to leave. He rarely spoke about himself, and especially not about his past. But over the course of our years together, I had managed to cobble together a fair amount of information about my enigmatic *sifu*.

Fu Han Tong was born in 1925 in Guangzhou (Canton) in the southern Chinese province of Guangdong. He was orphaned when he was nine years old, and spent his childhood migrating from one Kung Fu school—*kwoon*—to the next, being raised by their respective masters. This is how he learned his Kung Fu, and what explained his vast and varied knowledge on the subject. In particular, this was what lay behind his eclectic approach to martial arts, fully mastering a wide variety of different styles and related disciplines.

Fu Han Tong grew up in a deeply chaotic era of Chinese history. He was born as the nationalist Chiang Kei-shek consolidated his grip on large swaths of China, including Fu Han Tong's native Canton, thanks to his defeat of the warlords who had divided the country as the Qing dynasty languished in its final death throes. But stability under the nationalist party, the Kuomintang, was short-lived. By 1937 the Japanese spread from Manchuria to the rest of China and the Sino-Japanese conflict eventually became embroiled in the Second World War. No sooner had that global confrontation ended in 1945 than China plunged into its own civil war, until Mao's Red Army eventually defeated the Kuomintang in 1949. Living through those years of disruption was hard enough for all Chinese, and was all the more so for an orphan child and teenager like Fu Han Tong.

As the Maoist regime consolidated its power in the 1950s, Kung Fu increasingly came under the watchful gaze of the government, which saw it as a potential threat. Traditional martial arts slipped into the domain of illegality, becoming entangled with other illegal activities. But the connection between Kung Fu and the Chinese mafia did not begin then. The origin of this connection dates all the way back to the Ming dynasty, which ruled between 1368 and 1644, when Kung Fu fighters were used by criminal networks to control territory, for gambling purposes, and to protect business interests. But as Kung Fu became illegal under the Maoist regime, the connections with organized crime intensified. Perhaps inevitably, but tragically, under the Communist regime this noble art at the heart of Chinese history and culture was put on par with the basest of illegitimate activities.

Fu Han Tong was nineteen years old when the civil war broke out, and he became involved with the Triad, the Chinese mafia. As far as I know, he was not high up in the hierarchy. He was just one of the many young fighters the Triad used to carry out its dirty work. For reasons that remain unknown to me to this day, he eventually fell out with the upper echelons of the organization. His life was in danger.

In 1965, Fu Han Tong assumed a new identity and fled China. He first settled in Sydney, Australia. But after a little over a year, he had to flee again, because the Triad was close to discovering his whereabouts. His next stop was Los Angeles, where he stayed for a year and a half before he had to leave again. Fu Han Tong then crossed the Atlantic, briefly stopping in Marseilles before crossing over to Italy, first to Turin and finally to Genoa. Unlike Sydney and Los Angeles, Genoa was not a popular destination for the Chinese community. There were only a few Chinese families who had settled in my native city. Though this meant that Fu Han Tong's journey from Canton to Genoa had been long and torturous, he was able to settle with near anonymity on the Ligurian coast, and this was tantamount to safety. He was, after all, a fugitive, and the fewer Chinese people who knew where he was, the better. The large Chinese communities in Australia and the United States and the connections he found there had proved instrumental in his escape from China. But they were too big for him to be safe. In Italy his only contact in his early days had been Mr. Liu, with whom he eventually collaborated in the small import business of Chinese statuettes. Mr. Liu helped him settle in Genoa and find a job at the carpenter's shop. Fu Han Tong changed his identity a third time, and the Triad finally lost track of him.

Twelve years and three identities later, Fu Han Tong knew that it was safe enough for him to return home. In 1977, after five years in Australia, the United States and France, and after seven years in Italy, he was ready to go back to China. His dream had probably been to return to his roots all along. He did so when he knew he could return safely.

True to his dramatic life story, Fu Han Tong was enigmatic, an undecipherable man of extremes. His life was defined by a dramatic oscillation between roots and rebellion, East and West, Yin and Yang.

Fu Han Tong was deeply Chinese. Despite his meanderings across four continents, he was deeply rooted in his people, his country, his region and his hometown, Canton. Abroad, like most Chinese migrants, Fu Han Tong was magnetically attracted to his own community, even when it only amounted to a handful of families, as it did in Genoa in the 1970s. As I would discover over the years, his Chinese origins took on a different meaning when he was in Genoa versus Hong Kong or mainland China, and particularly in his native Guangzhou. It is no coincidence that after many decades, he eventually returned to the latter.

His rootedness in Chinese culture was enmeshed with his respect for traditional Kung Fu. Fu Han Tong was profoundly devoted to martial arts traditions and sought to instil the same respect in me from the first day we met. In part, this devotion and respect arose from the fact that, as an orphan, Fu Han Tong had looked to traditional Kung Fu for the emotional and material security and sustenance that he had been deprived of in childhood. In and through Kung Fu, Fu Han Tong searched for a surrogate family.

In fact, as I would later learn, there are astounding similarities between the Chinese family unit and traditional Kung Fu, notably the *kwoon*. Both are sacred to the Chinese and both are deeply hierarchical, with roles, rights, and responsibilities clearly defined in an unwritten rulebook. A Kung Fu school, like a family, provides its students with food and shelter. But the rules of the house must be respected to the letter. Those who live in the *kwoon* are not there simply to learn Kung Fu, eat, and sleep. They carry out a myriad of chores and work outside the *kwoon*, often in markets and restaurants. The students then hand over their earnings to the *sifu* who manages the finances of the *kwoon*. Only in his few remaining minutes of spare time does the resident student dedicate him or herself to the study and practice of Kung Fu. In traditional Kung Fu, as with everything else, there's no such thing as a free lunch.

At the same time, it was precisely those norms, rules, and traditions that Fu Han Tong rebelled against. Fu Han Tong was a radically free man. Because he lacked the mental and behavioural structures instilled by the Chinese family, Fu Han Tong felt that rules were a straight-jacket. As a result, while he constantly sought out structure for security, he also failed to permanently settle into one set of rules, migrating restlessly from one *kwoon* to another during his youth, and eventually from one continent and identity to the next in adulthood. It's one thing is to spend a few months or years fully immersed in the norms and rules of one school; it's quite another to dedicate one's entire life to a single *kwoon*, *sifu*, and style. Were his choices made according to nature or nurture? I'll never know, and it doesn't matter. What matters is that Fu Han Tong was an orphan in life as much as he was an orphan in Kung Fu.

Fu Han Tong never settled into a Kung Fu family, nor did he create one over the course of his life in China, America, Australia, or Europe. Even though he was raised in the world of traditional Kung Fu and could have established his own *kwoon* and *lineage*, Fu Han Tong never chose to do so. His spirit was too free, too wild and selfish to accept the responsibilities that came with running a school. He didn't want anything to defend, to stand up and to live for. The hardships he endured had been so traumatic that living his own life was the most he could bear. He was unable and unwilling to compromise; he gave no more and no less than what he felt like. His was a loneliness so entrenched as to make it incompatible with the lasting bonds created by any social structure, including a *kwoon*.

Over the course of my life, I only met two people who claimed to have been Fu Han Tong's students: Yun San Fa and

Hay Chen Liu. I met both many years later in China. Hay Chen Liu was only a few years younger than Fu Han Tong. When I first saw him in Shenzhen, he was already an old man. Yun San Fa was a few years older than me. Originally from Canton, he moved to Canada in 1982 and occasionally returned to his hometown, where we met in 1985.

But Fu Han Tong did feel the urge to pass on his art, deep down. Teaching his Kung Fu was a calling he felt in his heart and soul, not something that was motivated by the mundane necessities of everyday life. I don't mean that he didn't value money. On the contrary, Fu Han Tong was deeply materialistic. When, many years later in China, he realized that he could make money through Kung Fu, or more accurately through my Kung Fu, he had no qualms about doing so, including in the most despicable of ways. But I know this is not why he started teaching me Kung Fu. He made his living through disparate means, holding odd jobs and engaging in different businesses, but when he began teaching me Kung Fu, he did so for reasons pertaining to the heart and soul, not to his purse.

Perhaps Fu Han Tong saw a flicker of himself in me, that same combination of rootedness and rebellion. I wasn't an orphan, of course, but I was certainly a rebel within my own family. Despite the barriers of language and culture, Fu Han Tong must have sensed my rebellion from my parents and my rejection of rules I did not understand or relate to. At the same time, I longed for roots. I had an innate sense of discipline and respect. Unlike him, I was eager to plant my roots through the teaching of Kung Fu. It was that mix of rootedness and rebellion that we shared, and which lay at the foundation for the magical bond between us, a bond that eventually travelled from West to East, and saw as much joy, love, and devotion as hardship, violence, and cruelty. But we will return to this later.

On my own

Back in Genoa, when Fu Han Tong told me he was leaving, he said that he wanted to intensify our lessons before he did so. Time was running out and he probably felt that he needed to complete his teachings before I could stand on my own feet, and before he could make me a *sifu*. The amount of time I had available was the same given my teaching commitments, but the intensity of our training noticeably increased.

He became much stricter with me. There was a clear change in gears. In those last months I remember that once Fu Han Tong asked me to buy some marbles. I returned the next day with a small bagful. He shook his head. He wanted many more. The following day, I returned with a much larger bag. I handed it to him, and without saying a word about it, he began our lesson. It was a particularly tough one, and at the end I was exhausted. After the customary *Lai*, I was getting ready to leave, late in the evening. He asked me to wait, sat down at his desk and slowly poured himself two fingers of whisky. He then took out the bag of marbles, which he had stowed in his drawer. He dumped them all out onto the floor. Hundreds of marbles rolled off in every direction. He looked up at me, stone-faced, and asked me to pick them all up. Without saying a word, I knelt to the floor and started gathering them. It took me an hour and a half to return all the marbles to the bag.

From those last months with Fu Han Tong in Genoa, another incident remains vivid in my mind. At the entrance of the basement where our lessons took place, Fu Han Tong used to signal his presence by raising the grate thirty centimetres or so. When I arrived, I would slide through the narrow opening. One afternoon, I got there about ten minutes late. I found him sitting at his desk at the entrance, on the side of the staircase that led down to the basement where we trained. I apologized profusely for my delay and made my way to the stairs. He stood up, and without saying a word, gave me a side-kick—*pang tek*—that sent me flying down the stairs. Miraculously, I was bruised but intact. But he was unsatisfied with this punishment: no sooner had I picked myself up off the ground than Fu Han Tong greeted me anew with a cascade of punches and kicks. Our training session had begun.

I also remember how, before he left Genoa, we used to go to Bar Shanghai for lunch. Fu Han Tong was a drinker. The fact that I was only a teenager was of no concern to him, and he encouraged me to drink with him during meals. I remember our two-litre Chianti bottles followed by beer. I'd walk out of the café more than a little tipsy, and then our three-or-four-hour training session would begin. Whether through forms, technique, sparring, or *lop sao*—a controlled method of sparring in which each partner takes turns on attack and defence–I would sober up the hard way.

At the end of 1977, Fu Han Tong left. Shortly before, I asked his permission to start teaching Kung Fu. Not only did he grant it, but he also honoured me with the title of *sifu.* After seven intense years of an exclusive relationship between master and student, I was on my own. I felt disoriented and proud at the same time. *Sifu* Fu Han Tong was leaving, but he was leaving behind a *sifu.* If he was confident that I could stand on my own feet, I had to have that same confidence. In September of 1977, I opened my own *kwoon.*

But I knew that, sooner or later, I would be reunited with Fu Han Tong.

Curiosity

Curiosity opened the door for me to embark on the Way of Martial Arts.

Curiosity is an instinct that buds from the desire to know, discover, enrich and fulfil our being.

Curiosity is an emotional state, intrinsic to both humans and animals, which drives us to explore. It is born with us, manifesting herself in childhood, and walks with us throughout our lives.

It is precisely because of this instinct that we can grow through our experiences and strive to learn, research, and know. In every step of my martial arts, I have been accompanied by curiosity. Curiosity has been the fuel for my motivation to search for knowledge, consciousness and self-awareness.

Being curious means being alive.

CHAPTER 2
Perseverance

Curiosity had gotten me to where I was.

Perseverance would take me where I needed to go.

As explained 5000 years ago in the seminal Book of Changes—the *I Ching*—each symbol, quality or image gives rise to the next, which in turn opens the door for others along the journey. The seeds of martial arts were planted in me as a child by curiosity and my constant desire for challenge. Those seeds blossomed into a passion, which motivated me to put long and hard hours of work into my Kung Fu. When *Sifu* Fu Han Tong returned to China, everything I had so far—a mix of emotion, instinct, and natural ability—would not have been enough. Perseverance became essential, too.

In my journey, I knew where I wanted to go. That sense of direction meant that even in my hardest moments, moments of extreme loneliness and distress, I never lost myself, never lost my way. When young people lose themselves, there's never just one thing to blame. But perhaps they get lost more easily when they have no goal, no guiding light, no dream to pursue.

I had a dream. I used my full body, mind, heart and soul to make it happen. The vision was the goal, and perseverance the means to achieve it. I remember Angela, who eventually became my first wife, telling me when we first met that I put every cell of my body into everything I did, from the most frivolous to the most consequential. She was right. Whatever my objective was, be it as trivial as buying a sports car or as pivotal as establishing my *kwoon*, I never accepted second best.

This spirit, often described as the spirit of the warrior, does not mean that I always met the goals I set for myself. Life is a labyrinth of surprises, unexpected U-turns and unforeseen obstacles. But despite, or precisely because of this, what matters is that you not lose the way. Even if the finish line seems far, what matters is that we push as hard as we can to get there along the path we have chosen for ourselves. It is about living and dying on the path we walk, not wandering, distracted, without purpose and direction.

But the Way—*Tao*—is not a tunnel. Following the *Tao* means walking above, not below, the path we have chosen. Hovering above it means keeping our eyes wide open, staying alert to everything that surrounds us, aware of the many different Ways we could pursue, while choosing, and choosing again, the path we have traced for ourselves. Pursuing our goals while remaining centred means being enlightened by life, not blinded by ego, selfishness or ambition. There are two beautiful Japanese sayings which capture the essence of this state of being: *Tsuki no kokoro*—the spirit must resemble the moonlight that shines evenly upon all things; and *Mizu no Kokoro*—the mind must be still, like the water of a pond. This reminds me of a less high-minded but equally powerful scene in the classic movie "Enter the Dragon": when Bruce Lee points his index finger upwards and tells his student, "Do not concentrate on the finger or you will miss all of the heavenly glory!" The finger points the way towards the vision that we have imagined for ourselves, a vision that we must persevere in achieving. But we must do so keeping our eyes, hearts and souls wide open, retaining that same curiosity and sense of wonder that we had when the journey began.

Vision: My first real journey

I was seventeen. After seven intense years of training, my master Fu Han Tong had honoured me with the title of *sifu*. He had returned to China, leaving hardly any trace behind him. I had started teaching Karate two years earlier, but it was only in September 1977, a few months before his departure, that I officially opened my *Kwoon*, beginning my long journey in the teaching of Kung Fu.

Fu Han Tong had left. Once he was gone, what had once just been a childhood dream gradually began to take shape and became a concrete project. I wanted to travel East and visit China. The East meant so many things to me; and China in particular, the birthplace of martial arts, held a special place in my heart. China was the land of legend, home of all the history, culture and tradition that I had been so deeply immersed in through seven intense years of teachings, stories and life lived alongside my *Sifu* Fu Han Tong. China was the magical country of all the books I had read and all the movies I had watched over the years. In my imaginary China, everyone was, in one way or another, a martial artist. It was a country in which everyone was like *sifu*, or at least was a practitioner of martial arts. As Kung Fu became an all-consuming passion for me, I could not understand how anyone could feel otherwise with the luck and luxury of being born in the birthplace of Kung Fu itself. In Italy, being a martial artist was unusual. I was convinced that in China it was the norm. I was just as convinced that, as the mother of Kung Fu, China was an exceptionally powerful place. If I were to go there, that power would somehow rub off on me, too. I would have walked there if I could.

Of course, walking to China was not an option. And flying there in the late 1970s and early 1980s wasn't easy, either. It required a lot of organization, and a lot of money, too—money that I didn't have. It took several more years before I was able to physically visit China for the first time.

In reality, it wasn't my first trip there; it was my second. I took my first trip to China in my imagination, during a month-long experience that remains one of the most powerful meditations I have experienced to this day.

When I was fourteen, I started practicing meditation—*Tzu Chan*—an internal Kung Fu practice, like Tai Chi, and like Chi Kung, a vital breathwork practice. Since I was a boy, it had always been clear to me that martial arts were not merely about physical strength and technique. Ability, power, strength and energy didn't just require physical, "external" work; energy required internal practice above all, work on the mind and the soul of the martial artist. One of the meditations I used to practice often in those early years was made up of three parts, in no particular order. I would lie down in the dead man's position with my eyes shut—*savasana*. I would relax my body from my toes all the way up to the top of my scalp and concentrate on the day that had just passed. I would retrace my actions, inactions, my thoughts and feelings, discerning the positive from the negative, the good from the bad. In the second part, I would let go of all those thoughts, emptying my mind by concentrating on my breathing at first, and then gradually letting go of that too.

Finally, my imagination was freed. My body was thoroughly relaxed and would start feeling empty, almost ethereal. It was so light that I would float, hovering above the ground. I could get out of bed, leave my bedroom, open the front door and find myself outside the house. I would float down three flights of stairs, open the gate and suddenly be on the street. I would carefully observe every detail around me, every person I met and every object I saw. Once, during this meditation, my astral body ended up in front of the grocery store. I distinctly recall seeing an orange Fiat 127 parked there. When I eventually ended the mediation and left the house for real, I saw that very same orange Fiat parked in front of the store.

Fu Han Tong had only briefly trained me in this method of meditation, this way of controlling my mind through visualization; for the most part I invented it myself. It was my way of meditating while breathing life into my wildest dreams, to my innermost desires. Images from the heart would appear in my mind. My strongest wishes, as trivial, ephemeral or deep and long-lasting as they were, would materialize in my mind. It could be an object, a person, or, most often, an entire movie in which I was the star. It was my way of travelling and exploring the world while stretched out on the floor of my small bedroom in Genoa. Most of these visualizations came and went, but one was a constant throughout those years: my desire to travel to China. With my mind, I would wander into the most incredible martial arts adventures in the East. It was my special way of making my greatest dream come true.

One day, in the shimmering candlelight of my bedroom, something different and magical happened. I went on a journey, my first real journey to China. Just as I had during previous meditations, I left my room and little by little started making my way toward China. All the faded photographs, the movie scenes, the legends, and the facts I had read and studied began to come to life, as did all the anecdotes Fu Han Tong had shared with me over the years. That day, I found myself smack in the middle of Hong Kong's bustling streets. I was blinded by Kowloon's neon lights, my nostrils filled with the pungent smells of street food, and my skin was moist in the heavy, humid air. I elbowed my way through the crowds with a deafening noise all around me. Suddenly I stopped in front of a small door that was squeezed in between a shabby restaurant and a knick-knack store. I was magnetically drawn to the place and slid inside. All was still. All was quiet. I climbed up a steep narrow staircase and opened a small red door at the top. It was a *kwoon*. Inside I met masters and students. I plunged into their world, which became my own. Everything I saw and experienced made me euphoric, and I had no idea what would come next. Would there be new and life-changing opportunities for me? Or would I end up in danger? From the other side of the planet, my mind was able to transport me into totally unexpected scenarios. The same curiosity that I felt as a child was coming back to life in me once again, through a vision.

I eventually came out of that meditation and resumed my daily routine of working and training. The next day I began my meditation again. To my own surprise, my journey in China, the one I had begun the day before, picked up exactly where I had left off. My meditation continued that day, just like a dream that you sink back into after almost waking up. It continued the next day. And the one after that. It lasted for approximately one month, as though it remained uninterrupted by my day-to-day life. It was a meditation that was left deep impressions on me, spiritual, mental and almost physical too. I genuinely felt, and still feel, that I truly travelled to all those places. I fully experienced all the adventures of that intense and magical month. This was the power of martial arts.

It was my first and, in many ways, most important trip to China.

It was early 1979 and *Sifu* Fu Han Tong had left a year and a half earlier.

Perseverance: Back in Genoa

A few years would pass before my second, physical, trip to China. A lot transpired in the meantime. The word that best describes those years is perseverance.

I was only a young *sifu* without a *sifu* to guide him. Perhaps others at my age would have felt lost, but I did not. Fu Han

Tong had left me with knowledge that was so rich that I knew I had plenty of material to work with. My own personal training became even more important. I trained anywhere and everywhere. My Kung Fu practice adapted to the spaces that I chose or that chose me. I used to love running through the dark and silent streets of Genoa at night. I trained in squares, in parks, in alleys and on staircases. And naturally I trained in the schools where I taught.

But above all else, I loved training in nature. When I was fifteen, I discovered a beautifully secluded meadow with a pristine stream running through it up in the Genoese hills, surrounded by stunning mountains. San Felice was my treasured escape, and it was a mere forty minutes' walk from town. I went there often to train, alone or with friends, with or without my weapons or other training gear. After Fu Han Tong's departure, my stays in San Felice became longer and more frequent. I bought a tent, a sleeping bag, a grill, a camping cooker and various cooking utensils. Up there I found a hiding place for my belongings, which allowed me to come and go at will and with relative ease. My stays usually lasted a couple of days.

My nights alone in San Felice were special. I collected wood during the day and started a fire at dusk. I slept with a knife in case wild animals approached my campsite. I trained intensely, day and night. I remember training in the firelight. The stars shone above my head and the sounds of nature enveloped me. I used to enter an emotional state of pure fear as the noises of the wind and the wild animals grew ever more menacing in my mind. The shadows of trees in the firelight came to life, becoming my imaginary enemies. In that state of fear, I moved with the same explosiveness, rapidity and strength as I would have if I had truly been under attack. I repeated a form or a sequence of techniques countless times, each time driven by my ever-increasing fear and energy to match it. Finally, exhausted, I would crawl into my sleeping bag. But fear had gripped me so strongly during my practice that it still reverberated within me long after I'd stopped. There were many nights when I lay half asleep in my tent, gripping my knife tightly in case danger arose. One night, after my practice, I put out the fire. Shortly afterwards I heard the sound of wild dogs barking. I could tell they were close by, and they sensed I was there, too. Instinctively I climbed up a tree. The dogs continued to bark and roam around my campsite. I remained perched in that tree until the sun rose.

My perseverance was not confined to my personal practice. It also emerged in my teaching and the consolidation of my *kwoon*. I had begun teaching in September 1977, a few months before Fu Han Tong returned to China. I started teaching Kung Fu gradually, initially incorporating it into my Karate program; as my confidence grew, I made it more of a focus, and eventually it became the only martial art I taught.

The number of students steadily grew. Equally important, their quality rose as well. Training with me was not easy. It was akin to driving a sports car at two hundred kilometres per hour with no brakes. It was like getting on a rollercoaster you could never get off. Stepping off meant stopping for good; it was black and white for me back then. Training with me and learning my Kung Fu meant going through all the work, the effort, the discipline and the hardship that were part and parcel of my martial arts. My students needed to have ironclad integrity. The rules and norms of the *kwoon* had to be respected to the letter. My belief in the discipline of martial arts was total, and I expected no less from my students. Today I can better see how extreme, and yes, perhaps how crazy, it all was. I was little more than a boy, and I didn't have the experience to know that not everyone could live martial arts the way I did, or wanted to. At the time, I felt that if a student wanted to take a less serious approach to martial arts, it meant that they should abandon Kung Fu altogether.

Word soon spread about my *kwoon*, my teaching and about me, the young martial artist. This generally meant free publicity and popularity. Sometimes, though, it created odd situations that I had to extricate myself from as best I could. Like one afternoon back in 1978, when one of my students, Paolo, rushed over and whispered excitedly in my ear: "*Sifu*, there's a guy in the *kwoon* wearing a *gi* and a black belt, warming up on our tatami mat: what should we do?" For a second I thought it was a joke. What on earth was a *karateka* doing in our *kwoon* without having introduced himself or signed up for a trial lesson? Before entering the room, I peered through the window; lo and behold, there was a broad-shouldered man in a *gi* stretching on our mats. Paolo was nervous and agitated, at a loss as to what to do. I felt both perplexed and somewhat amused. I walked into the tatami room and firmly but politely asked the man: "Is there anything we can do for you?" Curtly, he replied: "I'm here to challenge you!" The guy must have seen too many martial arts movies, I thought to myself.

I paused for a moment and pondered how best to resolve this strange situation, while my students pushed their way into the room to see what all the commotion was about. I wanted to keep my students out of it, so I invited the man into the changing room. I asked him why he wanted to challenge me; had I inadvertently done something to offend him or his school? As the man struggled to respond, I realized he was bluffing, and only took a few minutes to persuade him to drop the charade. He eventually left the *kwoon*, and I was left feeling confused but satisfied that I had resolved the situation through the power of words rather than brute force.

Evening classes began and the bitter-sweet taste of that strange encounter quickly vanished. I didn't give it a second thought until one week later when, in the middle of a lesson, the front door of the *kwoon* flew open. There was a heavy thunderstorm that evening, and at first I thought a strong gust of wind had opened the door. But an instant later the same man in a *gi*, this time soaking wet, strode into the room. He dropped his bag and without further ado raised his guard. It seemed my words had not been enough after all; I had no choice but to act.

I asked my students to move to the edges of the tatami mats and invited the man to the center. I stood three metres away from him and performed the martial salute. He did the same. Neither of us said a word or clarified what rules, if any, applied to our fight. I was in no mood for a show that evening and was determined to put an end to that ridiculous farce as quickly as possible. The man wanted a fight and he would get one, but it would be as short and painless as possible. I attacked first, faking a low-kick and then immediately lifting my leg into a side-kick that struck him squarely on his chin. The man's head snapped back as he lost his balance and collapsed onto the floor. He lay there for a few moments, bleeding, in an almost religious silence. The air was thick with fear and excitement, and my students watched and wondered what would happen next. The man finally stood up, slowly, his white *gi* stained with large splotches of dark red blood. With one hand on his cut chin, he performed a martial salute, picked up his bag, turned around and left with his head held high.

It was only several weeks later that I discovered that the man, a well-known *karateka* in Genoa, had come to challenge me because of a bet placed at a bar, amongst martial artists. They had bet one hundred thousand liras on the fight, a small fortune at the time. Word of a talented eighteen-year-old *sifu* was spreading through town and some of the more seasoned martial arts teachers felt threatened. That fight, along with many others that would take place in the months and years that followed, put those feelings to rest. I tried to avoid those situations as much as possible. Like any true martial artist, I had been taught by my *sifu* to use my art only as a last resort. When those situations became unavoidable, however, I used my head. To me they seemed no different from the fights I used to have with the kids in the neighborhood when I was younger.

My reputation helped the school grow rapidly. But the difficulty of my teachings in those years inevitably meant that there was a high turnover of students. Many enrolled, but those who were looking for little more than another standard martial arts course eventually left. Many of my friends whom I had started teaching back in 1977 took different paths: they pursued other interests or studies, or became totally absorbed by their jobs and families. Whenever a friend left me and my *kwoon*, I was overcome by a piercing sense of loss. But it didn't last long, and I never had regrets or hard feelings. I had chosen my Way, my *Tao.* It was only logical that others would do the same.

Those who stayed had something special. They were truly motivated, and this imbued me with greater strength and determination to make my *kwoon* succeed. I owed it to all the ones who persevered and believed in me, as much as I owed it to myself. Two students were particularly important to me.

The first was Carlo, my older brother. Carlo had always been athletic. As a child he was passionate about artistic gymnastics, but he inevitably became acquainted with martial arts too. Carlo had lived every step of my martial arts journey alongside me, from the early days in which I monopolized our small bedroom with my private training sessions to those dreadful arguments with our parents because of the life choice I had made. We were very close as children and remained so as we grew up, often looking out for one another. We had our disagreements, but overall, our shared childhood was one of empathy and mutual support. Carlo was one of my first students when I started teaching Karate in late 1976. He continued with Kung Fu the following year. His choice to train with me meant a lot. Beyond brotherly love, the fact that someone who knew me so well chose to endure all the hardship that came with my *kwoon* meant the world to me. It meant that there was real value in what I was trying to build. As the years passed, Carlo became more and more passionate about martial arts. He had enrolled in university to study engineering once he finished high school, but after an illness interrupted his studies for several months, something changed in him. During his illness, I tried to help him by introducing him to *Tao Yin*, soft gymnastics and postural exercises to stretch the meridians and improve breathing. Luckily he got a lot out of that practice. When his health improved, Carlo resumed his martial arts practice and his desire to dedicate his life to Kung Fu grew exponentially. Several years later, I gave him the opportunity to do so through my school.

The second student was Angela. She too enrolled in 1979. Angela was passionate about martial arts; by the time I met her she had already experimented with different martial disciplines, including Karate and Jiu Jitsu. She was one of only a few women who had practiced Savate at the time, and she was curious about Kung Fu. A friend of hers, Gianni, had started practicing Kung Fu and took her to his school, run by master Shin Dae Wong. They soon found out there was another *kwoon* in town, led by a very young *sifu*: me. They were both curious to learn more and showed up one day to observe a class. Angela immediately enrolled. Her friend did too, leaving *Sifu* Shin Dae Wong's *kwoon*.

I was immediately struck by Angela's passion and dedication to martial arts. She was twenty-three, four years older than me. She had a boyfriend, a solid group of friends, and was pursuing a degree in the history of Eastern art. We immediately clicked: a friendship was born that eventually blossomed into a romantic relationship. Angela was at first intrigued and later fascinated by my life. It was so radically different from anything she had encountered up until that point. She was attracted to my passion and enthusiasm, to my quirks and rebellion, but also, perhaps unconsciously, to my inner suffering and never-ending quest for growth.

Angela too, in her subdued way, has always been on her own path to becoming. She would never be attracted to something or someone she felt was static, completed, arrived. Little by little and totally organically, she slipped into my world, until eventually she became a central figure in it. As she put it to me recently, she felt like there was an aura, a magnet, that drew her to me. She left behind most of her life, her interests, her friends, and her projects and immersed herself in the world of martial arts. United by that powerful bond, our relationship was serious from the beginning. We trained together and often went camping in the mountains of San Felice. Back in Genoa we would occasionally do what other young couples did, but always in a slightly different way. I remember going to the cinema with Angela, and in typical Asian style, we would bring along a full meal to eat while watching the movie, to the astonishment of those around us. She thought I was a little crazy, and she was probably right. But she loved the world that I had brought her into, that touch of the East we were both so fascinated by. I fell in love with her.

Angela and I trained together intensely. She was a committed student of the *kwoon* and followed me into every adventure. A good example of the craziness and dedication that I and my students had at the time, beginning with Carlo and Angela, was an experience we had together in San Felice, in 1982. It was one of the seminal moments in the history of my *kwoon*. I had taken my students to the mountains to train up before, but this was the first time that I had decided to organize a week-long retreat there. It was a special retreat. We all took a vow of silence. For the whole week, not a single word was uttered, neither during training nor at meals nor rest time. We trained at any time of day, and I cooked for the whole group; we ate and drank around the fireplace. There were around fifty of us when we started. The rule was that no matter what happened, we had to remain completely silent. Those who felt they could not take it were free to leave at any point, but they had to do so in silence, packing up their tents, collecting their belongings and leaving San Felice without speaking one word.

Half-way through the retreat, more than half the group had left. Those who remained saw the retreat through to the very end. As the hours and days passed, a gradual but noticeable change took place in each of us. Externally, we appeared to weaken. As time went on the group looked more and more tired, their clothes dirty, their hair ruffled, their beards long. Internally, though, a completely opposite transformation was taking place: their eyes gleamed with a new light. Our spirits were lifted and a magical peace spread around us as a special connection, an intuition, grew inside us, and bonded us powerfully together. Without the spoken word, we began communicating in different ways. Ours became a language of looks and gestures. It took a mere glance for someone to say that they wanted a sip of water, or a second helping of food. Words were no longer needed for us to understand one other, from the most basic physical needs to the deepest callings of the soul.

At the end of that week, we started talking again. That was when Angela and I announced that we were pregnant. She was twenty-six, I was twenty-two; we were both young. We had moved in together two years earlier, in 1981. Not even for one moment did I feel scared or anxious about having a child—as I would later discover, a baby boy. We both knew it wouldn't be easy. We were young and we couldn't count on our families to help us. Either they lived too far away or simply had too much on their plates. At the time I was solidifying my *kwoon* while pursuing my own practice, including what were becoming long and frequent trips to China. It wasn't going to be easy for Angela, either. She would have to slow down her own practice and spend a lot of time alone. She knew that when I was at home, in Genoa, I was one hundred percent present, and I helped clean, cook, shop, and take care of the many errands of daily life. But often I was away. And this was tough for Angela while she pregnant and especially during the first months and years with our son, Shan. I saw it at the time, and I see it even more clearly now. But we were young, in love, and had a big life project ahead of us. We were happy.

Desertion

Let's return to the late 1970s. My practice was intense and my *Kwoon* was growing. My relationship with my parents was improving too, as they began to realize that my life choice hadn't been a mistake. They saw that I felt accomplished, that I was talented and dedicated to what I did. Above all, they couldn't deny that my choice was paying off financially. At twenty, I was independent, living on my own and earning more than most of my childhood friends. In fact, I was earning more than many adults my parents' age. It was no coincidence or fluke: every step I took required hard work. My parents were finally beginning to take me seriously.

At that time, I had approximately fifty students enrolled in my school. I taught at two venues in Genoa: the cycling association in Piazza Martinez, and the gym of the Santa Maria Maggiore Church on Corso Sardegna. I later opened another course, at a school, and until 1978 I taught in Lavagna too. Eventually, I dropped the course in Lavagna and in Piazza Martinez and consolidated my teaching in Genoa at the church on Corso Sardegna. But that year I began to feel a growing need to find my own *kwoon*, a headquarters for my school.

In late 1978 it looked like I had found an ideal place, a

former coffee factory no longer in use, which I could have rented to finally establish my very own *kwoon*. I liked the venue and was enthusiastic about the project. But my dreams would soon be shattered.

On a grey and rainy morning, a letter arrived in the mail. The envelope bore the logo of the Ministry of Defense. I knew that this day would eventually come, but I had ignored it for a long time. My heart sank as I opened the letter: I was being drafted for my year of compulsory military service. I had been enrolled in the Navy.

I knew right away that military service would represent a tremendous loss of my precious time and energy. There was so much to do and so little time to do it. I felt like I had just learned to fly, and a year in the military would clip my wings. How could I continue to invest in my practice and my teaching? How could my school continue to grow and consolidate? The first casualty of my military service was the loss of the opportunity to open the headquarters of my *kwoon* in the former coffee factory. There was no way I could pursue that project from afar. I had to give it up.

I had little choice but to head off to the military. But after less than two weeks, I couldn't believe my luck: I was sent back home due to an excess number of recruits. I resumed my life of teaching and practice in Genoa, in those months my relationship with Angela began, and, with her help, I resumed the search for my *kwoon*. Seven months later, a second letter from the Ministry of Defense arrived. I took it even more badly than I had the first time. Not only did I have much more to lose, but this time they had called me to join the *Alpini*, a special mountain infantry, known as the toughest corps in the Italian army.

I was determined not to give up. I was not going to allow military service to cloud the vision that I was pursuing. I was going to persevere and fight back. And a year-long fight it became. In the main barracks of Borgo San Dalmazio, where all young recruits were sent for their first month of training, everything I saw and lived confirmed my worst assumptions. I detested the bullying by older soldiers and I refused to put up with it. One day, during my first month of service, I left the barracks; rather than return that evening, I showed up the next morning, to the scandalized stupor of my peers and fuming rage of my superiors.

As a result, I was sent to a punitive barrack in Boves, in Piedmont, which was rife with criminals, dropouts, and sheer lunatics. In charge of the barracks was a former marshal who had been demoted to a captain due to his own obvious craziness. The captain hated me from the start because of my refusal to accept the bullying, which was an unwritten rule of the club. He made sure he demonstrated this to me at every opportunity. I got into countless fights with my "seniors," which always ended with them in tears and, often, with broken limbs.

One evening, a group of older soldiers slipped into my barracks and poured a bucketful of mule urine onto my bed. When I realized what had happened, I was furious, but kept my calm. Without thinking twice, nor talking about it with anyone, I went straight to the stable nearby, where fifty-six mules were kept. I nonchalantly asked the farmers for two buckets of urine. They were surprised, not by of my strange request—to which they were clearly accustomed—but because it was coming from me, a freshman. Usually it was the older soldiers bullying the younger ones, not the other way around. I told them about my intentions: when the seniors were on leave later that evening, I would give them a taste of their own medicine. The farmers were shocked. "Are you crazy?"—they gasped—"haven't you learned the rules of the game?" I ignored their stern warnings, took the buckets, patiently waited for the seniors to leave, and snuck into their dormitory, pouring the urine onto eight beds. I returned to my own dormitory, where I had managed to get hold of a clean mattress, and lay down in silence, amidst my companions' disbelieving stares.

When the clock struck midnight, I heard the seniors raucously climbing the two flights of stairs above me to their dormitory. For a long moment, there was an eerie silence, followed by an outburst of screaming and swearing. My barracks-mates urged me to run away and hide, but I had no intention of doing so. On the contrary, I wanted to make sure those people found me, so we could settle the matter. I went to the bathrooms—large empty spaces were my best bet in those circumstances—and waited. When they finally stormed in, all hell broke loose. The eldest, who was clearly the ringleader of the gang, swore and tried to head-butt me. I skirted his clumsy attempt and reacted with an avalanche of techniques.

When the dust settled, I saw what looked like a cross between a horror movie and a battlefield. The white ceramic sinks were dripping blood, and scattered across the floor were eight young men, curled in the fetal position, with broken noses and ribs. Behind me there was a crowd of dumbstruck men who stared at me with their mouths open: I didn't have a single scratch. But the glory did not last long. My superiors blamed me not only for the outcome of that brawl, but also, worst of all, because I had broken the informal rules of the barracks. This, above all else, was unacceptable to them, as much as the reverse was indigestible to me.

Weeks passed and I could no longer take it. I desperately tried to get permission for a two-day leave, which was highly unusual for a young recruit, and particularly one who was in a punitive barracks like mine. So I developed a strategy. In Boves, I befriended a middle-aged lieutenant who was in love with his Suzuki. I was passionate about engines myself, and had learned a great deal about them over the years. I pretended to be a mechanic, wooing the lieutenant with conversation about his favourite subject. He warmed towards me, so much so that one afternoon he lent me his beloved Suzuki for a short ride. I knew that was my moment: I had to capitalize on his sympathy and act fast. After the ride, I asked him for a two-day leave, which he duly conceded to me with a wink and a smile.

As soon as I stepped out of the Boves barracks, I was seized by an irresistible urge to never return. I didn't have a plan, but I loathed the thought of stepping foot there again. And so, I escaped to my hideout in San Felice. On my way there, I managed to contact Angela, who arranged my tent, cooker, and cooking utensils there. She also brought food and other basic goods which I would need to survive. The police began searching for me. After five days of unauthorized leave from military service, I was considered a deserter. It was an offense prosecutable by military trial.

I knew I couldn't stay in San Felice forever. I wanted to get back to my ordinary life, not end up as an outlaw in the mountains. After seventeen days in hiding, I decided to return to the barracks. When I did, all hell broke loose. The captain, who didn't have much sympathy for me in the first place, was determined to prosecute me for desertion. I was facing up to six months in a military prison, only to then have to restart my compulsory military service from the beginning. Life in the barracks was a piece of cake by comparison.

There was no time to waste. I had to come up with a way to avoid the trial. The evening I was due in court I feigned illness and asked to be seen by a medical doctor. While I waited, Chi Kung came to the rescue. There are Chi Kung practices that can temporarily raise blood pressure. So, I put myself to work, increasing my blood pressure and simulating a heart dysfunction. As soon as the doctor had seen me, I was rushed in an ambulance to Cuneo, the nearest city, where I was immediately taken to a civilian hospital. I spent the night there, knowing full well that the doctors would realize that my heart was perfectly healthy the following morning. But I had to take it one step at a time. At that moment, all that mattered was avoiding the nightmare that was the martial trial scheduled for the following day.

The next morning my blood pressure had indeed returned to normal. From the various check-ups I received that day, it was crystal clear to all the doctors that my heart was fine. But I got lucky: they prescribed me one week off military service to recover. I was then sent to a military hospital in Turin for approval.

During my stay at the hospital in Turin, I began practicing Chi Kung again, achieving the same effect on my blood pressure. The high pressure didn't last long, however, and since I'd repeated the same trick twice, I had to change tactics. In the hospital, I understood that the surest way to obtain a longer-term leave was to be diagnosed with a psychological or psychiatric illness. This wasn't an easy approach, since many recruits tried to fake different psychological disorders, and doctors in military hospitals were well versed in spotting a bluff. But luckily, I succeeded: I was diagnosed with anxiety and depression and sent to the neurology ward, where I spent a week with genuinely disturbed patients. This was how I managed a two-week leave-of-absence back home.

As soon as I got back to Genoa, I resumed my training and teaching. I only had two weeks off, but I was determined to make the most of it. Towards the end of that period, I accidentally broke my nose while training. It wasn't intentional, but as soon as it happened I realized that I could use it to my advantage. I went straight to an ENT who told me that, while it wasn't urgent, I would eventually need surgery. But he also said that I would have to wait for several weeks before undergoing the operation under general anesthesia, which is what he recommended. Several weeks was too long for me; I only had a few days left before my leave was up and I would have to return to Boves, where the specter of a military trial awaited me. The only way to square the circle and be operated on immediately was to do it under local anaesthesia only. It would be far more painful, but it was my only way out of the conundrum. So that's what I did, earning myself another three weeks of leave.

Even though I was technically still in recovery, I continued my teaching and training during those three weeks. After the routine afternoon check-ups, I would escape from the hospital; Angela waited for me outside the entrance and brought me back through the emergency room before nightfall. I was almost recovered, and so I began again to devise new stratagems for avoiding going back to the barracks. I turned to my hands. Over the years, I had already hurt them many times, so I decided to rely on them again. I trained obsessively on a *makiwara*—a Japanese wooden board—which made my hands swell terribly. With my hands in that state I got an X-ray in the emergency room. I knew that my hand wasn't broken that time, but because I'd had so many past fractures, the technician couldn't tell which had happened when. It did the trick: I received another two weeks of leave and continued my daily escapes from the hospital.

It was in this period that Angela and my mother met. One day, I had been dismissed from the hospital but I was in a terrible state. My energy levels were rock bottom: I could hardly move or talk. I stumbled into the house and collapsed onto my bed. My mother rushed in to help, but all I could mutter was: "Call Angela and ask her to bring the needles." My mother was worried and bewildered. Why on earth did I need needles, and who was Angela? But I was in such a sorry state that she didn't ask me these questions. She rummaged through my drawer, found my phone book and dialled Angela's number. Angela, who was used to my escapes and knew the effect they had on my health, was fully equipped with my acupuncture set.

Angela rushed over and handed me my needles. I could hardly move but summoned all my strength and concentration to place them in the right spots to unblock the meridian I had voluntarily disrupted to get hospitalized. While I rested with the needles in place, Angela went into the kitchen to introduce herself to my mom. Half an hour later I was back on my feet and eager to take Angela out for a walk. My mother, who thought I'd been on my deathbed, was perplexed, to put it mildly. Though the circumstances of their meeting had been unusual, Angela and Lidia immediately hit it off. To this day, my mother's eyes light up when my ex-wife's name is mentioned.

I continued coming and going from the hospital with self-inflicted physical injuries for a few months. During that time I continued my teaching and training, and finally figured out a long-term solution to avoiding the trial and ending my military service. My parents knew a marshal in a Genovese barracks, and they contacted him, explaining my situation. He wanted to help, and introduced us to a woman who worked in the administrative office of Genoa's military hospital. She ended up solving my problem. She understood my predicament and figured out a way to transfer me from Boves to the administrative office of her hospital. This was how I ended up completing the remaining months of my service working in my hometown's military hospital, simultaneously avoiding the trial and resuming my life in Genoa: my practice, my *kwoon*, Angela.

After twelve hospitalizations over the course of eleven months, I was finally free again in late 1980. As soon as I left the military, my life picked back up again at full speed. With Angela's help, I found what eventually became my *kwoon*: an old convent that later became a high school in Salita delle Fieschine, not far from Brignole station in Genoa. It was a stunning location. Initially we rented only the ground floor and shared the space with a fencing association. Soon I realized that there was a room next door to ours that was completely empty. It was in bad shape and needed to be renovated, but when joined with the first room, it would give me a decent amount of space for my *kwoon*. I needed it badly. By then I had almost a hundred students and the school's program had evolved, with different levels and classes. Over time, I rented another two rooms on the second floor too. They had been the storage and laundry rooms of the convent back in the day, but we put a lot of work into them and they became two more rooms for my school. Lastly, we added more rooms on the second floor that had been used as machinery depots for the provincial government. Over the course of several years, I completely restructured all the space I had rented, outfitting it with several training rooms, bathrooms, showers and changing rooms. Spanning the two floors, I had two thousand square metres entirely dedicated to martial arts. The school lives on to this day. It is one of my proudest accomplishments.

Wider horizons

In 1979 my *kwoon* began spreading to central Italy.

In April 1979, during my time off from military service due to an excess number of recruits in the Navy, I planned a short holiday to Rome. I had never been to Rome before and longed to see the Eternal City. I went for a long weekend with two friends and we followed the classic tourist itinerary. I saw the Colosseum, the Forum, St. Peter's, and wandered around Rome's historic city centre, marvelling at its many churches, buildings, squares, and alleys. But I had also done some research into the martial arts schools in town. One evening, my friends and I decided to visit one.

A well-known and respected school in Rome at the time belonged to Karate master Augusto Basile. I located its address and telephone number in the phone book. Basile was sitting at the front desk when we arrived, and he assumed we were three nineteen-year-olds who wanted some information on Karate. He told us that unfortunately there was no Karate class that evening, but that a Kung Fu master was teaching a guest class instead. I reacted enthusiastically and he allowed us to sit in and watch the class. The Kung Fu teacher was Narciso Pula, whom I later discovered was a Franco-Italian master. We sat quietly on a bench and watched the class unfold. The room was packed, but what I saw was unfamiliar. It wasn't just the styles, forms, and techniques that looked different; the atmosphere of the class lacked the discipline, respect and magic that were essential to me in the teaching and practice of martial arts.

At the end of the class, Pula approached us to share some information about his school. He asked us some questions as well. I told him the truth about why we were there, which may have been naïve: I told him that I practiced Kung Fu and that, in fact, I was a *sifu.* I told him that my own *sifu* was Chinese and had returned to China. I talked about the styles I had studied with Fu Han Tong, which I now practiced and taught in Genoa. He looked at me with suspicion, hardly believing that a boy my age could be a master. Intrigued nonetheless, he invited me to his *kwoon* the next morning for a personal training session. I excitedly accepted.

I showed up the next morning at the agreed-upon time. Pula asked me to show him some of my Kung Fu, which I did, performing sequences from several forms in different styles. He then asked me to teach him something. I taught him part of a form in the Praying Mantis style—Tang Lang—as well as a sequence of the tiger form—*Tao Hu*—in the Shaolin style. He asked me to return that evening to teach his students. I agreed.

That evening he assembled only his most advanced students. He introduced me to them as if we were old friends. He asked me to teach what he had learned from me that morning. As I did, he corrected his students, pretending he had known the forms for years. With Pula's encouragement, I performed other forms for the class, who watched in awe. I was young, I was enthusiastic, and I was somewhat naïve. But I was not stupid. I knew that something wasn't quite right. There was something insincere about it; Pula pretended to be a master of the forms he had only just learned, from me, that morning. At the end of the class, he told his students that they would have other opportunities to train with me in the future. I said nothing, but I knew that would not be the case.

That same day something else happened that turned out to be a significant event in my life. After class, Pula invited me and my friends out to dinner. He told me that he and his colleagues were organizing a large Kung Fu exhibition for the coming June, and the most important masters in both Italy and France would be in attendance. He asked me to participate as a master, and explained that the presentation time allotted to each *sifu* would depend on the number of attendees who signed up for his session. Although I harboured doubts about Pula himself, I thought that the exhibition represented a wonderful opportunity for me and for my *kwoon*. The only *sifu* I had known was my own: Fu Han Tong. The only practitioners I knew were my own students from Genoa. I was curious to discover what else was out there, to broaden my horizons. The idea of being exposed to a Kung Fu gathering with masters and practitioners from both Italy and France, and of having the opportunity to teach my own Kung Fu to them, was a dream for me. My concerns about Pula notwithstanding, I accepted the invitation.

June arrived quickly. I travelled to Terni, in central Italy, where the exhibition was taking place. I brought along Luciano, one of my best students, who would be my sparring partner at the exhibition. One of Pula's students came to pick us up at the train station. I have a vivid memory of that moment: it was Roberto Macaluso who picked us up, the man who would later become my best friend, in his orange Super Simca. He took us to the hotel to drop off our bags. From there, we went straight to the stadium where the exhibition would begin the following morning. The stadium was crowded with masters and their students. I saw Pula, but he was extremely busy setting everything up, so I barely spoke to him. In fact, I hardly spoke to anyone that Friday afternoon. I listened carefully to the rules of the exhibition as they were announced. Given the number of masters present—twenty—each one would have only an hour to conduct their class. We would be called on stage when it was our turn, and once time was up, we would need to turn the stage over to the next teacher. In addition to the students who had enrolled, there were members of the press there, too. It was an excellent opportunity to gain some publicity in both Italy and France.

At 7:30 A.M. sharp the next day, Luciano and I arrived at the Terni stadium. The place was packed. Around three hundred students had enrolled in the exhibition. Alongside them, the twenty masters showed off the nicest gear I had ever seen. There were uniforms embroidered with tigers, leopards and dragons. I had nothing like this; I wore a plain black *yishang*. A few minutes before the hour, the organizers announced the class schedule. My timeslot was from 8:00-9:00 A.M.: I was going first. I had prepared a short session, knowing that I only had an hour. With over three hundred students in attendance, it was just a small taste of my Kung Fu. My class plan included short sequences of different Shaolin animals, with their respective applications, which I would demonstrate with Luciano.

Five minutes before my time was up, I performed a form: a little extra to leave the group wanting more. I performed my *Lai*, the martial salute, and the stadium broke out in a loud applause. I waited for my cue to end the session and leave the stage, but nothing happened. There was silence. After a few long minutes, I was called to the side. One of the organizers walked up to me, telling me that the masters had agreed to give me an extra hour, from 9:00-10:00 A.M. I was surprised but happy to have the opportunity to delve more fully into the lesson plan I had prepared. At ten, having performed my second *Lai*, I once again prepared to exit the stage. But the same thing happened again. The organizers asked me to continue, not just for another hour, but for the rest of the morning. I had to improvise a new program, which I did. Leaving aside Shaolin, I introduced some Wing Chun, as well as general hand and leg techniques. At nineteen, having started teaching Kung Fu only two years before, I led an improvised four-hour long exhibition in front of three hundred students.

At noon we took a break. The organizers took me out for lunch along with the other masters. They bombarded me with questions. Some were genuinely interested, enthusiastic and admiring. Others were more distant, suspicious and, I sensed, envious. I asked them what had happened. Why didn't the other masters show up to conduct their classes? What had gone wrong? Some looked at me in embarrassment. Eventually one of the organizers told me that after my first performance, the other masters didn't feel up to it. They were concerned that if they followed my performance, it would have ended up in negative publicity for their schools, so they had chosen to step back. A bit awkwardly, they asked me to lead the afternoon classes, too. Eventually, I led the entire exhibition for the whole weekend. Out of the twenty masters present in Terni, only two aside from myself agreed to teach one-hour long classes on Sunday afternoon. It was a triumph for me. As soon as the exhibition was over, I was literally pulled away, as if the organizers didn't want me to mingle with the crowd. Some students and masters managed to get my contact details, but not many relative to the huge crowd that had gathered around me.

No sooner had the exhibition ended than Pula asked me to establish a national Kung Fu association with him: the National Federation of Chinese Fighting. I didn't give him an answer right away, but my instinct was to say no. I returned home and mulled over the whole experience. While I was incredibly grateful for and proud of the experience in Terni, the level of Kung Fu I had seen was disappointingly low. Until then I had only been exposed to my *sifu* and to my students. I didn't expect every other master to be at Fu Han Tong's level, but I had hoped to see a similar discipline, passion and dedication to martial arts. But what I had witnessed in Terni, much like in Rome six months earlier, was a world apart from my martial arts practice. I politely declined Pula's offer. He tried to insist with repeated letters and phone calls, but I remained steadfast. Eventually he gave up. That was the last I heard of him.

After the Terni exhibition, the few who had managed to get my contact details got in touch. In particular, there was Tonino Cusenza, an instructor from Viterbo and Tuscania, who wrote to inquire about my Kung Fu. I had no memory of him from the exhibition, but he told me that he had been there. He invited me to Viterbo, where he wanted to host a meeting with a group of Kung Fu instructors who were interested in me and my school. I travelled to Viterbo in the winter of 1979. Cusenza told me he would meet me at the train station, where he would be wearing a beige coat, a moustache and holding a newspaper under his arm. I got off the train and sure enough I saw a moustachioed man in a beige coat holding a newspaper waiting for me on the platform.

He held the meeting at his house, where seven or eight teachers were waiting for us. I recognized a few of them from the exhibition in Terni six months earlier. Others had been brought over by Cusenza. All of them were much older than me. A lively discussion began. They started talking exuberantly about Kung Fu, about Bruce Lee movies, about tournaments and competitions. I listened quietly, noticing with dismay that no one talked about Kung Fu for what it actually was: a martial art. After a while, Cusenza abruptly interrupted the group. He said that I was there for a reason: the men gathered in the room were interested in following me and becoming my students based on what they had heard about me or seen with their own eyes in Terni. Cusenza asked me to take the floor. I talked about what Kung Fu meant to me, and about the culture and tradition of martial arts that lay at the heart of my *kwoon*. I spoke about the different Kung Fu styles, techniques and methods. Most importantly, I explained the values of Kung Fu. I did not mince words. I admitted that what I had seen and heard both in Terni and in that room had nothing to do with Kung Fu. They may have been masters and instructors, but that meant nothing to me. In Terni I had seen expensive uniforms that made them look more like kings or cardinals than martial artists. That was not Kung Fu. Kung Fu was not about fashion, business, or fame. Some nodded vigorously at my words; others raised their eyebrow and looked stung. I told Cuzenza and the rest of the group that I would only teach those who humbly agreed to start all over again: to set aside their titles and their convictions and begin from scratch. They were stunned, but these were my rules. Take it or leave it and make a choice. Four raised their hands. The others left the room. With those who stayed a new adventure began.

The next day, in Viterbo, I began teaching two of my four new students: Tonino Cusenza and Guido Politini, who were already teaching Kung Fu. I gave them a couple of lessons over the course of the next two days. Although they pledged total loyalty, I still had my doubts about whether they would actually stick with me. The next day, I would return to Genoa and would only be able to teach them occasionally. Following me would not be easy.

But they kept their word. No sooner had I returned home than my new students from Viterbo got in touch to arrange a visit to Genoa. Tonino Cusenza, Guido Politini, and a few others became my faithful students. Several months later, I received a letter from Roberto Macaluso, who had picked me up in Terni station all those months ago. He was teaching Kung Fu in Monterotondo at the time, but wanted to join my school too. I had great respect for these men, who had been practicing and teaching what they thought was Kung Fu for years, and still humbly agreed to join my *kwoon*, acknowledging to their students and above all to themselves that they had to start over from scratch. I was determined to reward their humility and commitment. Once my military service ended, I began travelling regularly to Viterbo, Tuscania, and Monterotondo to teach them as well as their students. Of course, they continued coming up to Genoa too. A long and intense relationship with them began, which allowed my *kwoon* to grow and consolidate in central Italy. Eventually, my school would expand to Terni, and by 1984 it would reach Rome too: I opened my first school in Italy's capital at a sports center near Porta Maggiore.

Looking east: my second journey

By the time my military service came to an end in 1980, my *kwoon was* growing in Genoa and Lazio and my life was full. Beyond the teaching and practice of Kung Fu, the size of my *kwoon* required that it have proper structure and administration. Little by little I established the rules, the structure and the programme of my *kwoon.* I had to do everything on my own, with no prior experience. *Sifu* Fu Han Tong had taught me everything I knew about Kung Fu, but he had never established a *kwoon* that I could look to as a model for my own. I had been his only student in Genoa and his other students were few and far between, scattered around the world. Fu Han Tong's model of teaching worked for one student. It would not work for a school that taught over a hundred students in six different locations.

This was how I established a structure for the school. My experience with Japanese martial arts helped me with this effort, since they are so well structured. I created different levels that students would graduate through if they passed their exams, which included both theory and practice. At first my theory exams were relatively simple. Students were asked about the meaning of Kung Fu, and about the categorization of different styles, depending on their geographical origin or school: internal—*Nei Chia*—or external—*Wai Chia*.

The very first theory exam was held in 1980. As my own studies intensified and my knowledge grew, the theoretical component of my teaching expanded, and with it so did the complexity of my exams. The levels of progression I'd established were essential, because they allowed me to delegate teaching to the most advanced students when I was away visiting other locations of the school around the country. I rotated constantly between different towns, and wherever I was, I held three classes per day. In addition, I taught the most advanced students in the mornings, and they eventually became the first instructors besides me at the school. In the evenings, I taught their students. In addition to this frequent domestic travel, I eventually began traveling to China two to three times a year for a few months at a time; keeping my *kwoon* tightly organized according to a hierarchy was crucial. There would have been no other way to hold everything together.

By the early 1980s, I was extremely proud of what I had achieved. My passion for Kung Fu had sprung from curiosity and blossomed into a vision. It became my reality through perseverance and hard work. I gave everything to my Kung Fu practice, to my teaching, and to the organization of my school. But as time passed, my long-held dream of going to China, which I first experienced through my month-long meditation, grew into an urgent desire. I felt a strong need to nourish my own practice through what would become my second, physical, trip to China, the land of dragons.

I had saved some money for the trip, but I had no idea where to begin. I was twenty years old, naïve and inexperienced. The furthest I had travelled was to Calabria, in southern Italy. China belonged to a different planet, even more so in the early 1980s when the country was all but closed off to the West. I didn't know anyone who could help me: neither my friends nor my family had any travel experience, let alone to China.

But I was determined to get there. I felt ready, both physically and emotionally. So, I got my passport in order to travel to Hong Kong. If I wanted to visit mainland China, I would have to obtain a visa in Hong Kong. In those days, getting a visa to travel to mainland China from the Chinese consulate in Rome would have taken up to a year, and I had no intentions of waiting that long. I went to several travel agencies for information, but the most I could find were a few uninformative leaflets. I decided to buy a one-way plane ticket to Hong Kong, and I packed a small bag and a First Aid kit. I knew when I was leaving, but I had no idea if or when I'd be back.

I wanted to see China to enrich my skills and find Fu Han Tong. I wanted to discover the birthplace of Kung Fu, continue learning from my *sifu,* and show him what I had become and what I had accomplished in the years since he left. I would go to China no matter what.

All I had was an address, scribbled on a scrap of paper by Fu Han Tong several years before. I had no clue what I would find there: maybe a house, or a shop, a restaurant, or a *kwoon,* or something else altogether. For all I knew, Fu Han Tong himself may not even have been in Hong Kong. He could have returned to his hometown, in the Guangdong province, or anywhere else. Looking for him would not be easy, not least because of his different secret identities, which he needed to keep hidden from both the Triad, which was probably still on his tail, and the Chinese government. I was aware of three of his aliases, but there could have been more. I knew he had a wife, but I didn't know anything about her, nor if they were still in touch.

But none of this mattered. I had my one-way ticket to Hong Kong, a passport, my First Aid kit and some clothes. Most importantly, I had an address.

This was all I needed to set out on my adventure.

Perseverance

Perseverance is a virtue that sustains us in our pursuits and reminds us of our intentions. Perseverance allows us to advance our goals, to master a subject, a job, an art.

Perseverance is close to the meaning of the word "Kung Fu": a great ability that is born of sacrifice, resolve and hard work.

Since I began martial arts over fifty years ago, I have never stopped persevering in my practice, my studies and my research. Perseverance has allowed me to become one with the art itself, and has shown me my path.

Insistence and persistence are the keys to always improving in life, and in Kung Fu. By persevering, we refine our bodies and our minds, and as a result, our souls.

Never lose sight of the guiding light of perseverance, even in moments of difficulty and duress. By persevering in martial arts, we not only improve our technique, but we also transform internally. Through the dynamic movement of our bodies, we enter a meditative state, getting to know ourselves and gaining a greater consciousness of our being.

Persevere with perseverance, with your eye on the horizon, and our hearts and minds will know no limits.

CHAPTER 3
Discovery

Finally, the time had come.

After years of fantasizing, meditating, and longing to travel to China, the cradle of Kung Fu, the day of discovery arrived.

Since I was a child, China had been the object of my desires, of my dreams, of the longest and most profound meditation I had experienced. China was the physical embodiment of the life choice I had made, the path I had embarked on and had persevered through day after day, in joy and hardship.

China was the birthplace of Fu Han Tong, my *sifu*. After his long years of exile in Australia, America, and Europe, it was to China, his home, that he had returned. To find Fu Han Tong, show him the progress I had made, and learn from him how to move forward, was the goal that I set out for myself the day he left Italy three years before. I planned my trip, stitching together all the fragments of information about China that I could gather. Month by month, I saved money. Year by year, I treasured that yellowing scrap of paper on which my *sifu* had scribbled a Hong Kong address. It was there that I hoped I could track him down; there, where my journey would begin.

At long last, the day had come when imagination and reality would meet.

On that trip, I discovered the stark contrast between the China of my dreams and the China of reality. The fantasy land of a twenty-year old Italian boy who had barely set foot outside his own country and the reality of early 1980s China were starkly different.

In my mind, I had imagined that Kung Fu was widespread in China, with masters, students and schools at every corner. This turned out to be true. In Hong Kong alone there were over two thousand *kwoon* at the time. On every street, often tucked away in a small building, there was a Kung Fu school. In fact, there was a much higher concentration of Kung Fu schools in Hong Kong than on the mainland, because many masters had been forced to flee the wrath of the Maoist cultural revolution. Hong Kong, like Macao and Singapore, was often where they escaped to. Many martial artists settled there. Others, like Fu Han Tong, travelled further afield to the West.

I thought Chinese Kung Fu would be similar to the martial arts I knew back home, and to the myriad of Kung Fu films and books I had devoured over the years. I thought that things in China would be exactly like that, and that there would be many more teachers, schools and students than in Italy. On the first count, I later discovered, I was completely wrong.

In my mind, Chinese Kung Fu masters looked the part: well-built, well-toned, and muscular, with elaborate uniforms, fearsome looks and imposing postures; they would have, in short, the *physique-du-rôle* of a *sifu.* Fu Han Tong himself, though he never wore expensive uniforms or showed off the art he had so skilfully mastered, certainly had the build of a *sifu.* I expected everyone to look just like him. I expected that all Chinese masters would dress and behave like him, too.

I also imagined a Chinese *kwoon* to be big, spacious, pristine and well-organized. I thought the lessons would be meticulously planned and structured according to different levels of ability and experience. I expected to find strict hierarchies of students who followed a well-defined curriculum, taught by experienced masters, who taught their classes at consistent times of day. In all honesty, this is not what I had experienced with Fu Han Tong. But I knew that my experience with him had been unique. I knew that, while he was a *sifu*, he had chosen not to teach formally or open a *kwoon* during his years abroad. As a fugitive, he had carefully concealed his identity in the anonymity of a carpenter's shop in Genoa. I knew that I had been Fu Han Tong's only student in Italy. So there had been no need for him to structure a school or a curriculum the way I gradually learned to do with my own *kwoon*.

The reality I discovered in Hong Kong on my first trip was dramatically different from what I had imagined. Masters rarely looked like masters. They were old or middle aged, and some had small builds, rounded shoulders and protruding bellies. But when they started to practice, their martial skills became clear: they were masters, without a doubt. Their unorthodox looks notwithstanding, their *Chi* was apparent in every move: power, explosiveness, agility and speed. But unless they chose to reveal themselves, they passed for average Joes. Rarely, if ever, did I see them wearing Kung Fu uniforms: no *yishang*, no belts. What they wore to teach and practice was what they wore in the streets: tracksuits, jeans, shirts and sweaters. There was no difference between how they looked inside or outside the *kwoon*.

The Hong Kong *kwoon* were equally lowkey. On the highly congested island and tip of the peninsula, space was a rare commodity. Shops, restaurants, offices, apartments and hotels were all, invariably, small. There were simply too many people squeezed onto such a small strip of land. Just like everything else, *kwoon* were rarely larger than one room. Along the edges of the room, stacked messily on shelves, hanging on walls, or simply piled on the floor, was a myriad of objects: weapons, training tools, punching bags, sandbags, woodmen (*muk yang chon*), lion masks, weights, boxing gloves, and perhaps a mirror or two to check one's form. Most important of all, in each and every *kwoon* there was an altar. It could be as small and bare or as large and ornate as space allowed. But on all altars there were the typical statuettes of *Fu*, *Lok*, and *Sao*, the gods of happiness, richness, and longevity, respectively; there was the statue of Kwan Kung, the legendary warrior, god of protection over the people; there were pictures of the *sifu*, often standing next to his seated master (*si gong*); and there were offerings of fruit, incense, and the unmistakable red envelopes with money for the master and for the maintenance of the school. In these small and crammed spaces, there was everything you could need for a lifetime of growth in the practice of martial arts. You didn't need anything else.

Kung Fu lessons were also very different from what I had imagined. Rarely, if ever, was there a structured lesson with a group of students, with a clear beginning and end. Students came and went from a *kwoon* throughout the day. The *sifu* did the same. He didn't arrive at set times to teach a group of students; rather, the *sifu* would drop by the *kwoon* when he happened to be around, stopping to teach or correct any students who happened to be practicing at the time. He would concede as much or as little time as he saw fit. Students appeared to have no expectations or demands; they simply took what the *sifu* offered. The rest of the time, they would practice on their own, at times for hours, at other times for a few minutes. The more time the students spent training in the *kwoon* and the more likely they would be to bump into the *sifu* and be present for his teachings, and therefore the faster their progress would be.

Not everything was casual, however. At times, the *sifu* would arrange to meet a student. But there seemed to be no standard rule to these private lessons, either in terms of frequency or duration. It depended entirely on the time, will, and whim of the master. As I had learned from Fu Han Tong in Genoa, the student would offer the *sifu* a bag of oranges and a red envelope with money inside as an exchange. The amount of money varied depending on the expectations of the master and what the student could afford. In my case, over the course of my first two months in China, I offered approximately three thousand Hong Kong dollars in red envelopes. Thanks to these offerings, I learned, trained, slept, and ate. Since life in the *kwoon* was all-encompassing, the money in the red envelopes essentially went towards an "all inclusive" stay.

In traditional Kung Fu, the *kwoon* served as the *sifu*'s home, library, and office. Often the traditional Kung Fu *sifu* was also a professional practitioner of traditional Chinese medicine, including acupuncture, acupressure, moxibustion, and similar treatments. Mastery of martial arts and knowledge of traditional medicine were intimately related. Sometimes it was precisely his expertise in Chinese medicine that drew him to Kung Fu. Often his main profession was doctor, while teaching Kung Fu was something he did on the side.

This was the traditional way of martial arts. As Kung Fu became popular in the West, particularly with the popularity of Bruce Lee movies, "Western" Kung Fu schools started popping up in Hong Kong and eventually in mainland China. Westerners interested in martial arts flocked to these schools, which were similar to Western gyms. Like in the West, a teacher taught classes at set times and with set payments at these schools. The students could pay for monthly membership or for a specific course, usually a Kung Fu form. These *kwoon,* which began to spread across Hong Kong in the '80s and through mainland China in the '90s, became money-making machines. The business attracted many real masters, and many charlatans, too. Fortunately, not all the serious masters went this way. Around three-quarters of the schools in Hong Kong at the time stuck to the traditional way of Kung Fu. As a Westerner, it was extremely difficult, if not impossible, to find, let alone be accepted, into these traditional schools, and to therefore experience the real Kung Fu.

I never encountered another Westerner at any of the various *kwoon* I visited in Hong Kong during that first trip. I was extremely lucky to be given access to that world, which is all but gone today.

The thread that united masters, schools and practitioners was the holistic and all-encompassing nature of Kung Fu. In the West, martial arts, or any sport for that matter, is self-contained, detached, and insulated from everyday life. To practice a sport or a martial art, one changes into separate clothes, at predetermined times, in specific locations. Once the time is up, clothes, activity and place change again, and life resumes its natural flow. The external, physical, and superficial dimensions of sports and martial arts in the West are paramount: appearance is key. In China, by contrast, there was no line that separated traditional Kung Fu from ordinary life: Kung Fu was ordinary life itself. The clothes were the same; practice and teaching time blended into the flow of the day; and the location was the same as for eating, sleeping, and working.

Moreover, in China, there was nothing separating the external and internal dimensions of martial arts. The physical ability of a martial artist was naturally connected to his or her talent and hard work. But these, in turn, were connected to the martial artist's character, from passion to perseverance, from determination to resilience, from generosity to humility. Most importantly, this all stemmed indistinguishably from the internal energy cultivated by the martial artist. Traditional Kung Fu in China was enmeshed into culture, tradition, religion, and habit. Kung Fu was simply life, and life itself was the essence of Kung Fu.

A bad start

It was the end of 1980 and I had just turned twenty. I hadn't travelled much before; I only spoke a few scattered words of

English; and I had a one-way ticket to Hong Kong and an address to search for. But three years had passed since I had last seen my *sifu.* I had no idea whether I could find him. I felt anxious, worried, and even bit scared, but I would not be deterred. Before I knew it, I had landed in Hong Kong.

I felt exhausted. I booked the cheapest itinerary I could find, so I had travelled for thirty hours, with several layovers across Europe, the Middle East and East Asia. I was jet-lagged and had never changed time zones before. When I stepped outside Kai Thak, the old Hong Kong airport, I was overwhelmed by the heat and humidity, by the crowds of unfamiliar Asians, by the languages I could not understand, and by the intensity of the smells in the air: a unique mixture of food, incense, and smog. The streets were packed with people, cars, bicycles and motorbikes. I felt lost and terribly lonely. I had no idea what to do, where to go, or whom to call.

But it was precisely these feelings that triggered my survival instincts. Amidst the crowd, I spotted a Western-looking couple who also appeared to be leaving Kai Thak. I ran up to them and asked them in broken English how to get to the city center. I was totally unfamiliar with the landscape of the city, and didn't know if that was anywhere near the address I was looking for. But it seemed like it would be a good place to start to get my bearings. The couple knew Hong Kong well. They knew that there was a city center on both Hong Kong island and on the tip of the peninsula in Kowloon. They escorted me to a taxi and asked the driver to take me to Tsim Tsa Tsui, the business and touristic neighbourhood of Kowloon.

It was early evening by then. The taxi dropped me off on bustling Nathan Road and I started wandering around with my bag on my shoulder. I began looking for a place to spend the night and recover from the exhausting trip before I began my search for Fu Han Tong in earnest the next morning. But all the hotels and guesthouses I encountered were either full or way too expensive for my tight budget. By midnight, I was still meandering down the streets of Tsim Tsa Tsui.

Suddenly, two young Chinese men walked up to me and shoved a business card in my hand. They spoke Cantonese, but I figured out they were recommending a guesthouse where I could spend the night. In that moment I felt relieved. I didn't have the time or energy to consider whether the two men looked trustworthy or not, what their intentions might be, or whether they meant trouble. I felt that I was in trouble already and whatever looked like a helping hand was no less than godsend.

The two men led me into a large building. At the entrance was a flashing neon sign proclaiming the building's name: Chum Kim. Inside was a veritable Babel of different nationalities: Vietnamese, Pakistani, Iranian, Iraqi, and, naturally, Chinese. The place was downtrodden, filthy, and sketchy, to put it mildly. Seeing the look on my face, the two men tried to reassure me, saying they would help me find a cheap room for the night. I had little choice but to follow them. We started walking through what felt like a maze of stairs and corridors, elevators and floors, through different sections of the building separated by gates. In the rooms we passed I saw gambling, prostitution, shady massage parlours, alcohol, and drugs. Had it been daytime, or had I been anywhere else back home, I would have turned on my heels and left. Nothing good could come out of such place. But I was there, exhausted, on the thirteenth floor of a labyrinthine building that I had no clue how to escape from. The two men opened a small gate, walked me through it, and closed it behind them. On the other side of the gate, a third man was waiting for us.

No sooner had the gate closed than the three men began shouting at me, ordering me to give them my money. Those petty criminals had probably pegged me a lost-looking Westerner who had just landed in Hong Kong and had some

US or Hong Kong dollars on him, which indeed I did. Easy prey. I pretended not to understand what they were saying. Bracing for the worst, I put down my bag. Then one them grabbed my arm and instinct kicked in. With a side kick—*pang tek*—I hit him hard in the ribs. I jabbed the second man in the face. The third man jumped back, his back to the wall. Right at that moment, a door flung open. An old man in a vest with an authoritative look on his face began shouting at the three men, visibly upset by what was going on. The three stepped back and froze. Whoever the old man was, he obviously commanded their respect. I seized my bag, hurrying to the gate. The door was locked. With a nod, the old man signalled to the third man with his back to the wall to unlock the gate for me. As soon as he did, I slipped out, and didn't look back once.

Lost in the dark alleys of Chum Kim, I looked for a way out. After many flights of stairs, endless corridors, and several dead ends, I finally bumped into a prostitute, to whom I somehow managed to explain that I was looking for the exit. With an understanding smile, she invited me to follow her through several more gates that she unlocked for me and up to an elevator that finally took me to the ground floor.

I was back at square one, only more tired, stressed and distressed than I'd been a couple hours before. Despite, or possibly because of my martial arts practice, I rarely found myself obliged to use it out on the street. In fact, apart from a few playful skirmishes back home, I only remember one significant episode that had taken place a year before. It was Easter Sunday, and I was in Genoa waiting for a bus in front of the Augustus cinema. A gang fight broke out before my eyes, and I was attacked and pushed into the mix. I tried to extricate myself using my Kung Fu. The fight ended with two ambulances being called in for the six boys who had attacked me.

But back then, I was in the comfort zone of my hometown. Now I was on the other side of the planet, with no one to help me and nowhere to go. With my bag on my shoulder, I started wandering around the streets once again, lost in a starless and eerily silent Hong Kong night. I finally came across a small park and sat down on a bench. I slipped my money and passport in my underwear, lay my head on my bag and fell asleep, exhausted.

Finding Fu Han Tong

I opened my eyes a couple of hours later with the first rays of misty morning light. I had hardly slept, but at least it was morning and I had a full day ahead to find the address I carefully guarded in my pocket. I did have a map, but it turned out to be completely useless. I needed help. I began stopping passers-by, asking them for directions as best I could. As I did, I found myself walking up Nathan Road, past Tsim Tsa Tsui and into the depths of Kowloon. I walked and asked for help, asked for help and walked some more. No one seemed to be able to help me.

I had been wandering around for six hours when finally a young man recognized the neighborhood where the street name I was after might be: Sam Sui Po. That was a first step at least. A while later, I made it to Sam Sui Po. I began looking for the right street once again. After countless other enquiries, I found the right address. There was no recognizable sign there. No shop or restaurant, let alone anything remotely related to Kung Fu. Apparently, no one was there. There was a small gate ajar that led to a staircase. On the first floor, there was a door and to its side was the street number I had desperately searched for hours on end. I waited there for a while, hoping someone would show up. Eventually an elderly man did. I approached him, but he waved me away, as if to say that he could be of no help.

Half an hour later, another man walked up the stairs. This time, I wasn't going to let him go. I held my yellowed note up to his face. He nodded, suggesting that I was in the right place. Relieved, I muttered, "Kung Fu." To my joy, the man nodded again, pointing to another door nearby with old painted characters on it. With a rush of newfound energy, I knocked on the door. After a few long moments, a man peered out, eying me with suspicion. I pronounced Fu Han Tong's name, hoping he would recognize it. He did not.

My dreams started crumbling before my eyes. The address was correct. In one way or another, that place was related to Kung Fu. It was obvious that Fu Han Tong had meant for me to come here. But my *sifu* was no longer there. Three years was a long time in the life of a fugitive. He could have been anywhere by then. Had I not found any clues in that place, tracing him down in a country the size of a continent would have been next to impossible.

In a last desperate attempt, I whispered the second name my *sifu* used in order to conceal his identity. Taken aback, the man looked up at me. Yes, he recognized that name! We stared at each other, his bewilderment matching my excitement. The man told me that Fu Han Tong was not there, but would probably arrive later that afternoon. He showed me in, inviting me to sit down on a low wooden stool. I could wait there if I so wished. That was the first time I entered a Chinese *kwoon*. It was a small room, packed with old weapons, a couple of worn-out punching bags, and several paintings on the walls of characters and other symbols. There was the unmistakable altar, with its typical statuettes and offerings.

I walked in and sat down. As I looked around the *kwoon*, the countless times I had imagined my reunion with Fu Han Tong came flooding back to my mind. I tried to reconcile those fantasies with the reality I was living then and there, exhausted but excited. One hour passed, followed by another, and another. I felt anxious, but not impatient. I was in the right place. Sooner or later, Fu Han Tong would show up. A few hours made no difference to me in the big scheme of things. After three long years, I was going to see my *sifu* once again.

Finally, at 3 P.M., after I'd waited four hours, the door opened. Two Chinese men walked in. One was Fu Han Tong. I immediately stood up and performed my *Lai.* We were across the room from each other and I wanted to run up to him, hug him, show him all my joy and excitement. But to my dismay, when I looked him in the eye, I received a cold and blank stare back. Rather than walking towards me, he turned away and headed towards a small door to the right of the room.

I froze. Was he angry? Was he upset or annoyed to see me? Or, worse still, did he not recognize me at all? Did Fu Han Tong, the man who for eight years had been a teacher and a second father to me, who was perhaps the most important person in my life, not even know who I was? Could three years have erased all his memories? Did everything we went through together mean nothing to him?

Stunned and desperate, I sat down on my stool. I felt lost, and I didn't know what to do. A few minutes later, the two men walked into the room again. Instinctively, I stood up and walked to Fu Han Tong. I introduced myself to him, assuming he did not remember me. With the same blank look, he replied that he knew who I was. I didn't know whether to be relieved or even more upset. He remembered me alright, but obviously was not very pleased to see me. That seemed like the only possible explanation. Fu Han Tong asked me when I had arrived in Hong Kong and why I had come. I told him the plain truth: I had landed the day before and spent all my savings in order to visit him and to continue to walk the path of a Kung Fu student. I reminded him that he had given me that address three years ago, telling me that it would have been the best way to reach him. He nodded, finally appearing to remember. But just as stone-faced as before, he explained that that was not his home, nor his *kwoon*. It was his friend's *kwoon*. He asked me coldly where I was staying. When I told him that I had nowhere to stay, he appeared completely unmoved by the fact that I had travelled the world to see him and had nowhere to lay my head.

At that point, his friend, a total stranger to me, and obviously the *sifu* of the *kwoon* where I had been patiently waiting, came to the rescue. With a sympathetic look, he told me that there were several cheap guesthouses in Sam Sui Po. He kindly offered to escort me to one so I could settle in and get some rest. I accepted gratefully. The two of us left the *kwoon*, but Fu Han Tong stayed behind. *Sifu* Chan Wan Li, as I eventually learned was his name, helped me check into a modest but decent guesthouse. On his way out, he proposed, almost as an afterthought, that we have dinner together that evening. I naturally accepted.

That evening I dined with *sifu* Chan Wan Li, Fu Han Tong and a few of their acquaintances. Finally, my *sifu* slowly began opening up. The ice between us very gradually started melting. He asked me about my life in Genoa, my practice, and my school. I replied to all his questions and tried to convey to him how happy I was to see him. There was so much more that I wanted to say. I wanted to tell him every detail about my *kwoon* in Genoa, about its expansion to the rest of Italy. I wanted to recount all the sacrifices I had made in those years, but also all my accomplishments. I wanted him to know how much I had longed to visit China, how much I had been looking forward to my reunion with him. I wanted to share my anxieties and fears about that trip, and my steadfast determination to pursue my dream nevertheless. I wanted to tell him all this, and much more. But partly because of language constraints and partly because of the jovial atmosphere of the evening, I didn't. I limited myself to conveying the basics, hoping that future opportunities would allow for more in-depth conversation. I was grateful enough to be with him. As if reading my mind, before saying farewell that evening, he reassured me that we would have other opportunities to catch up.

Discovering Kung Fu in Hong Kong

During my first week in Hong Kong, I was allowed to attend *Sifu* Chan Wan Li's *kwoon*, a traditional school of the southern style of Choy Lee Fut, while I stayed in the guesthouse nearby. Back in Genoa, Fu Han Tong had introduced me to Choy Lee Fut, a highly effective combat system featuring wide circular movements, which had become popular during the mid-19th century, during the British Opium Wars and the revolts against the Manchurian government. In those first weeks in Hong Kong, I deepened my knowledge of the style significantly, learning forms from different *lineages* from the ones I knew, with the specificities of their techniques, systems, and secrets. My daily routine revolved around the *kwoon.* In that small space, I learned from *Sifu* Chan Wan Li and occasionally from *Sifu* Fu Han Tong as well. I trained on my own or with the students of the school, I studied, and, in my spare time I hung out, ate, and drank with the people I encountered there. Soon I was fully immersed in life at the *kwoon.* I did what I was told and went with the flow of life around me without demands, expectations, or wishes. I was there to learn, to absorb, and to embrace everything that came my way. It was all new to me, from the precious pearls of knowledge about Kung Fu to the most mundane aspects of social life: it was all an experience to be cherished.

After a week at *Sifu* Chan Wan Li's school, Fu Han Tong introduced me to another *kwoon* in the same neighbourhood, this time specializing in Loon Yin, a style traced to the Hakka ethnic minority in southern China. Inspired by a dragon with magic and esoteric powers, the Loon Yin moves like a reptile and a cat at the same time, with quick and precise moves that are mostly performed with the arms. This style was entirely new to me. Luckily for me, *Sifu* Wong Kwook's *kwoon* was better organized and had more students than the Choy Lee Fut school, which helped me learn this new style quickly. I was also allowed to sleep in a small room in the *kwoon* itself.

My days in Hong Kong were extremely busy. I was happy because I was training in Kung Fu and learning from my *sifu* and from his colleagues. I felt accepted by them, and at times even welcomed. The training was difficult, but it didn't scare me. I was very used to it. Most of all, I knew I was extremely lucky to be having an experience that was almost unheard of for a foreigner. I knew that without Fu Han Tong's introductions, the traditional world of Kung Fu in Hong Kong would have been inaccessible.

But my stay was not easy. And not only because of the language barrier (I knew very little Cantonese); I had developed good relationships with the masters, but I couldn't say the same for their students. Among my fellow practitioners, the atmosphere was hostile to say the least. I felt rejected: they saw me as an alien and an in intruder. Some were extremely distant and reserved with me; others eyed me with suspicion; others still condescended to me. I often felt lonely, confused and at a loss as to how to behave. During trainings, they made me uncomfortable by deliberately putting me on the spot: they liked to show off while pointing out my mistakes.

As long as I trained on my own, repeating the sequence of a form, training with a weapons, or using punching bags, I could deal with this dynamic. The problems began when we trained in pairs. My peers made it crystal clear to me that I was not welcome, and this annoyed me tremendously. They acted lazy, avoided me, or deliberately overdid it, losing control over their techniques with me. I struggled to find the right balance in my reactions. On the one hand, if I behaved in the same way, the situation would get out of hand. On the other, I could not allow myself to be disrespected in this way by my peers. As much as I could, I avoided getting into sticky situations, but when it happened, I had no choice but to react.

As weeks passed and my training in the two schools intensified, the situation became increasingly tense and untenable. I had to speak to Fu Han Tong. I suspected that he knew about the situation, but I wasn't entirely sure. He came and went from Hong Kong and may not have been aware of my daily travails. Either way, I needed his advice. When I opened up to him, he was uncharacteristically warm. He explained to me that as a foreigner, my fellow students considered me to be a *Kwai Lo*: a "white devil." A white man had never set foot in those traditional Kung Fu settings. Had he not recommended me to his colleagues, it would have been unthinkable for me to stay there. So while the masters had accepted me, as a personal favour to Fu Han Tong, the students had not, and were trying their best to get rid of me without explicitly breaking the formal rules of the *kwoon.* Fu Han Tong told me that, though he wasn't aware of any details, he had known all along that this would happen. It was simply the price I had to pay to be there. This, he said, would be theme of my stay in China, now and going forward.

Fu Han Tong warned me not to trust the students, and to never lower my guard with them. He told me never to appear weak or defenceless, and to always put maximum effort into anything I was taught there, into any technique I performed. At the same time, I should show my unconditional respect for the school, the *sifu*, and the style. He told me never to show off my ability or demonstrate all I knew, as it would have only made things worse. Above all, I had to avoid revealing my knowledge of styles other than the one practiced in the school.

Doing so would have made me object of derision and scorn; knowing more than one style was considered blasphemous.

That was one of the few occasions on which Fu Han Tong made explicit reference to his own life and upbringing. True, he was Chinese and was never considered a *Kwai Lo* like me. But he had had a unique education, migrating from one *kwoon* to another, from city to city, region to region; he came into contact with many different styles and lineages over the course his life. Plus, he had lived in the West and was well aware of the many ways in which life there was different from life in China. But his story was the exception, not the norm. Most of the people I would encounter in the world of traditional Kung Fu in China had never left their country, region, or even city. Most of them had never set foot outside their neighbourhood or had official schooling, and had lived within one *kwoon* all their life. For them, the *kwoon*, the *sifu*, and the style were the only things they knew. So it had to be, by definition, the best. When they were exposed to difference and novelty, their typical reaction was to shut down and become defensive and disparaging about anything beyond the narrow confines of their world. It was simply a natural defence mechanism that I had to accept.

Given this, it wasn't easy to strike a balance in my interactions at the *kwoon*. I was there to learn and much of the Kung Fu I was exposed to in Hong Kong was new to me. This was particularly true at the Loon Yin school. I had to learn and train on my own before I could demonstrate my ability and be on par with my fellow students, who had been practicing those forms and techniques for many years. At the same time, I couldn't stray outside the boundaries of what I was taught, lest I betray my knowledge about different styles, which would further complicate my relationships with my peers. During group training sessions, it was obvious that different students had different levels of skill, but these differences were seen as normal. There was no risk of the situation getting out of hand.

But during freestyle sparring, when instinct and experience inevitably come into play, it was difficult for me to stick to the techniques I had just learned rather than draw on my full breadth of knowledge of Kung Fu. As a guest, I tried as best I could to always honour the school and *sifu;* but when I had to defend myself, it became clear to everyone around me that my Kung Fu toolkit was far richer and more varied than theirs. I was constantly seeking the right balance between paying respect to others, and commanding respect for myself. It was a lesson I learned during that first trip to Hong Kong and which I have carried with me since.

The underground scene

One day, about a month into my visit to Hong Kong, *Sifu* Wong Kwook asked me to fight against his best student. There were a lot of people present at the *kwoon* that day, including Fu Han Tong. At first I didn't know whether it was meant to be a competitive fight or a free-sparring session. But as soon as the fight began, I realized that my opponent's goal was nothing less than a K.O. My instinct and experience kicked in as I shed all the stylistic limitations I'd imposed on myself in the previous weeks. Without overdoing it, I quickly prevailed over my adversary. I was winning. Once *Sifu* Wong Kwok saw the writing on the wall, he ended the fight. Fu Han Ton congratulated me and praised me to his colleague Wong Kwook, who also had warm words for me. That was my last day in the Loon Yin *kwoon*. It was probably the first day Fu Han Tong started seeing me as more than just a student. I didn't see this at all at the time, but it became clear to me later: in that moment, the seed that would eventually poison our relationship was planted.

The following day, Fu Han Tong took me to a third *kwoon*, this time specializing in Wing Chun, a style that was created by two women in the seventeenth century and stemmed from the Shaolin tradition. With its emphasis on speed and continuity of attack, Wing Chun had become one of the best-known self-defence systems worldwide over the centuries. Wing Chun was not new to me; *Sifu* Fu Han Tong had introduced me to it in Genoa. At the school of *Sifu* Chang Chen (also known as Chang Fai) in Hong Kong, I continued the study of Wing Chun in the same *lineage* as the one I'd studied with Fu Han Tong. Originally developed in Foshan, in the province of Guangdong, this *lineage* derived from Luk I Chay and Lam Chun, unlike the Wing Chun I would eventually learn on my later visits to China, which derived from the lineage of the iconic Ip Man, who is credited for popularizing Wing Chun in the rest of the world.

I left my room in the Loon Yin school and settled in another guesthouse a few minutes' walk away from the Wing Chun school. For the last few weeks of my visit, I stayed with a family, who were apparently acquaintances of Fu Han Tong's. In those days, I also intensified my training with Fu Han Tong himself. We used to meet at dawn in a small park in the Sam Sui Po neighbourhood. It was then that I discovered the beauty of Hong Kong's green corners, where hundreds of people would gather each morning to practice their Kung Fu, normally Tai Chi, as well as Chi Kung and other internal practices.

Sifu Chang Chen's *kwoon* often organized sparring tournaments, gathering the best fighters from his and other Kung Fu schools. In Hong Kong in those years, Wing Chun and Choy Lee Fut fighters were known as the strongest. Fu Han Tong explained to me that the tournaments were an important feature of the Kung Fu world both in Hong Kong and in mainland China. The spirit and approach of these tournaments were very different from sporting events in the West. In China, the aim of these gatherings was to determine an unspoken hierarchy between styles, schools, and masters. Fighters from different schools, practising different styles and following different masters, would challenge each other to determine which style, school, and *sifu* came out on top.

The tournaments were necessary for honouring a style, school, and master. When Fu Han Tong first explained this to me, I was immediately fascinated and intrigued. I didn't see anything wrong with these tournaments. On the contrary, I believed they provided meaning and value to the practice, which was, after all, martial. The value of a school, I thought, should be determined not by its size and wealth, but by the strength and ability of its students. I also understood the risks and dangers involved, but this was an integral part of Chinese the Kung Fu, and so I immersed myself in it.

Of course, it turned out to not be so straightforward.

On a much more practical level, the hierarchies that emerged from these tournaments determined territorial control over the city. In a city with over two thousand *kwoon*, the competition was fierce. The tournaments became a necessary means to achieve territorial conquest, legitimacy, and mere existence. The most successful schools, which brought the best fighters, could have control over the smaller schools in their neighbourhood. But this "patronage" and "protection" did not come for free: regardless of the style they practiced, the smaller schools had to pay their dues to exist in the same neighbourhood as the larger ones. For any master and school just starting out, it was an uphill struggle; the better their fighters, the quicker their school's name and status would rise. Alliances were often formed between schools to consolidate power. This is where the expression "Kung Fu brothers" came from: a joining of forces to strengthen one group of schools against others. It was a mafia-style "survival of the fittest." No one could escape this system. Even highly respected figures, such as the legendary Ip Man, had to fight for their space, reputation, and status this way.

At a baser level still—as was often the case in China, where materialistic culture prevails—money was a factor in these tournaments, too: masters bet on their respective students. As I would learn over the course of my regular trips, these fighting matches were a veritable business; the vicious cycle of money and power overshadowed the ethics of Kung Fu. An entire generation of masters made their living this way. When Fu Han Tong saw me fight at the Loon Yin school, he probably realized for the first time that I was not only a talented student he could show off with pride, but that I also represented a business opportunity for him. In Italy, this dimension of our relationship had been completely absent. No wonder had he never mentioned this underground world to me during our years together in Genoa. When he rediscovered me in Hong Kong, he understood that I had the physical, mental, and spiritual characteristics of a successful fighter. Fu Han Tong was faithful to neither style nor *kwoon*. In addition to pride, it was money that reignited his interest in me as a fighter.

But it took time for me to truly understand the world of the underground Kung Fu scene in China. At the time, I could only see the positive side of my master's explanation to me, and not its underbelly. Fu Han Tong explained that these tournaments were very common, not only in Hong Kong but also in mainland China. He had often participated in them before his escape from China. He did not deny the illicit nature of that world, but justified it in the context of Maoist China's ban on traditional Kung Fu. This explained why the tournaments were more common in Hong Kong, Macao and Singapore than in authoritarian mainland China. But that didn't change the fact that the tournaments were illegal in Hong Kong and in the rest of Asia. They were held in secret, in warehouses, on the rooftops of skyscrapers or in the basements of restaurants and shops, hidden from the watchful gaze of the authorities. They were also considered illegal because that there were no rules and no protections. It was not unusual for the fights to end in serious injuries. At times, they ended with death.

At the time, I only saw the romantic, even ethical, side of that world. In the West, competitions were highly individualistic: with all their cups and trophies, they were about personal pride and satisfaction, which often spilled into egocentrism and selfishness. In contrast, the fighting scene in China was communitarian and relational: it was about paying respect to and demonstrating the value of a style and its centuries-old genealogy. In the West, tournaments were highly regulated and protected, with strict rules, referees, judges, and physical protections. Just like its shiny gyms and fancy sporting gear, Western competition was insulated from the untidiness, ugliness and risk of real life. In China, fighting was unruly and lawless, it was violent, it was dark, and it was dirty. It was certainly dangerous. But precisely because of this, it was true to the essence of life itself.

I was nearing the end of my first stay in Hong Kong. I had been there for almost two months and the time had come for me to go home. My family, and Angela in particular, missed me tremendously. I missed them too. Over the previous eight weeks, I had managed to phone home only twice. Telephoning the West from the East in those years was not a simple affair, even from the relatively open Hong Kong. There were only a few international telephone centres, and they were always extremely busy. I had to queue for hours on end to get minute or two on a bad connection with Genoa. This meant that Angela was constantly worried about me. She later told me how much she panicked after days and sometimes weeks went by without any news from me. She feared the worst and often contemplated jumping on a plane in a desperate attempt to find me. It was time for me to return. Plus, I had gone two months without any direct oversight of my *kwoon*, which by now had expanded to many cities.

A few days before my return home and after his long explanation of the underground Kung Fu world in China, Fu Han Tong announced that he had organized a fight for me: it would take place in two days' time, in a restaurant storage room. That was all he told me. He didn't say one word about who my adversary was or the rules of engagement. In fact, he told me that he and my adversary's *sifu* would agree on the terms on the day of the fight itself.

I arrived at the restaurant around 4 P.M. on fight day. We walked down a narrow passageway into a dimly lit basement that held extra tables and chairs. These had been stacked to one side, clearing the spacious room with its unpaved cement floor. Sitting on stools along each side of the room were approximately fifteen middle-aged men. I had no idea whether they were Kung Fu masters, friends or random acquaintances. The only extra bit of information I managed to glean that day was that my adversary, and therefore his school and *sifu*, specialized in Nam Siu Lam, or southern Kung Fu styles. The actual style itself was unspecified. After exchanging a few brief words with his colleague, Fu Han Tong told me that he and my adversary's *sifu* had agreed that the fight would be relatively relaxed: if one of us fell after a hit, we would pause the fight and the two masters would decide whether or not to continue. He also told me that I was free to draw on all the techniques I knew, and did not need to avoid hitting any body part; the only prohibited move was the snake-head or spear-shaped hand (*tour se*), which aimed at the eyes.

Five minutes before the fight, I finally laid eyes on my adversary. I had no time to study his build and attitude. We performed the ritual salute, *Lai,* standing five metres apart. A referee signalled the start of the fight. It lasted a few minutes. After a few exploratory moves from both of us, I faked a low kick and then landed a circular kick (*chull tek*) on his head. He stumbled, disoriented, and as he did, I hit him a second time, finishing him off with a K.O. The fight had ended. My adversary was quickly helped out of the room; I never saw him again. My blows had been strong, but I knew that he was not badly injured.

To my surprise, his *sifu* remained in the room. Even more surprisingly, the group who had watched the fight, including my adversary's master, was gathered upstairs in the restaurant within an hour, eating jovially together. Fu Han Tong was in high spirits and, by his standards, extremely warm and congratulatory with me. I didn't grasp every word he said, but I understood that he was praising me to his friends and telling them the story of how we knew each other, dating back to his years as an exile in Italy. I felt proud and happy. I thought I had defended my *sifu*'s honor, demonstrating to him and to everyone present the value of his teachings, my ability and perseverance, and my unconditional commitment to Kung Fu. On top of that, it was fun: it was a game, after all, and I had won. The fact that Fu Han Tong's happiness that day was due not only to pride but also to the money in his pockets didn't even cross my mind. As I said before, it was only much later that I began to see the other side of the coin.

My first adventure comes to an end

My trip to Hong Kong was a first taste of the world of traditional Kung Fu. I was a foreigner, and I didn't come across a single other Westerner in those months who had been as fully immersed in it as I had. I had entered a mysterious and fascinating world, a world that had been the object of all my dreams and desires since childhood.

The journey also allowed me to discover a new side of Fu Han Tong, a far more "Chinese" side than the one I had known during my childhood and adolescence in Genoa. My *sifu* had always been a tough and unsentimental man. During the eight years I spent with him in Genoa, I had rarely seen him smile, open up, or display even the slightest emotion, particularly in front of me. He had always been strict and not particularly talkative. But the man and master I discovered in Hong Kong was different. By comparison, what I'd seen in Genoa was his human side. Back in his homeland, any bit of softness was gone. He was back in his world and wanted to make sure I knew it. I had to adapt to him, not the other way around. He left the city five days before my departure. He barely said goodbye, and didn't even ask me how I was going to get home.

But the uniqueness of my first experience in Hong Kong was not limited to what I saw and learned. Above all, I learned something about myself. In those two months, I discovered the full extent of my love, passion, and dedication to Kung Fu. I appreciated more fully my perseverance and, most of all, my resilience, which was a quality that would emerge ever more clearly as the years went by. During those weeks in Hong Kong, far more than in my previous twenty years in Italy, my capacity to bend without breaking was put to the test. I knew I had that gift. It had grown during the harshness of Fu Han Tong's teachings that I endured when I was little more than a child, to the years of friction with my family, to the many hardships during military service, and to the hurdles I encountered while setting up my school.

In Hong Kong, however, my resilience became fully apparent in all its power. Just as certain metals can bend but not break, so can human beings. It's a quality that is cultivated through experience and hard work. My first stay in Hong Kong presented a series of situations that repeatedly tested my resilience: I came in contact with food, culture and traditions that were unfamiliar to me, from my traumatic arrival story of getting lost, conned, and attacked, to Fu Han Tong's ice-cold greeting after three years of longing to re-join him, to the hostility of my fellow Kung Fu practitioners, to the dangers of the underground fighting world I had set foot in. My ability to adapt and react in the face of difficulty was put to the test like never before.

But beyond what I lived in Hong Kong, it was what I missed there that represented the biggest challenge. The trip was not just a discovery of the Kung Fu world in the East; it was also a trip within myself, of self-discovery. For the first time in my life, I made contact with my emotional and sentimental side. It was a part of me I had never fully encountered. It was revealed to me by being so far from home, the homesickness I felt and the emptiness it created in me, made even more acute by the harshness of my life in Hong Kong and the difficulty of communicating with my loved ones.

After two months, I was ready to go home. The trip had been so intense that there were a few moments where I told myself I would never visit again. I was exhausted. At the same time, I was filled with an energy I'd never had before. I had lived through the many hardships of that world, but I had found myself in the process and loved every second of it. And I still had yet to notice its dark sides: the jealousies, materialism, and corruption of the Kung Fu world in China had escaped me altogether. Despite its harshness, I had only seen its purity, value, and honour.

Yes, I was happy to return home.

But deep down I knew I would be back soon.

Discovery

A sense of discovery is innate in human beings. We seek to discover that which is unknown to us or simply a figment of our imagination. I wanted to see with my own eyes what I had heard from others or imagined myself. It was time to discover my magic, Eastern world.

Human beings have always sought to discover new horizons, to take a risk that might land them in paradise or hell, in peace or at war, Yin or Yang. Without the desire to discover, we would not gain knowledge or power; the desire to know and conquer illuminates the path that leads us to discovery.

My first trip to China, lived through meditation, finally became a reality.

With a sense of stupor that swung from joy to disappointment, I discovered that the real China was different from my imaginary East. Much of what I saw reflected my master's stories or my many readings about the country, but the differences were enormous nonetheless. I was disappointed to see that not all Chinese people were martial artists or respected the values of Kung Fu. At the same time, I was amazed by many marvellous discoveries that I could never have imagined. On that first trip and others that came later, I saw the authentic culture and traditions of the Chinese. Most importantly, I discovered the attitude that allows us to discover: the physical, mental, and spiritual Zen of emptiness, void of images and expectations, pure, present, and ready to soak in everything that comes our way. This is precisely the attitude we learn when we practice martial arts: through our emptiness, we become open to receiving the message and treasure of discovery.

CHAPTER 4
Enrichment

When I landed in Genoa, I was exhausted. My mind and body were caught in a whirlwind of memories and emotions, struggling to digest everything I had seen, done, and lived during those intense months in Hong Kong. At the same time, I was happy. In Hong Kong, I had missed my family, first and foremost Angela, whom I had only had the chance to speak with twice. I was looking forward to seeing her, eager to tell her all my stories. I was also excited to pick up where I had left off at my *kwoon*, and I was anxious to see how my students had done during my time away.

But the most powerful memory I have of that first return from Hong Kong has to do with my *Chi*. Even though I was exhausted, I felt like I had been imbued with newfound energy. I felt like a tank that had been refilled to the top, like a car that was ready to roar to life with fresh fuel. I was recharged.

I was keen to channel this energy into my school. My journey had enriched my Kung Fu practice significantly. And my Kung Fu was part and parcel of my *kwoon*, with which I wanted to share that enrichment. The standard curriculum of the school remained unchanged: the point was not to import new techniques, forms, or styles from Hong Kong to Genoa via a conveyor belt. Over time, I certainly did enrich the program by drawing on my martial experiences in China, but not after that first trip. It was a different form of enrichment I sought to convey. It was more intangible and diffuse, and had more to do with culture, tradition, and symbols than with techniques, forms, and styles. I was eager to convey the essence of what I had learned in Hong Kong, not its practical, superficial, and material aspects.

After a few days of rest, I was on the road again. My constant travel between my students in Genoa and in central Italy resumed. I was pleased to see my students, reassured by their unwavering commitment and devotion, and delighted to witness their newfound curiosity and enthusiasm. I focused my teaching on the most advanced students, since I had relied on them during my frequent absences. My life on the road was hard work, but the buds were blooming. There was now a substantial group of advanced students who were determined to make Kung Fu and the *kwoon* a central part of their lives. Those were the students I had to invest in: they were the building blocks of the edifice I was constructing. Someday they might become instructors at the school and contribute firsthand to its growth. They were key figures for the *kwoon* as well as for my own personal growth: I would count on their presence the next time I left.

As the weeks passed, what had been a faint intuition on the day of my return from Hong Kong solidified into a conviction. My personal enrichment in the world of martial arts, and therefore the development and success of my school and students, meant that my trip to Hong Kong could not be a one-off. Travelling to the East was no longer simply the realization of a childhood dream; it would be a place of repeated nourishment for me as an adult martial artist, with an insatiable desire to learn and grow.

In early 1982, only eight months after my return to Genoa, I headed to Hong Kong once again.

A sharp contrast

This time I felt no anxiety about the trip. At home, my *kwoon* was fairly well-structured and organized. Unlike the first time, the thought of leaving my school unsupervised for a few months did not worry me. My advanced students were sufficiently on top of things. They would manage without me for a while. Moreover, Hong Kong was not an unknown to me anymore. Although it would take years, not months, for me to really get to know the vibrant city I had fallen in love with, I left for my second trip with much more than just a scrap of paper in my pocket. I was as curious, excited, and eager to learn as I'd been the first-time round. But I had clearer ideas of where to go and what I would find. For one, I knew where to locate *Sifu* Fu Han Tong. At the end of the day, that was all I needed.

Upon my arrival, I easily found my *sifu*. We spent a few weeks together in Hong Kong, following a similar pattern as the last time. He introduced me to different masters and their respective *kwoon*. I learned new forms and techniques. I trained alone and with other students. Most importantly, I met with Fu Han Tong regularly, enriching my Kung Fu through his teachings in the magical atmosphere of Hong Kong's parks at dawn. What I did not do in those first, somewhat easy-going weeks in Hong Kong was step back into the city's underground Kung Fu world. Fu Han Tong had not arranged any fights for me, nor had I asked him to.

One morning, three weeks into the trip, *Sifu* Fu Han Tong greeted me with an uncharacteristic smile. He proudly announced that he had obtained a residence permit on the mainland: the time had come for him to go home. Even though he was from the mainland, he had fled, changed his identity and therefore lost his Chinese papers. Now he had new documents. As a "new man," he could finally return home. Beyond the question of legality, he must have known that it was safe for him to return.

I wondered what this meant for me. True, I was now acclimatized to Hong Kong. I knew my way around town and had more than a handful of *kwoon* I could rely on. But my entry point to every school had been Fu Han Tong. With him gone, I wasn't sure if I would still be welcome. Moreover, while I was always keen to know new schools and masters, Fu Han Tong was the one from whom I learned and wanted to learn the most. He was my *sifu*, and aside from my unconditional commitment to him, I strongly believed that he was unrivalled amongst the masters I met.

I was just beginning to mull these questions over when, to my delight, Fu Han Tong asked me to join him in mainland China. Without thinking twice, I accepted; it was another important part of my dream coming true. The only problem was bureaucracy: my visa only covered Hong Kong, not mainland China. Fu Han Tong reassured me in his typically nonchalant way. He knew a travel agency in Hong Kong that would fix our problem.

Indeed, a few days later I had a freshly minted visa for the People's Republic of China. The rules and regulations for a tourist's entry into communist China in the early 1980s were stringent. It was only in the second half of the decade that Deng Xiaoping's opening of the country to the West took hold, particularly after the 1984 agreement with the United Kingdom whereby Hong Kong would return to Chinese rule in 1997, though maintaining self-government for fifty years. But in 1982, movement between Hong Kong and the People's Republic was heavily restricted and regulated. In order to obtain my visa, I had to sign endless declarations documenting in minute detail all the possessions I brought along with me, from clothes and personal accessories to cameras and camera lenses. I also had to obtain and carry the Chinese tourist currency: Fan. As a Western tourist, it was illegal for me to possess and use Chinese Yuan. The Fan severely limited foreigners' ability to move freely around the country, as only a few scattered places accepted the tourist currency. The Fan allowed the government to keep track of foreigners, monitoring their movements so as to be able to intervene at the slightest indication of politically suspect activity. No less problematic for me, using the Fan was terribly expensive. Everything was three or four times more expensive than the equivalent in Yuan. Fu Han Tong reassured me once again: once we were in China, we would work something out.

We were ready, and set off by train for Guangzhou/Canton. The minute we crossed the border into the People's Republic, the difference hit me like a cold shower: I was in a different and completely unfamiliar world. Up until then, Hong Kong to me had been as Chinese as it got. To me, the hustle and bustle, the chaos, the bright neon lights, the crammed tiny spaces and the exhilarating sense of freedom of Hong Kong represented China.

I found none of this in the "real" China. The crowds were there, of course. But unlike in Hong Kong, people were all dressed in the same dull and dreary uniforms. There were no smiling passers-by or couples holding hands in sight. The only colours that stood out were the red collars and stars on the caps of the unmistakable Red Guards eyeing scared and weary-looking citizens.

The wealth of Hong Kong was nothing but a memory in Guangzhou. Though I immediately noticed floods of people walking and an endless stream of bikes, there were no cars or other vehicles. The buildings in Canton were on average much larger than those in Hong Kong, but they looked dull and run-down. We were only a few hours away by train, but even the temperature was different, much cooler in Canton than in the hot and humid Hong Kong.

After a painfully slow visit to customs, in which all my possessions and documents were carefully inspected, I finally arrived in Canton. In town, I settled in a plain but decent guest-house. The place was relatively cheap, but Fu Han Tong explained almost apologetically that it was costing me about four times as much as the equivalent price in Chinese Yuan. I had just arrived in the People's Republic and knew those were the rules. But I trusted that my *sifu* would soon figure out a way for me to get around like a local.

That experience in Guangdong, in the early 1980s, was difficult and terribly lonely. By comparison, Hong Kong had been a piece of cake. Hardly anyone spoke a word of English and written signposts were exclusively in Chinese. More difficult than the language barrier was the human one: people were extremely closed-off, suspicious, and reluctant to answer even the most basic of questions, let alone to socialize. I felt unwanted and left to fend for myself.

Perhaps most shocking of all was the way Fu Han Tong changed when we crossed the border. During my first trip the year before, I had come to terms with the Hong Kong version of Fu Han Tong: colder and less humane than the Genoese Fu Han Tong of my childhood. In mainland China, my *sifu* became even more detached and likely to leave me on my own. In Hong Kong, we often ate and drank together. In the People's Republic, our training intensified, but Fu Han Tong disappeared as soon as our session was over. I slept, ate, and spent almost all of my free time alone. This was partly because in Canton, Fu Han Tong was back home. He had a life to return to, pieces of his past to pick up and reconstruct and others to carefully conceal. It was a past that had nothing to do with me, and it was understandable that he kept me away. But this, I suspected, was not the whole story. In addition to his past, there was the present: Fu Han Tong returned to being his true self and re-entered the world that raised him. In Hong Kong, as in the United States, Australia, and Europe, he had been a foreigner. As such, he had adapted to local customs, traditions and lifestyles. I could accept this rationally, but not emotionally. Yet I had little choice: I had understood that it was necessary for me to always look on the bright side of things.

I had to figure out how to get by. Driven by need, I soon found out how to get a hold of Chinese Yuan. It was a risky endeavour, for me as well as for the currency exchangers operating on the Dollar-Yuan black market. In addition to the risk of being caught by authorities, you might also be pickpocketed before or after the exchange took place. Fortunately, I never had such problems, though I was horribly ripped off in several of my early exchanges. Because they were illegal, these exchanges had to take place very quickly, and I didn't always have the time to count the Yuan that I was given in return for my Dollars. But I soon got the hang of how to conduct these exchanges and get my value for money.

In the weeks that followed, I alternated my stay between Canton and Foshan, a town on the outskirts of Guangzhou. Both places had been pivotal in the history of Kung Fu, notably of its southern styles, particularly those deriving from the southern off-shoots of Shaolin—Nam Siu Lam—such as Hung Gar, Hap Gar, Lau Gar, Wing Chun, and Choy Lee Fut, amongst many others. Guangzhou, the capital of Guangdong, had for centuries been the largest city in southern China and the cradle of Cantonese culture. It had been the destination of many pilgrimages over the years, including by many Kung Fu masters. Often they settled in Canton, and in the neighbouring Foshan, and spread their Kung Fu teachings, including iconic figures of the 19th century such as Chan Heung, the founder of Choy Lee Fut, or the legendary Ten Tigers (*Sap Fu*) like Wong Fei Hung, Wong Kei Yen, and Ti Kiu San, and the founder of Hap Gar, Wong Yun Lum, who had bravely fought against Western colonizers. I knew I had made it to one of the most important locations in the history of Chinese martial arts, a far more mysterious and historic one than Hong Kong. I was excited and eager to absorb all I could. Tough as it was, I was now in real China and was determined to make the most of it.

But here is where I encountered a paradox. Predictably, the

contrast between Hong Kong and the People's Republic of China was not limited to politics, economics, society, and culture. Precisely because Kung Fu is such an integral part of life itself in China, martial arts in the People's Republic is profoundly different from what I had seen in Hong Kong. Just like the rest of mainland China, Kung Fu had been shaped by the trauma of the Maoist revolution. The difference, however, was exactly the opposite of what I expected. The "Westernized" Hong Kong had actually retained and fostered traditional Kung Fu in a way that had seemingly been lost on the mainland. In "real" China, the People's Republic had tried, and often succeeded, in erasing martial arts, replacing this ancient art with a modernized and soulless proxy: Wu Shu.

Upon reflection, this was actually not a paradox. I knew that the Maoist regime had viewed Kung Fu as a threat, much like it viewed all other forms of art, tradition, religion, and culture. Any individual expression, let alone a martial one, was seen as anathema to a regime which sought to forcibly regiment and communize society. Well aware that uprooting a five-thousand-year-old tradition was impossible, the regime created a proxy instead. Wu Shu is essentially a form of gymnastics, which makes use of acrobatic martial gestures. Creating Wu Shu was a strategic ploy. On the one hand, it allowed the regime to promote physical education in schools in a way that drew upon China's beauty and proud history. On the other, Wu Shu enabled the government to control and erase the essence of Kung Fu. In fact, Wu Shu lacked the martial and potentially lethal dimension of martial arts, and ignored the cultivation of the martial artist's *Chi*. The regime, did not only ban traditional Kung Fu, in fact. While it accepted elements of traditional Chinese medicine such as acupuncture, moxibustion, cupping, traditional massage, acupressure and natural remedies, it side-lined Chi Kung, hypnosis and traditional Chinese orthopedics, *Tee Taa*. As a result, many traditional Kung Fu masters escaped China in the 1960s and 70s. Hong Kong had been one of their main destinations. This explained not only the high concentration of *kwoon* in tiny Hong Kong, but also the fact that these schools had retained their traditional nature.

In Hong Kong there were thousands of schools specializing in different styles, often relegated to the tiniest corners. I bumped into such schools all the time. Over the years, I met hundreds of traditional Kung Fu masters. In Canton and Foshan, everything was larger and more dispersed. I did see Kung Fu schools, but they were fewer and farther between. And they were much harder to find. The *kwoon* of mainland China were incomparably larger than their counterparts in Hong Kong. They lacked the traditional feel of Hong Kong schools, from the altar to the incense to the training equipment and weapons stacked in all corners. The atmosphere was cold and at times even antiseptic. In a place so far from home, mainland Chinese *kwoon* actually reminded me of Western gyms. Yes, in some *kwoon* I did see some of the typical signs of traditional Kung Fu, beginning with the altar, but these were the exception, not the norm.

Kung Fu itself was different on the mainland. Setting aside the schools that explicitly practiced Wu Shu, the external, aesthetic, and acrobatic sides of martial arts tended to be privileged over the martial ones even in official Kung Fu schools. Many of the styles that I had already studied were practiced here, but were modified to accentuate and, at times, exaggerate the choreographic beauty of a form or a predetermined combat. Teams of martial artists from different schools trained and competed with one another in parks and huge gyms. Given that Wu Shu was heavily promoted and subsidized by the state, it had an advantage over traditional Kung Fu, whose schools struggled to compete financially and politically. In a traditional Kung Fu school, the *sifu* supported himself and his school through his teaching. A Kung Fu *kwoon* is a private enterprise, a heresy in Maoist China during those years. So official Kung Fu schools, even if they were not explicitly practicing Wu Shu, inevitably underwent a creeping "WuShuization" to survive.

Fu Han Tong was not a Wu Shu master. Born in 1925 and orphaned as a child, Fu Han Tong had grown up among various traditional Kung Fu *kwoon,* well before the communist victory in the civil war in 1949. By then, he was a young man with almost twenty years of traditional martial arts experience. It was not until 1966, at the start of the Cultural Revolution, that the regime's purge of traditional Kung Fu took place, alongside the codification and imposition of Wu Shu. By then, Fu Han Tong was a full-grown man in his early forties. His personal history explained why he did not know or teach Wu Shu and, more importantly, why he actively disdained it. He often told me that Wu Shu is an artificial, denatured and emasculated Kung Fu: a Kung Fu that had lost its effectiveness, power and spirituality. It had lost its essence. This was not an accident: it had been the product of a conscious and carefully implemented policy to physically tame the masses, as well as to politically eradicate the Kung Fu families and clans whose power represented a lethal threat to the regime.

When I understood all this, I was deeply disappointed. I had expected to find an even more authentic Kung Fu in mainland China than in Westernized Hong Kong, but precisely the opposite was true. Over the course of my stay in Canton and Foshan, during that second trip and the many more that followed, my disappointment faded somewhat.

As Fu Han Tong had rightly pointed out to me, a five-thousand-year-old tradition could not be erased in a few decades. Over the course of China's tumultuous history, with its endless successions of dynasties, wars, and disruptions, Kung Fu had lived through many golden and dark ages. We were—and still are—clearly in the latter, but rosier times will come. If history teaches us anything, this is all but certain. Brighter days are ahead; even at the height of the Maoist repression of Kung Fu, some traditional schools lived on. These schools were extremely hard to find, but they existed, and the fact that they survived the political convulsions sweeping across the country gave them an exquisitely mysterious, almost magical, allure. Some were over a century old, and in the early 1900s were transformed into museums and historical sites. Once again, Fu Han Tong was my key to this secret world.

Not unlike in Hong Kong, in the rare traditional Kung Fu schools in Guangdong, the *sifu* or *si bak*—the next in line after the master—taught in a somewhat unorganized manner. Here too, there were no set times for large group lessons, although the *si bak* and *sisook*—advanced students—did arrange meetings with the master either for individual or small group lessons. As opposed to modern Wu Shu or Wu Shu-ized schools, which combined different styles, traditional schools remained faithful to one style. At the most, usually as the result of theoretical and practical exchanges between different masters, a traditional school could introduce elements of a second style. In that part of the country, the traditional *kwoon* naturally specialized in southern styles, particularly those that had become popular more recently such as Hung Gar, Choy Lee Fut, Wing Chun, Pak Mei, Tang Lang, and Loon Yin, amongst others.

Here, too, an underground fighting scene existed. Fu Han Tong had not mentioned anything to me in Hong Kong, but after a few weeks in Guangdong, he informed me that he had arranged another fight for me. Today, I look back and wonder whether he decided to bring me with him on that trip precisely for that reason. As before, Fu Han Tong was scant on details. I only knew that the fight would take place in a park on the outskirts of Foshan, and that my adversary was a Choy Lee Fut fighter. It was a full contact fight, with no rules, regulations or limitations.

That morning, when Fu Han Tong and I arrived at a secluded

green area tucked away in Foshan, only my adversary and his master were present. The fight began right away. It was as quick as it was dirty. My opponent attacked me with the wide circular kicks and punches typical of his style. He was strong, but he employed no strategy with his moves, no precision in his attacks. It only took me a few seconds to figure out the right distance and the right moves to attack him. I won the fight with a K.O. without much trouble.

After the fight, Fu Han Tong invited me to celebrate with him and some friends over dinner. At the time I thought we were only celebrating my martial victory, but we were probably celebrating his financial win too. But I did not see this then, just as I hadn't in Hong Kong. I was happy to have honoured my Kung Fu and my master once again. That night, I can clearly remember my elation as one of Fu Han Tong's friends escorted me back to my guest house on his scooter. Driving the wrong way down a one-way street, we provoked the ire and insults of oncoming bikers. In the cool Foshan night, the wind hit my face and ruffled my hair, and I smiled.

Between two worlds

After a month in Guangdong and another week back in Hong Kong, I returned to Genoa. I was satisfied with my progress and felt deeply enriched by my experience on the mainland. It's true that the lifestyle and the martial world that I had discovered in the People's Republic were a disappointment compared to Hong Kong. But it had provided a crucial piece to the Kung Fu puzzle I was cobbling together in those years, with all its positives and negatives.

Thanks to Fu Han Tong, I had discovered some of the authentic, traditional schools in Guangdong, a key region in the history of martial arts. Though I had encountered a colder and more detached Fu Han Tong there, my training with him had intensified. Last but not least, I had learned how to enter mainland China and get by on my own there.

This was a precious victory, as I knew it would be essential for me to continue following my *sifu.* It became clear to me during that trip that I was far likelier to find Fu Han Tong on the mainland than in Hong Kong in the future. Now that he had received his residence permit, he would make Canton his home once again. This did not mean that my Hong Kong experience was over. Not only was there a rich Kung Fu world there that I wanted to continue exploring, but Hong Kong would also still be my first port of call to travel on to the People's Republic.

Back in Genoa, I got back into my routine immediately, although this time I knew that it would be only a matter of months before I set off again. In fact, I actively worked to structure my *kwoon* based on that assumption. My trips to China would become regular from then on, taking place two to three times a year for a few months at a time. Over the next twenty years, I spent a third of my time in China. My school had to be organized accordingly and my students had to know not only that my absences would be regular, but also that they were essential for the continued success of our school. In truth, I did not struggle to get this point across. My students and instructors were extremely devoted and respectful towards me. They were proud of the fact that they had the opportunity to constantly grow, develop and improve thanks to the new experiences of their *sifu.*

When I was away, they held the *kwoon* together as best they could. Naturally, it was inevitable that they make mistakes in front of the less experienced students. But they always tried their best, and on the whole I was satisfied.

When I returned from my trips, my students loved hearing about my adventures and mishaps in a far-away land. They were honoured to be part of my inner circle, and we had many laughs as I told them the strangest stories over drinks. But they also understood the risks and dangers involved, the sacrifice and the hardships that I endured. Every time I left, I could sense their anxiety. Every time I returned, they rejoiced and were eager to hear about what I had done. They were curious about my deepening knowledge of the Kung Fu world in Hong Kong and Guangdong, as well as my widening understanding of Asian martial arts and related disciplines as I travelled across China and beyond, notably to Thailand.

On my travels through mainland China, Fu Han Tong remained my key contact and guide. He was always my first point of entry into a place, a school or a master. Everything that happened between us over the years notwithstanding, it is thanks to him that I developed a holistic approach to martial arts and its disciplines, cultures, religions, traditions, and medicine. Without *Sifu* Fu Han Tong, an outstanding martial artist with unparalleled intelligence, open-mindedness, and spiritual strength, and yet capable of an almost inhumane coldness, even cruelty, my becoming would have taken a very different path.

My second guide

Over my years of travel in China and the rest of Asia, I met countless masters. I am and will always be grateful to each and every one. The experience I gained from them, no matter how long, precious, or intense, added a brick to the foundation of my Kung Fu. But at the top of the pyramid, almost on par with Fu Han Tong, there is only one other *sifu.* He is the main, but not the only, reason why 1983 was a milestone year for me.

On March 16th, 1983, my son Siao Shan was born. Though I was only twenty-two at the time, my life until then had been rich and tumultuous, and I was a mature man at a young age. Angela and I had been together for four years and our solid marriage was further reinforced by our shared passion for Kung Fu. When we found out she was pregnant, I felt blessed: not even for a second did I panic at the thought that I would be a father so soon. The day that Shan was born will always be one of the most joyful and memorable of my life. I will return later to Shan and my relationship with him over the years.

Mature as I may have been, I was still young and in midst of my ascendence in the world of Kung Fu. I felt a strong need to reconcile my growing family with the imperative to keep apace in the martial world. I also became increasingly eager to bring Angela along with me to the East. I'd been taking trips to Hong Kong and China for two years by then, and they had become an integral part of my life. To share the experience with her would mean a lot to me, and I knew how much it would enrich her, too, as a martial artist.

In September of 1983, Angela and I decided to go to Hong Kong together. I would leave before her, in order to get settled and find an appropriate *kwoon* for both of us to train at during her first Hong Kong experience. She would join me forty days later, and we would spend three weeks there together. Shan, who was six months old by then, would stay with Angela's parents. It was a difficult choice to leave Shan behind when he was little more than a baby, but that trip was important for both of us.

As always, when I arrived in Hong Kong and then travelled on to Canton, I reached out to *Sifu* Fu Han Tong to seek his advice and resume my studies with him. He told me that he was travelling to Hong Kong a few days later and proposed that I join him. That was absolutely fine by me; I followed him wherever and whenever I could. But after a week or so, Fu Han Tong told me that his plans had changed: he was headed to Shanghai. He travelled often throughout the country, for reasons that by and large were unknown to me. I was used to his sudden change of plans and usually adapted to them. This time, however, he did not suggest that I follow him. Angela was scheduled to arrive in three weeks. Had I travelled all the way up north to Shanghai, I would have probably not made it back in time to meet her. Fu Han Tong reassured me: he would introduce me to a good Hung Gar school led by one of the most well-known and respected *sifu* of Hong Kong: Grand Master (*Tai Sifu*) Chan Hon Chung. I was happy and relieved. If Fu Han Tong recommended a school, I followed his suggestion without hesitation.

When Fu Han Tong left for Shanghai, I made my way to the address he had given me—729 Nathan Road, Mong Kok—armed with his letter of recommendation. There I would find *Sifu* Chan Hon Chung's *kwoon*. While I hardly knew anything about *Sifu* Chan at the time, I felt nervous that day, as if I sensed that this school and master were different from the others.

When I got there, I thought I had the wrong address. After two years, I knew how to spot the unmistakable signs of a Hong Kong *kwoon*, but there were none to be found at 729 Nathan Road. All I saw was a small shop selling ties and watches. I entered and walked through the shop, only to end up at a tailor's shop. From there, a small door led to a medical clinic, and to the right of that was a room: *Sifu* Chan Hon Chung's *kwoon*. The *kwoon* was not unlike other traditional schools I had seen. On the right was a punching bag attached to a ladder. Next to the bag, a weapons rack and cement weights sat on the floor. On the left there was a *Muk Yang Chon*. At the front, as always, was the altar.

I was in the right place.

A young man approached me, and I immediately reached out to hand him my letter. But he explained that neither *Sifu* Chan Hon Chung nor *Si bak* Cheon Yee Keung were around.

Edward, the master's son, was supposed to arrive shortly. I sat down and waited.

An hour later, a group entered the *kwoon*, dressed in the traditional uniforms of the lion dance (*Mou Si*), with their drums, cymbals and, naturally, the lion's head. They were tired and sweaty from their performance elsewhere in town, and initially they paid no attention to me. Several minutes passed before the most authoritative looking one among them, who I soon discovered to be the *si bak*, asked me who I was waiting for. Deferentially, I handed him my letter. He told me to return the next morning when I would have the opportunity to show my letter to *Sifu* Chan himself.

I found a cheap guesthouse in Mong Kok for the night and the next morning I showed up at the *kwoon* at nine-thirty sharp. This time, an elderly man greeted me: it was Chan Hon Chung himself. He scanned my letter and gave me permission to attend his *kwoon*. He escorted me to a room where I could leave my belongings and sleep, and explained the school's schedule for eating and training. I was not the only one sleeping in the *kwoon*. *Si bak* Cheon Yee Keung, several tailors and a few other students slept there too. *Sifu* Chan explained that boarding students were expected to pay a monthly fee, which went toward food and accommodation. As per tradition, payment for trainings were made on the basis of the student's offerings as well as by carrying out different chores in the school. Finally, *Sifu* Chan asked me about my Kung Fu, and I answered honestly, without concealing my knowledge of other styles or my experience with Hung Gar itself.

That first day in *Sifu* Chan's school, I simply acclimatized myself, watching students train, patients enter and exit the clinic, and streams of people flowing in and out of the tailor's shop, whose working hours seemed to be from 10 A.M. to 2 A.M. with only a few minutes' break for meals. I also discovered an interesting little bookshop in that building. During the weeks that followed, I spent a fair amount of my free time there, leafing through books and journals about traditional medicine and treatments. On that first day, I lunched and dined in the *kwoon* and went to bed early. My meeting with *Sifu* Chan the next morning—as it would be every morning thereafter—was scheduled for five-thirty sharp.

I arrived at the entrance of the clinic right on time. A few moments later, *Sifu* Chan walked down the steps and invited me to have breakfast with him. As we made our way to a small restaurant nearby, several people in the neighbourhood stopped to greet him. He stopped at a news kiosk, where he bought no less than seven newspapers. He was obviously a cultured man, and well-regarded in the community. His open attitude with foreigners—I had never been invited to a meal during my first encounter with a master—the reverential attitude of passersby toward him on the street, and his keen interest in current affairs all suggested he was very different from the other *sifu* I had met so far. During our meal, *Sifu* Chan read through his papers while I ate in silence.

When we returned to the *kwoon* half an hour later, *Sifu* Chan asked me to get ready for my training. It would be just the two of us. I wasn't sure what to get ready for, so I started an easy warm up. I was ready for whatever he asked me to do. When he returned, he looked me in the eye and called out, "*Sei Pi Ma.*" I knew this was Cantonese for *Ma Bo*, so without needing clarification, I performed the horseman stance. He then asked me to hold the position for as long as I could and walked out of the room and into his private study. As the minutes passed, *Sifu* Chan occasionally came in to check on me. I was like a statue. Forty-five minutes later, he walked back in, grabbed a small stool and sat two metres away from me: I held *Ma Bo* as he watched. After one hour and five minutes, I gave up. He stood up and congratulated me. "You have a good

Kung Fu," he said. He was satisfied and didn't need to see anymore: he would teach me Hung Gar.

I was thrilled, but my joy soon faded when I realized I could no longer stand up straight. My muscles had endured the hour-long squat, but my joints had not. *Sifu* Chan escorted me to his clinic, where he mixed up various medicinal herbs and wrapped them around my knees to soothe my sore joints. Miraculously, twenty-four hours later I was on my feet again. My lessons with *Sifu* Chan could begin. In the weeks that followed, I plunged body, mind and soul in the world of Hung Gar.

Sifu Chan Hon Chung's Hung Gar derived from the dominant lineage of the style, which originated with Ti Sin Sin in the second half of the 17th century. Legend has it that Ti Sin Sin, also known as Chi Shin, was one of the few monks who had survived the destruction of the Shaolin temple in 1642. History, however, places him in a later period connected to the tradition of the southern Shaolin temple. Either way, he is known as having passed down his art in his old age—notably the tiger's movements and dragon's breath—to Jiu Gu Chan, a tea merchant. In 1768, Jiu Gu Chan was a wanted man and he travelled south, settling in Guangdong and changing his name to Hung Nei Kung, in honour of the first Ming emperor Hong Wu. It is from him that the name Hung Gar—literally, the Hung family—derives. Hung Nei Kung's school was passed down to Lok Ah Choy, and from there, for three generations, it passed to the Wong family: Wong Tai Ying, Wong Kei Yen, and finally Wong Fei Hung (1847-1924), the famed hero and one of the legendary ten tigers of Canton, together with his father. Originally a butcher, one of Wong Fei Hung's disciples was Lam Sai Wing (1860-1943), who eventually moved from Guangdong to Hong Kong. *Tai Sifu* Lam Sai Wing's lineage in Hong Kong passed to his nephew Lam Jo and to his right-hand man: Chan Hon Chung.

Sifu Chan's curriculum began with the style's basic forms: the Plum Flower Form (*Mui Fa Kune*) codified by Lam Sai Wing, and the form honouring the Lau family (*Lau Gar Kune*). It progressed to the form Dominating the Tiger (*Gong Ji Fook Fu Kune*), the Butterfly's Palms (*Wu Dip Jueon*), the Double Way of the Tiger and the Crane (*Fu Hok Seon Yin*), and the Form of the Five Ways (*Mg Ying Kune*), which represents the five animals of the Hung Gar style: the dragon, the tiger, the leopard, the snake and the crane. Finally, the most advanced students were taught the form of the ten styles (*Sap Ying*), codified by Wong Fei Hung to create a bridge to the lineage of another historic Hung Gar master and fellow member of Canton's ten tigers, Ti Kiu San, the creator of the mystically powerful form the Iron Thread (*Tit Sin Kune*). The Ten Hands that Kill (*Sap Juet Sao*) was yet another form, containing deadly techniques and codified by Wong Fei Hung. Beyond the teaching of forms, *Sifu* Chan's program focused heavily on working in pairs, technique, physical conditioning and the use of many weapons. Beyond the clear organization of the school's curriculum, what struck me most was *Sifu* Chan's almost obsessive attention to detail in every stance, technique and movement. Nothing went unnoticed, not even a single centimetre in the wrong direction.

I quickly established a daily routine in *Sifu* Chan Hon Chung's *kwoon*. After our five thirty breakfast each morning, my lessons with him began at six thirty sharp, lasting between two and three hours on average. By nine, *Sifu* Chan went to attend to his patients in the clinic next door. Around midmorning, he called me in to watch him perform physical manipulations and *Tee Taa* treatments. For the rest of the day, I trained, either alone or with other students in the school. They were surprised by the speed at which I seemed to digest *Sifu* Chan's private lessons. In fact, *Sifu* Chan had skipped teaching me the most basic forms in his curriculum, having decided that I was sufficiently advanced in Kung Fu. Instead I learned them from *Si bak* Cheon Yee Keung in the afternoons, notably *Mui Fa Kune* and *Lau Gar Kune*. *Sifu* Chan began by teaching me the *Gong Jee Fook Fu Kune*, a long and complex form codified by the founder of the style Hung Nei Kung and based on the teachings of the Shaolin monk Ti Sin Sin. The form holds within it the essence of over two thirds of the Hung Gar style, focusing as much on the internal aspects of Chi Kung through the use of breathing and sound, as on the external toning and strengthening of the body. An ancient proverb says that he who performs the *Gong Jee Fook Fu Kun*e every day will be able to lift all of China with just one finger.

My fellow students were curious about me and my Kung Fu. They were more accustomed to westerners and didn't treat me with the suspiciousness, aloofness and aggressiveness of other martial artists I had come across in China in those years. This encouraged me to open up, so much so that, when they asked me to, I occasionally demonstrated my Kung Fu, which I had never done in other Chinese *kwoon,* as per Fu Han Tong's wise advice. Perhaps with the exception of the *Sibak,* in whom occasionally I sensed a tinge of envy, all the other students struck me as genuinely curious, surprised and interested. Still, I was extremely cautious and always paid the utmost respect to the *kwoon* and to *Sifu* Chan. I never had any problems in the *kwoon*, and I always felt welcome during that first stay and in the many years that followed.

In those first three weeks in *Sifu* Chan's *kwoon,* the atmosphere was remarkably serene. I didn't become close with every student, but those who spent more time at the *kwoon* eventually became my good friends. They included *Sibak* Cheon Yee Keung, Mr. Po, a kind-hearted novice, Bro Liver, and Miss Sanny, who came from an important Kung Fu family in Hong Kong whom I would meet on later visits. In addition the students and visitors at the *kwoon*, I gradually got to know the tailors and other shop owners who shared our roof. Each day flowed into the next with a consistency, harmony and serenity that I hadn't experienced before in Hong Kong or China.

Enrichment in Thailand

In those weeks I also made my first contact with Thai boxing. It was a humid afternoon, and I was practicing kickboxing techniques at the *kwoon.* Kong Pun Wai, a student in Chang Hon Chun's school who was passionate about ring sports, watched me dispassionately. After a while, he walked up to me with an uncharacteristically determined look. There was a good kick-boxing school in town, he said, led by a Muay Thai master named Alex Sing. I knew nothing about Muay Thai, and neither did Kong Pun Wai, who called it "kickboxing." But as usual, I was curious and eager to seize any opportunity to enrich myself further in the world of martial arts.

The next day, after my daily lesson with *Sifu* Chan, I made my way to the Wan Chai neighbourhood to visit Sing's school. I found it easily, and immediately noticed a fairly open attitude to foreigners like me. During that trip, I only trained at Sing's Muay Thai school a few times, but I immediately liked it. Though it was my first Thai boxing experience, I had a fairly broad understanding of freestyle fighting and boxing, and so Sing immediately took an interest in me. He suggested that on one of my next trips to the East, I should stop over in Bangkok: he would put me in contact with some good Muay Thai camps there. I took him up on his offer. By the mid-1980s, a first stopover in Thailand for a few weeks before continuing on to China became part of my travel routine.

My trips to Thailand were deeply enriching. There I learned another noble martial art, which contributed to my technical, practical, and theoretical martial knowledge. Through my immersion in the Muay Thai world, I dove into Thai customs and tradition, savouring the many differences between Chinese and Thai culture, character, and behaviour, the former being far less open and less well-rounded than the latter. As I learned to navigate the world of Muay Thai, I increasingly spent my time in traditional—as opposed to Westernized—camps such as Chooky Gym, Bong Bang, Spartonwee, Maimuangkorn, and Kausay Galaxi. Not unlike China, there was a distinction between Westernized and traditional martial arts schools in Thailand, with the former gradually prevailing over the latter as time went by. Westernized Muay Thai camps were money-making machines where Western students were often taught precious little technique, while being bombarded with endless hours of heavy training on *pao*. In traditional schools, on the other hand, not only were the teachings infinitely richer, but spending time there also meant soaking in the essence of Thai culture. Generally, these camps were sealed to the *falang*—foreigners. Despite being a *falang* myself, I managed to gain access to this traditional world over the years, which was an immense honour.

Of course, it wasn't all roses. While it wasn't as acute as it had been in traditional Chinese Kung Fu schools, professionals in traditional Thai camps eyed me with suspicion at times, eager to prove their superiority in sparring encounters. I remember one incident, many years after my first trip to Thailand: after several days of tough training in a traditional camp, I noticed a strange-looking fellow with scars running across his face watching me with equal menace as curiosity as I trained. As the days went by and he saw me bond with fellow martial artists, his irritation grew palpably.

It came to a head on a warm festive day, when the camp emptied as students and trainers travelled to visit their families, and the master decided to take a day off work too. There were only a handful of us left, including the strange man with the scarred face. He proposed that we train together, which I duly accepted, ignoring the obviously unfriendly look on his face. After a short warm-up, one of the trainers strode towards us, inviting—or more like ordering—us into the ring for a three-round training match. We weren't wearing extra protection other than our eight-ounce gloves, mouth-guards and protective cups. But neither of us hesitated as we made our way into the ring.

We began in the typical Thai fashion, with a few moments of reciprocal study through light techniques aimed at unsettling one another. Suddenly, literally from one moment to the next, the scarred fighter changed gears and began bombarding me with a cascade of low-kicks to my legs. I was taken aback at first, but quickly reacted. Despite my relatively limited experience with professional Muay Thai fighting, I had many freestyle Kung Fu fights under my belt, which had exposed me to far greater risk and danger. I knew I had the technical skill, the physical training and, above all, the psychological predisposition to confront any martial situation I was exposed to. That day, I was fast on my legs and agile with my arms, skirting his kicks, while occasionally closing the distance between us and using my boxing techniques. After several punches, I inserted a few kicks into the mix that strayed from the strict—and rather limited—Muay Thai skill set. These always landed, not least because they were unexpected by my adversary. Unnerved, he renewed his attacks on me, but to no avail. I was habituated—all too well—to full contact fighting and responded with equal grit. The third round ended early with my K.O. against the scarred man, thanks to a kick and a hook punch that hit him squarely in the jaw.

From that moment on, we became good friends. I had earned his respect and we both guarded the secret of our encounter as an unspoken pact between us. Had the master found out what had happened in his absence, my scarred friend would have received a good scolding, while I would have been expelled from the camp. So, neither of us whispered a word about it, while everyone else watched, bemused, as a sudden bond formed between two former "enemies."

This, like all my experiences in Thailand, gradually became an important part of my cultural understanding. It was only natural that I convey it to my own students back in Italy. I began doing so through ad hoc Muay Thai workshops and eventually through a stand-alone Muay Thai course beginning in 1995. Today, I look back on those trips to Thailand with fondness, not only because of the martial and cultural enrichment they provided, but also because of the people I met. In Bangkok, as in Hong Kong, I made long-lasting friends. World famous Muay Thai champions like Pechindee Sakat, Payakaroon Samart, and Sengtiennoi, as well as great masters like Sennanan Seeyutong, remain close friends to this day.

Sharing my enrichment

Let's return to Hong Kong in 1983. My days flew by with an intense and steady rhythm, and Angela's arrival was fast approaching. Over breakfast one morning, I asked *Sifu* Chan if my wife could attend his *kwoon* as well. I explained that it was her first visit to China, and that she herself was a martial artist who was eager to explore the Kung Fu world in Hong Kong. With his unique grace and kindness, *Sifu* Chan rejoiced at her arrival and immediately accepted her into the school. I thanked him profusely. All was set for Angela's smooth landing.

Everything, that is, except the weather. The day before she arrived, a major typhoon swept across large swaths of Asia and was headed from the Philippines to Hong Kong. The mood in the city was tense, as the wind howled and the sky darkened, with grey-black clouds amassing on the horizon. Angela's flight was scheduled to land at three o'clock the following afternoon.

The next morning, I woke up at dawn, startled. I peered out of the window. The sky was almost as dark as the night before and the wind raced at a speed hitherto unknown to windy Hong Kong. Unlike the constant breeze in town, this wind was different: it was menacing, and roared to all that calamity was approaching. The city was deadly silent: the lights were out, shops were closed and the streets were eerily empty. It seemed like the end of the world.

I hurried out of my room and used my best Cantonese to find out what was going on. After a few unsuccessful attempts, I bumped into *Sifu* Chan's son, Chan Ka Wa, also known as Edward. He told me that the city was in total lockdown because of the typhoon. The airport, too, was closed and would remain closed until the typhoon passed.

My panic soared. By then Angela was on her way. She had departed from London the afternoon before, with a stopover in Abu Dhabi. The plane must have already taken off from the Gulf. I had to find out where my wife was, and only way to do so was to go to the airport. Of course, I knew she wouldn't be landing in Hong Kong anytime soon, but going to Khai Tak was my best bet to get some information. When I told Edward about my intentions, he almost ordered me to not go. He rebuked me: there was no way I could actually reach Khai Tak, since all public transportation had been closed down. On top of this, it was terribly dangerous to be out on the street. Edward also sought to reassure me: there was no way her plane would land in Hong Kong that day. It had most likely been redirected somewhere else in Asia. As soon as the storm passed, I could go to the airport.

Rational as Edward's explanation was, I could not stay put. He was probably right. But on the off-chance that he wasn't, it would be a disaster: I couldn't risk Angela landing in Hong

Kong without my being there to greet her. She would be completely lost, on her first trip abroad, in the middle of a typhoon. But *Sifu* Chan had locked the door to the *kwoon*. Asking him to unlock it was out of question; he would have strictly forbidden me to set foot outside. I had to find another way.

Luckily, there was a window. I stealthily snuck out, somehow managing to climb down to the ground. I looked around, trying to discern a living soul amidst the storm. There were no buses or taxis on the streets. The roads were ominously deserted. I started walking. I walked and walked, as the wind and rain pummeled me and I dodged flying street signs, bamboo sticks and other objects that swirled around me. Using my map, what street signs remained intact, and my intuition, I reached Khai Tak airport after several hours, soaking wet and exhausted.

The airport was closed. The door into the main hall was open but I didn't see any staff. A large billboard at the entrance reported information about inbound and outbound flights. There were dozens of flights inbound to Hong Kong, but none of them would land that day. For almost all of the flights, the board showed where they had been rerouted. But for two of the flights, nothing showed under "status": a flight from San Francisco, and Angela's flight from Abu Dhabi.

With all the offices closed and no one there to ask, all I could do was wait. I waited all afternoon and all evening. I was not alone, but as the hours went by, most other people left, having realized that there was no point waiting it out at the airport all night. I had nowhere to go. Walking back to the *kwoon* was not an option. Even if it had been physically possible for me to leave the airport in the midst of the storm, I couldn't leave Khai Tak before finding out where Angela was. I lay on the floor and tried, unsuccessfully, to sleep.

By dawn, the typhoon had passed. The sky was still grey, but the wind had calmed down, and the monsoon had mellowed into a drizzle. At seven, the blank space on the billboard filled up at last. The flight from Abu Dhabi had landed in Bangkok. It would reach Hong Kong at three that afternoon, twenty-four hours after its scheduled arrival.

The city was slowly waking back up. I walked out in the light drizzle and took a taxi back to the *kwoon*. At 729 Nathan Road, *Sifu* Chan was waiting for me, and he was furious. It had been irresponsible of me to walk all the way to the airport in the midst of the typhoon. The city had been in lockdown and for good reason, he snapped. He was right, but in retrospect, I would do the same thing again. I was extremely anxious and needed to know where Angela was, no matter what.

For her, on the other hand, it had not been such a tragedy. When Angela landed that afternoon, she was radiant. She had been rerouted to Bangkok and spent the night in a luxurious five-star hotel. She met a young couple on her flight and spent a nice evening with them, in spite of the delay. And so she landed in Hong Kong well-rested, happy to see me, and excited about the adventure to come.

We made our way to the *kwoon* together. As soon as we walked in, the stress and anguish of the previous twenty-four hours disappeared as *Sifu* Chan greeted us with his memorable smile. He welcomed us in, and generously offered us his own room. We could stay in his room, which was larger and more comfortable a couple, for the entirety of Angela's stay. In all my time within the ironclad discipline of Eastern martial arts, I had never witnessed such spontaneous display of generosity by a master. Moved by his offer, we accepted.

Angela was welcomed warmly by the students and bonded immediately with Sanny. She trained with *Si bak* Cheon Yee Keung, with Sanny and with other students. She had the honour of being taught the *Lau Gar Kune* form by *Sifu* Chan himself. In the two weeks that followed, we trained often, but we also enjoyed the city together. *Sifu* Chan invited us to his home in the country, to the theatre, and out to dinner on several occasions. He gave us a lot of free time to explore Hong Kong together.

The days flew by and before we realized it, we were heading back to Genoa, enriched by our experience and excited to hug our baby boy once again. When I saw Shan in his grandmother's arms at the Genoa airport, my jaw dropped: with his long hair and baby shoes, he had grown so much in those two months. I hardly recognized him. An instant later, my heart swelled as I melted in his tender embrace.

Looking back, looking forward

Those two months in Hong Kong will always have a special place in my heart. I had been blessed to meet *Sifu* Chan Hon Chung. In his *kwoon*, I had enriched my Kung Fu through a noble lineage of Hung Gar. I had not only learned new forms and techniques; I had also experienced also a new method of teaching and training. Only years later did I feel confident enough to incorporate *Sifu* Chan's teachings into my own *kwoon*, initially by opening a dedicated Hung Gar course, and eventually integrating it into my broader Kung Fu program. But after my first meeting with *Sifu* Chan, I knew it was a question of when, not if, I would do so. At 729 Nathan Road, I had met new people who, in contrast to the diffidence I had encountered so at other traditional schools, welcomed me as a brother in Kung Fu. I had witnessed a different way of organizing a *kwoon*, which was highly traditional but also open to the West. It was that mix of tradition and openness that I cherished and have sought to replicate at the heart of my own school ever since. I had seen and lived all of this with my wife Angela by my side, with whom I shared the passion and life project of Kung Fu.

I felt honoured by the fact that my relationship with *Sifu* Chan Hon Chung was not limited to the *kwoon*. From our daily breakfasts together to our evenings out dining or at the theater, from the weekend at his country house to the selfless way he had offered us his private room, I knew that I had met a special *sifu* and a special human being.

Sifu Chan Hon Chung was a remarkable person. He was well-known not only in the martial world, but in wider Hong Kong society as well. Born in 1909 in Guangdong, *Sifu* Chan moved to Hong Kong when he was twelve. At eighteen he began studying with Lam Sai Wing, eventually playing a pivotal role in promoting Hung Gar in Hong Kong. By the late nineteen-twenties, *Sifu* Chan's martial skills were renowned: in 1936, in the run-up to the second Sino-Japanese war (1937-45), he was invited to train the Republic of China's army in the use of weapons such as swords and spears. He founded his Hong Kong *kwoon* in 1938 and taught there until 1987, when he gave up the venue. He was one of the first traditional masters to officially accept non-Chinese students, thereby contributing to the spread of traditional martial arts in the West. In the many months I spent at *Sifu* Chan's *kwoon* over the course of eight years, I met several international students, mostly from Europe, the United States, Mexico, and Israel. In 1970, Chan Hon Chung helped found the Chinese Martial Arts Association and served as its first president, an organization that coordinated the many Kung Fu schools in Hong Kong. He also advised and took part in many martial arts films and documentaries over the years.

As I mentioned, *Sifu* Chan was also held in high esteem in Hong Kong society. An expert in the traditional treatment of *Tee Taa*, he had been at the forefront of the fight against drugs in Hong Kong and was elected President of the Anti-Drug Association. He was member of the exclusive Hong Kong Rotary Club and founder of the high-end Waterloo restaurant. In 1973 he was awarded a gold medal of honour by Queen Elizabeth II for his service to Hong Kong.

Until 1983, my only *sifu* had been Fu Han Tong, even though I had met many other masters along the way. Through his rough and rugged style, I had learned the essence of Kung Fu. *Sifu* Chan Hon Chung was Fu Han Tong's polar opposite: he was *Yin* where Fu Han Tong was *Yang*. Unlike Fu Han Tong, Chan Hon Chung was a true gentleman: well-mannered, kind-hearted and disarmingly polite. His Kung Fu was more limited than Fu Han Tong's, but his program was still rich and highly structured, resting on the solid foundations of a centuries-old Hung Gar lineage. Tough as the training with him was, there were none of the risks and dangers I encountered with Fu Han Tong. In Nathan Road, never once did I get a whiff of the underground Kung Fu world that Fu Han Tong had introduced me to. Without detracting an inch from my commitment to Fu Han Tong, whom I continued to follow assiduously for many years, I knew that Chan Hon Chung would be an important figure in my life going forward.

In a completely different but equally powerful way from Fu Han Tong, Chan Hon Chung took me under his wing. Over time, I gained his trust and respect. In his characteristically generous way, he enriched me tremendously over the years.

In Chan Hon Chung, I found a second, very different, Kung Fu father figure, one to whom I will be indebted forever.

Although I had been introduced to one by the other, I never saw Fu Han Tong and Chan Hon Chung together. True to their diametrically opposite natures, I like to think of them as two distinct pillars, each supporting one side of the same bridge.

Enrichment

Enrichment marked my life in the 1980s, when my first trips to Asia exposed me to people and places that contributed enormously to my knowledge and spiritual development.

Enrichment does not arise spontaneously; it requires conscious commitment and sacrifice. I had the opportunity to visit incredible places, meet remarkable people, and live unique experiences, but without my own conscious work none of it would have germinated. We can follow an instinct, enchanted by an image or a novelty, but it becomes true enrichment when coupled with hard work. We enrich ourselves through our intelligence, using to the fullest our ability to expand, strengthen and enhance the meaning of our lives.

We can appreciate fully the value of our knowledge by living with an open heart and true passion, which, fusing together within us, generate love for our lives and for the universe around us.

CHAPTER 5
Risk

The 1980s flew by punctuated by my journeys to Asia. Guiding me through my growth and development in the second half of the decade was Fu Han Tong, alongside Chan Hon Chung. Whereas Chan Hon Chung became a source of pure enrichment for me, my relationship with Fu Han Tong was characterized by something else.

Risk.

The risk Fu Han Tong exposed me to was complex. It was a risk engrained in his nature as a radically free man. His radical freedom meant that he neither had nor saw boundaries. Likewise, there were no limits to the situations he repeatedly exposed me to. Risk was an essential quality of these exposures, and of his life. Some of his reasons for putting me into those situations were noble: his own open-mindedness, selflessness, and generosity, as well as his belief in me and my abilities. Thanks to his methods, I experienced some of the most enlightening moments of my life. But he also had less noble motives: opportunism, selfishness, and greed. All of these complexities coexisted as a coherent whole in him, and they shaped my life in those years, for better or worse.

Risk and darkness

As the years went by, I experienced many new things. Every trip was a discovery. With every region, city and school I explored, I added another piece to my Kung Fu puzzle. I met countless people, learned many styles and techniques, and studied hundreds of weapons and methods. But there was one thing that remained consistent throughout: my fights in the underground world of Chinese martial arts.

Oddly, it was the sameness of those fights, their tedious repetition over time, that gradually awakened me to their dark side. The more I understood the risks of these fights for me and for my adversaries, as well as for the broader Kung Fu community, the more I perceived the darkness in that underground world, in Fu Han Tong, and, finally, in my relationship with him.

The level of risk changed from fight to fight. Symbolizing the danger was a ring that lay on top of a small velvet red cushion at the fight venue. When a silver ring was placed on the cushion, the level of risk was the lowest. The freestyle fight had a few rules governing it and a referee. The fights normally took place with no protections and often led to serious injuries. But in theory, at least, these fights were not lethal. A gold ring represented a level higher on the ladder of risk. When the gold ring was laid on the cushion, it meant there were no rules, no regulations, no referees or judges. The goal was to knockout your adversary, but when this happened or when the fight was nearing the point of no return, the loser's *sifu* could, if he wished, throw in the towel and interrupt the fight. A fighter's *sifu* could prevent his total defeat. Then there was the riskiest level of all: the jade ring. When the jade ring was placed on the cushion, no rules, regulations, referees, or judges were allowed. And, only the winning fighter's *sifu* could interrupt the fight. Each fighter placed his life in the hands of a stranger. The violence of those fights was extreme.

Their physical risk was obvious, but the darkness of those fights was not limited just to gratuitous violence. As time went by, I understood that the reasons behind these fights had little to do with the purity of martial arts, and more to do with the greed and cruelty of mankind. There are both vice and virtue in all things, and likewise the underground fighting scene represented the dark side of a noble art. Those two sides of the coin had always coexisted. Martial arts throughout the centuries have been a path to enlightenment and freedom, but they have also, sadly, been a tool for subjugation and possession. In those years in China, the underground fighting scene was where the distortion of Kung Fu showed its ugly face. Yes, occasionally the fights displayed the purity and ethics of tradition, and the fighters tested their ability to honour their style and master. Most of the time, though, a noble art was put in service of greed and cruelty, through gambling and the sheer pleasure of indulging in violence.

The underground fight scene put at risk not only the physical and mental health of the fighters, but also the Kung Fu community as a whole. Serious fines, possible prison sentences for those who organized the fights and their respective schools, and—worst of all—the violence and the gambling represented real danger for the integrity of Kung Fu. These fights soiled the purity of martial arts: they became a vehicle to establish a mafia-like hierarchy within the Kung Fu community, and a source of power and money for masters, earned on the backs of their unaware students.

As I mentioned before, I did not understand this in my early years in China. Blinded by naivety and enthusiasm, I had only understood the superficial meaning of my first fights: they were a way of testing my Kung Fu skills and honouring my art and my *sifu.* I didn't ask myself many questions, and I asked Fu Han Tong fewer still. I was excited to fight and proud of my victories. But as I won fight after fight, the excitement and pride faded. The fog of enthusiasm lifted and suddenly I could see in the dark. I began to see the tediousness, pointlessness and brutality of it all. What was the point of those fights? What was it I was proving over and over again with that uncontrolled aggressiveness? Why all that violence? Couldn't masters test their students' abilities in a safer way? Why the extreme informality, secrecy, and careful cover-up in those situations? What was there to hide? And why was Fu Han Tong so happy about my victories? Was it pure pride for his only student, or did the fights offer him status, respect, and money? And if he was earning money by putting my life in danger, what did it say about our relationship? I had known Fu Han Tong for two decades by then. I was a child when we first met. With him, I grew into a man and a martial artist. To me he was like a father, and in many ways he was more important. Was I not a son to him? Why did he put his son's life at risk? Was it just for money? And then there was the most painful question of all: Why did I agree to participate in these fights? If I had these doubts, if I took no pleasure in the violence, if I saw no point to the brutality, why didn't I say no? What did that say about me? Did I, too, have a dark side that took pleasure in these situations? Was I simply too cowardly to say no to my master?

As months and years went by, these and other questions churned in my head. At times, I dismissed them. At other times, I belittled them. But the more time that passed and the more fights I participated in, the harder it became to quiet these questions and ignore the dark side of Kung Fu, of Fu Han Tong, and within myself. As each fight approached, my anxiety soared. When the fights ended in victory, I was swallowed by an unbearable emptiness.

Those fights stole part of my precious time in China, which I could have dedicated to the discovery of new and hidden secrets of Kung Fu. A lifetime was not enough to discover them all. That feeling of lost time made me feel desperately empty and lonely. Being away from home, with a young son, a wife, and a school on the other side of the planet was hard enough. But I also knew that spending time in China helped me grow, tap into new energy and, most of all, find meaning. But when I participated in those underground fights, the pointlessness and loneliness were suffocating. What the hell was I doing there, thousands of miles from home, risking serious injury and even death?

The feeling of loneliness didn't disappear when I returned home. I brought it back with me, and I had no one I could tell about those experiences and the emotions they triggered in me. I fought alone, and I was alone in digesting them afterwards. My mother and father knew nothing about this. In those years, my dad was losing his long and courageous fight against cancer. My mother was by his side and in deep anguish. The last thing they needed was to know was that I repeatedly and voluntarily put my life at risk on the other side of the planet. Angela knew only a little more. My travels to Asia were hard for her to endure. I knew how much worry they caused her and her emotional detachment when I returned made me suffer tremendously, even though I knew that it was her way, perhaps her only way, to protect herself. I felt responsible and this exacerbated my pain. Of course, she was not oblivious to my traumas. I couldn't completely hide the stress that the fights caused me. But I wanted to protect her as much as I could, and spared her the details. It was the least I could do. I did share a few stories from the fights with some of my advanced students, notably with Roberto Macaluso and Gianfranco Galluccio. I felt I could be more open with them, but all they saw was the excitement and adventure in those experiences. They were proud of me and wanted to hear more. They didn't fully understand the risk of those fights, nor the darkness they sank me into. In some ways, talking about those experiences made me feel even lonelier.

In the 1980s, I participated in dozens of such fights. Most are bundled together in my head in a blurry, dark haze. Three fights stand out, however, that were milestones in my gradual awakening in those years.

Fighting, armed

The first one took place in 1984. One day Fu Han Tong told me that he had scheduled my next fight, and that it would include the use of a weapon. We, or at least I, was not presented with a choice of weapon. Fu Han Tong told me that I would have a two-headed stick—*Seon Tour Kwan*—while my adversary would use a single-headed one—*Yat Tour Kwan*. I had often sparred with weapons during training, including different types of sticks—*kwan*—but this was the first time I was entering an official fight with a weapon.

This novelty made me more anxious than usual. Anxiety was a typical prequel of my fights, just as emptiness was their inescapable sequel. But while the emptiness increased as the years went by, the anxiety lessened. The risk, of course, was always there. The more fights I participated in, the more I appreciated the risk involved. But humans adapt to everything, including risk, danger, and uncertainty; the more time passed, the less anxious I felt before each fight. But not this time. Fighting with a weapon increased, and not insignificantly, the risk of someone getting seriously hurt. My only source of confidence was my fighter's spirit. I knew I could always count on that, no matter how dangerous a situation became.

The fight took place on the rooftop of a high-rise building under the scorching sun. The space was fairly big and framed by a one-metre-tall wall. A young man pointed to the walls, indicating that we had to steer clear of it. If we approached the edge, the fight would be interrupted. The man was not a referee; his only duty was to keep us away from the roof's edge.

As with most of my fights, it was all over in a few intense

minutes. I gripped my two-headed stick at its centre, so as to be able to attack my adversary with both ends. My adversary clenched his single-headed stick at its base. While I had a greater variety of potential techniques to use against him, his weapon was considerably longer than mine, and he had the advantage when it came to distance. I had to adapt my strategy accordingly: instead of aiming for his head, torso or legs, I focused on his arms, which he held out in front of him as he clutched his *kwan*. I could strike them more easily. This was a strategy I had often used in fights against an opponent who was taller than me: I would concentrate on hitting his limbs as he extended them, especially when he leaned towards me with a punch or a kick. It was a strategy that had proved effective many times, and I instinctively turned to the same one in this fight. As my adversary advanced, holding the end of his stick, I struck the back of his hand with my *kwan*. He immediately dropped his weapon: I had broken his left wrist. The fight was over. There was no way my opponent could continue in that state, and he was escorted away. As with all the other fights, I never saw him again. Fu Han Tong and a few others who were gathered on the rooftop congratulated me, praising the smart strategy I had used as well as the precision in my technique. In the end, the fight had not been hard; it was perhaps one of the shortest I had fought. But the great anxiety I felt about it beforehand was equal to the emptiness it left behind once it was over.

Fighting in Macau

I had a second revealing experience in Macau one year later, in 1985. In the case of the *kwan* fight, my pre-fight anxiety shed light on the pointlessness and harmfulness of those experiences; in Macau, it was the sheer difficulty of the fight that was the eye-opener. Fu Han Tong had warned me: my opponent was strong and experienced. Strength and experience went hand-in-hand in that world. An experienced fighter was, by definition, a strong one too. These fights often ended in serious injury or death. The more fights someone had under his belt, the more victories, and many victories suggested unrivalled strength. In this particular case, my adversary actually made a living by fighting: any material gain went not just to his master, but to him, too. He was known and feared on the underground fighting circuit not only in Macau and Hong Kong, but in mainland China and throughout southeast Asia, too.

Normally, Fu Han Tong would let me know that I'd be fighting one or two days ahead of time. In this case, he gave me a whole week of warning. It makes me smile to think that a week's warning seemed like a long time in those days. Today, on the professional circuit, fighters train meticulously for months ahead of a match. But in the underground fighting world in China, there was no preparation involved. You were thrown into the deep end. One's technical skillset, mental and physical strength, resilience, and, above all, one's fighting spirit, were all one could rely on.

On that occasion, the week-long advance warning was partially due to the fact that the fight required us to travel to Macau. The island of Macau was governed under a special statute, and at the time was still a Portuguese colony, which it remained until 1999, when it was returned to Chinese sovereignty after 442 years of Portuguese rule. I had never been to Macau, but knew that it was famous for its gambling, good Kung Fu schools and, thus, its clandestine fights, in addition to being a renowned tourist destination. During that week, I worked on my physical strength and concentration, taking extra care to not injure myself, but by and large I continued my normal daily training routine. Fu Han Tong left for Macau a day before me to settle a few loose ends. I was scheduled to arrive two days before the fight.

As soon as I got off the ferry in Macau, Fu Han Tong and I visited several Kung Fu schools, mostly specializing in Choy Lee Fut and southern styles of the Praying Mantis, Tang Lang Chuan. It was on that occasion that I met Wong Hon Fun, one of the greatest Kung Fu masters of the 20th century, whose specialty was the Mantis of the Seven Stars: Chat Sin Tang Lang. In the years that followed, I returned often to Macau to learn from *Sifu* Wong Hon Fun. But that was not the moment to do so.

I got settled in a small guesthouse on a narrow alley in the historic center of Macau, which had a boisterous mix of Portuguese architecture and culture with a touch of Chinese kitsch. It was a bad choice. I was on a low floor, and the nightlife was particularly raucous that evening. Noise and anxiety kept me up all night. The fight took place in a gym, and a large crowd of around forty or fifty people had gathered to watch us. Unlike the rooftops, warehouses and basements I was used to, the setting here seemed to be almost official, and therefore safe.

Or so I thought. I learned that morning that my adversary was well-versed in both Tang Lang and Choy Lee Fut. He may have been a Tang Lang student of Wong Hon Fun, but I never found out for certain. Seeing as how he made a living from these fights, he seemed like more of a freelancer than someone acting on behalf and under the wing of his *sifu.* There was no master with him at the fight. It was a "golden ring" level fight. This was actually the first time I noticed the traditional red cushion in the fighting venue, with the ring placed on top signalling the rules of the fight, or lack thereof. We were told that we could only fight standing, never on the ground: if one or both fighters fell, the fight would be interrupted. The fight would take place over two rounds, but no one specified how long the rounds would be. Amazingly, we were permitted hand wraps and genital protections. But the golden ring indicated that beyond this, there were no rules, regulations, referees or judges. Fu Han Tong, as the only *sifu* there, could have interrupted the fight if I got in trouble. As for my adversary, he would have to signal himself if and when to concede defeat.

Unlike other fights in which the real action began almost immediately, in this fight my adversary and I spent a fair amount of time studying one another through a rather low-key exchange of techniques. Neither of us made a deliberate attack at first: we each sought to tease out the other's strategy and tactics. After a minute or so, my adversary made two attempts to hit me with more aggressive techniques. Having seen those, I figured out he was mainly a Tang Lang fighter. He targeted my limbs, attempted to block and break them, and performed wide circular kicks: it all pointed to the typical attitudes of the Praying Mantis. I had gained a precious piece of information about him and I had to make use of it.

From then on, our exchanges became more intense, but we limited ourselves to two or three techniques at a time and then distanced ourselves again. There was no continuity in our exchanges: neither of us felt secure enough to completely close the distance.

Many minutes later, we were stopped. The first round was over. Unlike in a professional fighting match, the break between the first and second rounds was unnecessarily long. Fu Han Tong advised me to attack my adversary with greater continuity rather than stepping back after only a few techniques. I concentrated on his advice.

As soon as the second round started, I sought to create a situation in which I could carry out a longer sequence of attacks. It was not easy. My adversary was agile. As he darted from one point to another, I struggled to close the distance between us. Many minutes and several failed attempts later, I finally got my chance. He was the one who struck first. I managed to hold my ground and dodged his attack by getting closer to him. He missed me because I was too close: he did hit me, but not exactly where or as strongly as he wanted. I had protected my most vulnerable parts, and, more importantly, I made use of my proximity to him to counterattack. He didn't K.O., but, remembering Fu Hạn Tong's advice, I continued to strike him. Here was the moment to create the continuity my *sifu* had advised. The fight went up a gear as the techniques on both sides became noticeably more powerful. We each endured the others' blows.

At one point I gave him a low kick and, immediately after, without setting my foot back on the ground, I aimed a high circular kick at his head. I made contact and did not stop. The instinct for continuity kicked in and I followed through with several punches. I elbowed him in the face, sent him to the ground and soon followed, having forgotten that the rules prohibited ground fighting. It was a mistake. The fight was interrupted because I'd broken the rules, and the pause allowed my adversary to gather what was left of his strength and get up. I had to quickly capitalize on the situation or else I'd lose my temporary advantage over him. I had to recreate a situation of continuity to finish the fight off as soon as possible. Otherwise, having understood my strategy, he might do the same to me. He was by far the strongest opponent I had met in my twenty odd years of martial arts.

Fortunately, my opportunity arose a few moments later, as I back-kicked him in the stomach and punched him hard in the face as he was doubled over. He fell. I stood still. Seconds passed and still he did not get up. I had won.

Usually, once a fight ended, I rarely thought twice about it, besides a detached analysis to help me refine my fighting strategies. Less still did I like to think about the fate of my adversaries. To do so brought psychological pain on top of the physical scars that even the easiest fights left behind. It was a pain and anxiety I could not bear. But no matter how hard I tried not to think about it, I couldn't avoid the dark emptiness each fight left inside me. This time, probably because of the intensity and violence of the fight, that emptiness was darker and more deafening than ever before.

After the fight in Macau it became increasingly difficult for me to silence the questions and doubts that crowded my mind. Yes, I had won the fight, just like I had won all the others. Yes, it had been the most difficult fight I'd experienced. I bore the marks of it all over my bruised body. Yet I felt no satisfaction, no joy; if anything, I felt sadness and remorse. From then on, I started realizing that rather than adding to my Kung Fu, those fights were actually weakening it. But for many years, I nevertheless continued to expose myself to that danger, sadness and emptiness.

The Five Goats

The third and most dramatic experience of all took place in 1988, a year after my father's death. That trip to China was special in more ways than one. With the exception of the trip to Hong Kong in 1983 when Angela joined me, I had always travelled alone to Asia. But in 1989, I proposed to Roberto Macaluso that he come along with me. I had met Roberto at the major martial arts exhibition in Terni in 1979 and in 1980 he joined my school. By 1989 he was an instructor in my *kwoon*. He was a difficult character, but nevertheless he had become one of my best friends. In January of that year, Roberto and I landed in a grey and drizzly Hong Kong and immediately went to call on *Sifu* Chan Hon Chung. Roberto had heard so much about him and it warmed my heart to see his enthusiasm and emotion at the prospect of meeting my *sifu*.

By then, the eighty-year-old *Sifu* Chan had closed his historic *kwoon* on Nathan Road. But despite his ailing health, he still practiced *Tee Taa* in his small study. It was in that same study that he had taught me the legendary iron thread Hung Gar form—*Tit Sin Kune*—a couple of years before.

After two weeks of training and carefree exploration in Hong Kong with Roberto, I received a message from *Sifu* Fu Han Tong. He asked me to meet him in Canton immediately because he had a special treat in store for me. I assumed it was yet another fight. Given the illegal and secretive nature of the fights, I knew I had to travel alone. Roberto would have to stay in Hong Kong alone, and he felt uneasy. It was his first trip to Asia and he did not speak a word of any foreign language. But he knew about my underground fights and understood my predicament.

When I arrived in Canton, Fu Han Tong told me what that special treat actually was. From whom, exactly, I never found out, but I had received permission to participate in the legendary Quest of the Five Goats. I had heard about the Five Goats, which were the symbol of Guangdong, but I didn't know any details about the challenge. It was a Kung Fu legend shrouded in mystery that dated back to the late 1700s. Unlike other Canton legends, such as the heroic Ten Tigers—*Sap Fu*—the quest of the Five Goats was a closely guarded secret. It consisted of a series of trails that only a handful of top fighters had the privilege of being exposed to. While the Ten Tigers were popular heroes who had publicly proven their worth as martial artists over the decades, no one really knew what the Five Goats quest consisted of, nor who had undertaken it or beaten it. I did know that the trials were aimed at probing not only the physical and technical strength of the martial artist, but above all his psychological strength and resilience, by subjecting him to extreme risk and danger. The first of the trials were developed in the 1700s, and new and more difficult ones had been added in the ensuing two centuries. The goal was to conquer all five goats, thus gaining entry into the mysterious hall of fame surrounding this legend.

It was a tremendous honour. Not only was it extremely rare to be invited to attempt the Quest of the Five Goats, but I also knew that I was probably the first Westerner to do so. I knew what I was up against. These feats promised to be not only physically and psychologically strenuous but very dangerous too. But my *sifu* believed in me, and this filled me with strength and pride. I was ready for the challenge.

The quest took place on the outskirts of Foshan. After four days, I had conquered the first three goats. Up until that point, I had not had to fight; my physical ability, concentration and inner strength had been tested. In some cases, the difficulty was a technical one, while in others, it was physical, and in other cases still, I was exposed to extreme risk. In faithfulness to the secret legend, I cannot reveal all the details of the tests, but I can give a few small examples. In one instance, I was asked to squat for as long as possible in *Ma Bo*, the horseman stance, with a thirty-kilogramme bag of rice on my head. In another, I was blind-folded and positioned in front of a stack of bamboo sticks that were tied together on both ends. I was told to break through the stack using the hand technique of my choice. My technique—the Eye of the Phoenix—punched through to the other side and I succeeded.

When, on the afternoon of the fourth day, I was told that my next test would be a fight, I was oddly relieved. I had been subjected to three and a half days of strenuous trials. I was physically, psychologically and emotionally exhausted. Ironically, a fight, even one without rules or protections, would be comfortably familiar. It was the first test I could actually anticipate and visualize, its intrinsic unpredictability notwithstanding. But of course, no matter who my adversary was, I knew I was starting at a considerable disadvantage compared to him:

I had just spent the last three and a half days undergoing the most extenuating martial experiences in my twenty years of practice.

That fight brought to an end not only my Five Goats Quest, but also my years-long winning streak. It was the first time I lost a fight, and I came dangerously close to losing my life, too. My adversary was strong and smart, with an evil twinkle in his eye. Several minutes into the fight, we were grappling in a head-lock. With his arm around my neck and his wrist under my chin, he threw me to the ground, and as I fell, he jerked my neck violently. I remember vividly that, as I fell, my mind was focused on how approach the mat fight that was about to begin. I didn't anticipate that violent twist to my neck, which had clearly been aimed at inflicting irreparable harm upon me. We hit the ground and I tried to move. But I just lay there, paralysed. My adversary straddled me, but as soon as he realized that I couldn't move, he stopped and stepped away. Everyone else in the room crowded around me. Fu Han Tong was not among them that afternoon, for reasons unbeknownst to me. I only knew one of the men in the room, but in that moment, as my eyes filled with tears and clouded my vision, I failed to recognize him. I was paralysed, aware of the commotion around me but unable to move or speak.

The men around me were talking and shouting animatedly at one another. No one tried spoke to me or touched me, maybe because they thought my neck was broken and that I was about to die. But rather than call for help, they threw a blanket over me and slowly pushed me to one corner of the room. A few moments later, there was silence and darkness. Everyone had left.

At first I didn't understand. I thought they had gone to get help and that in a few minutes they would be back, with an ambulance or at least a doctor. I don't know how long it took before I realized that nothing of the sort would happen: they had abandoned me. Those men must have thought there was no hope for me, and that in a matter of hours, I would be dead. Panic clutched at my throat. I felt like screaming but couldn't make a sound. They had dumped me in a corner, unable to speak or move, thousands of miles away from home. There was nothing, absolutely nothing that I could do. Maybe those men were right that I had fractured my cervical vertebrae, and would die then and there, or remain paralysed for the rest of my life. I didn't know what was worse: to die in a shabby warehouse in China, without my family on the other side of the planet ever knowing what happened to me, or to live immobilized for the rest of my life, deprived of Kung Fu, my lifeblood. I felt trapped in a nightmare, at a crossroads between bad and worse, unable to choose between the lesser of two evils. I was at the mercy of a cruel fate. As I developed a fever and pain numbed my body, I lay in that twilight zone separating life from death.

I had been there once before, many years prior, in 1974. I was camping with friends while in Manarola, a sea-side town in Cinque Terre, in Liguria. One day we decided to climb down from the beach onto the side of a steep cliff, in search of ocean treasures. Along the way I decided to take a break on a rock facing the water to meditate; I sat there with my legs crossed, practicing Tzu Chan, while my friends continued hunting for sea urchins along the rocky coast. After a few minutes I sensed a deep rumbling above me and felt the warm sand shaking beneath my feet. I lifted my gaze and saw a few pebbles rolling down towards me. Suddenly the pebbles became stones and then large rocks: I was in the middle of a massive landslide. The beautiful Cinque Terre, that jagged strip of Ligurian land between the turquoise Mediterranean and the rocky hillside, had turned into an abyss that was ready to swallow me. As the rocks tumbled down, I started to run towards the sea, but a large rock hit me in the back. I fell face down into the water. I tried to move, but could not lift a limb: I was paralysed. Luckily, the water was shallow enough for me to stretch my neck above the surface and breathe. As I lay in the water, conscious but immobile, I watched in horror as rocks continued tumbling down and heard voices screaming in the distance as people caught sight of me, stuck in the midst of that horrifying rock shower. I knew I was there, on that imperceptibly narrow stretch separating life from death, and there was nothing I could do to influence the outcome.

That day, in Manarola, I knew I wouldn't be forgotten on the beach. My friends would rush over as soon as the landslide ended and done what they could to save me. They would have taken care of me, in a place, in a language and in a context that were familiar. And that's exactly what happened. As soon as the landslide was over, my friends and several onlookers ran over and rushed me to the nearest hospital, in La Spezia. The doctors saw me immediately, concerned that I had broken my backbone. I lay there, covered in cuts, bruises, with the dried blood on my paralysed back sticking to the bed sheets. Much more than the physical pain, I remember the sheer fear of being unable to move again or practice my Kung Fu. But it did not last long. The doctors told me that the rock had narrowly missed my vertebrae and had not done irreparable damage to the nerves around them. I was discharged a week later, and my parents drove me back to Genova where I stayed with an aunt who could take care of me while my mom and dad worked. My spirits soon lifted. I was being lovingly cared for and was on the road to recovery. I rejoiced at the thought that I would soon be reunited with Fu Han Tong, who would help me with his cures and practices. Practicing "Eight Pieces of Brocade"—*Ba Duan Jin*—as well as the Taoist postural exercises *Tao Yin* were an enormous help, and I made a full recovery in a matter of weeks.

But that night in Foshan, I was paralysed, alone, and

abandoned to my fate. I remained fully conscious and concentrated on my breathing. By breathing into my abdomen I was able to keep my lungs still and control the excruciating pain in my neck. I took small comfort in the complete stillness of my body.

The hours that followed were a haze. I lay there for what felt like both an instant and an eternity; I lost all sense of time. Only by the light filtering through the door did I know that it was morning when I heard voices approaching the building. The door opened and I glimpsed out of the corner of my eye the men entering the room. Fu Han Tong was amongst them. I felt a surge of joy and relief. I was still alive, and Fu Han Tong had come to save me.

As the men approached me, they probably thought I was dead. I may have been paralysed, but I was fully conscious. I hadn't broken my neck and my medulla was intact. But my cervical joints had suffered severe whiplash. Fu Han Tong immediately understood what had happened, but I saw neither grief nor relief as he looked into my eyes. He didn't say a word to me but gave matter-of-fact instructions to the others on what to do. They gave me some water by squeezing a sponge into my half-open mouth. I was very gently turned onto one side so Fu Han Tong could examine my spine. Once he confirmed that neither my back nor my neck were broken, three men lifted me from my armpits while Fu Han Tong held my neck still. I was eased on to another blanket, which they used as a stretcher to carry me to a van. I assumed I would be driven to a hospital, but instead I was taken to a guesthouse. Looking back on it, I see now that if I had been taken to a hospital, the truth about the Quest of the Five Goats would have been revealed. Who knows, there may have also been illegal bets placed on the Quest. The Chinese bet on anything and everything that fights, from cocks and mantises to human beings. The gambling can be a game, or it can be a business. Both were illegal. Plus, we were in mainland China, where traditional Kung Fu was strictly prohibited by the regime: if we had been found out, everyone would have gotten into deep trouble, me first and foremost.

A doctor came to visit a few hours later. He and Fu Han Tong spoke amongst themselves. Neither said a word to me. I understood from their conversation that the doctor practiced traditional Chinese medicine. Sure enough, he pressed needles into my aching body, poured two spoonfuls of a sour syrup between my slightly parted lips, and gently massaged a cream onto my neck and back. Before they left the room, I looked intently at Fu Han Tong. With my eyes, I begged him to say something to me, just one word of comfort and reassurance. He looked at me and understood. With a faint twinkle in his eye, he repeated three times in Cantonese: "*ng gan yiu*"—"don't worry, don't worry, don't worry." That would be the only thing he ever said to me about the near-death ordeal I had been through, both at the time and in the years that followed. But that was just the way he was. I had known him since I was eleven. Language, culture, and personality all explained why my relationship with Fu Han Tong was never about words. Those three words were enough for me. They were all I needed: there was no reason for me to worry. I was going to be okay.

Indeed, in the days that followed, I slowly began to get better. I stayed in that guesthouse for six days, during which I was treated with acupuncture, acetaminophen to lower my temperature, and herbal creams and syrups. After two days, my fever was gone and the pain in my neck had calmed significantly. Very gradually, I regained my facial mobility, and then mobility of my body. Miraculously, in less than a week I was on my feet. I walked badly, but at least I could walk.

As soon as I was able to able to move with relative ease, I returned to Hong Kong. Roberto, unaware of what had happened to me, had been growing more anxious by the hour, and balked at the sight of me. I was alive, but I was not in great shape. I had only regained about thirty percent of my mobility, I had sprained my wrist, and I had a gash above my eyebrow. In Hong Kong, thanks to Roberto's company, I recovered not only physically, but psychologically too. But my wounds were deep. This time it was not just a physical wound from the violence of a fight. It was not just the damage I inflicted upon my adversary, nor even the greater damage he had inflicted upon me. It was not about losing a fight. In sports, as in life, learning how to lose is part of the beauty of it all, even more so than learning how to win. It was not even about the betting that may have been behind the Quest.

I suffered for another reason: the sheer inhumanity of the men who had abandoned me in that room. Fu Han Tong had not been there. I was convinced and needed to believe that no sooner had he found out what had happened, he had rushed to my rescue. But those men who had seen me fall and lie motionless on the ground knew what had happened. Maybe they hadn't known what to do; maybe they feared being caught; but no rational explanation satisfied me. I simply could not digest their total indifference to my fate. In communist China, individual human life has little value; that, I already knew, in theory. The collective always comes before the individual, no matter what. But it's one thing to know the theory and quite another to live it in practice. If I had died, it would have only meant another life gone to those men. They would have felt no responsibility, no remorse. Ultimately, I had chosen to participate in the Quest of the Five Goats. I was aware of the dangers involved and had voluntarily placed my life at risk in a traditional and therefore underground setting against the law. Had I died, as they probably thought I would that night, it would have been nothing more than a hassle to them. I tried to make sense of all this and acknowledge my part in it.

But I simply could not swallow the crude facts. The inhumanity of that abandonment echoes within me to this day.

In our world, risk and danger often arise unexpectedly, spontaneously. Good can transform in evil, and vice versa, in an endless cycle of transformation. I accepted that risk was a part of the life path I had chosen, that danger was intrinsic to my destiny. Risk, hardship, and loneliness I could bear. These were the testing grounds for the resilience I was building in my becoming as a martial artist. My experiences in China were almost never carefree. Entering, discovering, and becoming accepted in the world of traditional Kung Fu was never easy. Incidents and misunderstandings were the order of the day. But there must be a meaning, a purpose behind the risk, and there was neither in gratuitous violence and inhumanity. There was only sadness, loneliness and darkness.

Risk and light

But it was not all darkness. Risk brought with it dazzling light too. I associate such light particularly with my experiences in the field of internal practices, including Chi Kung and *Tzu Chan*, as well as traditional Chinese medicine and treatments. Happily, my experiences in China were not limited to Kung Fu schools and underground fights.

When I was in China, I dove into the country's culture and tradition. I ate red scorpions at dawn, dined on "snake blood"—which was actually snake bile—and tasted a myriad of insects supposedly meant to reinforce the body, mind and soul. I attended traditional rites and animist ceremonies, some of which were characterized by an unspeakable brutality. I participated in folk festivities, beginning with the typical *Mou Si* dances during Chinese New Year. All this was an integral part of my life in China. While only loosely connected to martial arts, these experiences gave me a fuller and more rooted knowledge of Kung Fu. They also enabled me to learn and improve my Chinese, especially Cantonese. To make the most of these situations, I had to accept risk.

This was also true for my immersion in the world of traditional disciplines related to but distinct from martial arts. Fu Han Tong was my entrypoint into this mysterious world. As with everything he did, risk was an essential element in this, too.

One of the most moving experiences I had in this realm dates back to 1986, when I was in Canton. Early one morning, Fu Han Tong approached me with some news. He had managed to retrace one of the most meaningful masters of his life: Tien Sin. Tien Sin was a special man. He had taken a vow of silence and had not spoken a single word in many years. He was a hermit and lived in a secluded hut in the middle of a forest on the border between Guangdong and Guanxi, near Zhaoqing and the town of Liu Zhou. After a long time searching, Fu Han Tong tracked him down and planned a visit. He proposed that I go with him.

Meeting one of Fu Han Tong's masters was a dream come true for me. In the case of *Sifu* Chan Hon Chung, I had a clear idea of his origins and where he was located in the history of Hung Gar; as for Fu Han Tong, on the other hand, placing him in the context of a specific lineage was nearly impossible. His knowledge of Kung Fu was vast and varied, and I only had vague and scattered information about who his masters had been and where he had learned his Kung Fu. Were it not for his unparalleled ability, one might have questioned his legitimacy as a *sifu*. Finding out more about Fu Han Tong's past was immensely valuable to me. Like a child learning more about his family tree, learning more about Fu Han Tong's history meant discovering my own origins as a martial artist. Meeting one of my *sifu*'s masters, and especially a mysterious one like Tien Sin, represented pure bliss to me. Exactly who Tien Sin was and what Kung Fu he practiced were not important. Fu Han Tong said nothing about him, nor did I ask. His style or method seemed like futile details that added little to my knowledge. And, as I was about to discover, it wouldn't change anything about the experience I was about to have.

We set off to meet Tien Sin, whose name means "star of the sky" in Cantonese. Reaching him was an adventure in and of itself. We took several trains from Canton heading west, towards Guangxi. At dawn the following morning, we got off the train at the last stop and started walking. We walked all day, first through the open countryside and then a thick forest. After fifteen hours of walking, a small hut appeared through the trees. It was dusk and the hut was barely visible, camouflaged as it was in the thicket. It was a small traditional Chinese house. As we approached, we saw a fittingly small and slender-looking man squinting at us in the twilight. Fu Han Tong raised his hand in salute. Tien Sin stood still. He may have raised an eyebrow in recognition, but it was already quite dark, and I could not be sure. What I am sure of is that Tien Sin looked intensely in our direction and straight in the eye of his student, Fu Han Tong. The intensity of his gaze pierced through the dusk like a ray of light. He knew who had come to find him. In the presence of those two souls meeting one another, I felt as if I disappeared, vanishing into the sunset. For Fu Han Tong and Tien Sin at that moment, I was simply not there.

Regardless, I performed my *Lai* as a sign of respect. As if only just then realizing that I was there, Fu Han Tong turned to me, and, acting as a surrogate host, showed me a corner in the hut where I could leave my belongings. Without uttering one word, he encouraged me to sit down while he served his master and me some tea, which we sipped in silence. But the silence was thick: master and student exchanged looks that spoke more than a thousand words. As they observed one another, they said without words everything they had lived during their decades apart. I sat there, enthralled. Time went by. As darkness enveloped us, Tien Sin stood up and led us to the patio outside the hut. A fire was burning there, with a stone barbeque and a couple of pots on top. In one, there was some steamed rice. In the other, more tea. In a bamboo basket, some steamed vegetables. It may have been fatigue or perhaps the magic of the atmosphere, but that simple meal was one of the most delicious I've ever had.

As I ate and blood started flowing back to my brain, a number of questions arose in my mind. There was so much I wanted to ask Fu Han Tong about Tien Sin and their relationship. As if he read my mind, Fu Han Tong stared sternly at me. In Tien Sin's refuge, not a word was to be spoken. Tien Sin's vow of silence became ours too as long as we remained there. Silence was the only method of communication.

Tien Sin slowly raised his arm. Like a painter delicately stroking his canvas with a paintbrush, he began calmly stirring the embers on the fire. I watched him, hypnotized. Right at that moment, Tien Sin stood up and started walking. But I saw not one Tien Sin walking—I saw two. As if he had doubled himself, one Tien Sin made his way towards the hut, and the other towards a tree. I pinched myself and rubbed my eyes in disbelief. I was wide awake, and yet I saw a man split in two before my very eyes. I gasped. With a quick gesture, Fu Han Tong silenced me. The two Tien Sins disappeared into thin air.

Fu Han Tong and I remained sitting by the fire a while longer, in silence. I mulled over what I had seen and felt. All the questions I had been pondering a few moments ago suddenly lost meaning. I didn't know and didn't need to know anything about Tien Sin. I had met a unique master. This much was crystal clear to me and nothing else mattered.

The fire went out and we were swallowed by a dark, starless

night, black as tar. Fu Han Tong eventually stood up and pointed out a straw mat where I could sleep. It was a hot and humid night and the mat was anything but comfortable, but as soon as my head hit my bag-turned-pillow, all the tension and fatigue left from my body and I fell into a deep and dreamless sleep.

I woke up with the first rays of light filtering through the windows. The forest was slowly reawakening from its sleep, but in the hut, there was total silence. I assumed that Fu Han Tong and Tien Sin were still sleeping, so I stayed put on my mat. Half an hour or so later, I got up and started wandering aimlessly outside the hut. I found Tien Sin meticulously ploughing his small vegetable garden. Fu Han Tong was nowhere to be seen. Since I couldn't ask Tien Sin any questions, it took a few minutes before I understood: Fu Han Tong had left. He must have left the hut silently, in the dark, before I woke up. He had accomplished what he'd come for. In that evening of silence, Fu Han Tong had said all there was to say and heard all there was to hear from his master. I was another matter. If Fu Han Tong had left me there, there had to be a reason. Unlike him, my time getting to know Tien Sin had just begun. I had no idea how it would unfold and when it would end. And I didn't have the faintest idea if or when Fu Han Tong would come back to get me.

Tien Sin paid absolutely no attention to me. Not only did he not speak, but he also didn't look at me, or try to communicate in any other way. He only did three things. First, he showed me where I could find the steamed rice bowl and the tea. I would be on my own: he had no intention of sharing meals with me or the like, but he made sure I had what I needed to survive.

Second, in the evening of my first day alone there, Tien Sin removed the straw mat I had slept on the night before. He gave me another one to replace it, but the catch was that the second mat was unfinished: it was only twenty centimetres long. The rest was a bundle of knotted straw. He clearly signalled that it was time for bed. Weaving my own bed was up to me. It goes without saying that he gave me no clue as to how to do it. Left to my own devices, I tried to braid the straw into something resembling a mat. The alternative was to sleep on the dirt floor. The result was barely decent: it looked more like a piece of swiss cheese than a bed. For the entirety of my stay, I slept on the edges of my swiss cheese mat. It was obviously one of the house rules.

Third, and most important, Tien Sin led me to a tree with a wide trunk and protruding roots, winding branches and rich silvery green foliage. It must have been hundreds of years old. I couldn't recognize its species, but I sensed its wisdom. Tien Sin gazed at the tree, and it seemed like the tree gazed back at him. With a slight nod, he suggested I observe the tree too. That was what I was there for.

I quickly settled into a routine. The rhythm of my days was marked by internal practices, training and cautious exploration of my surroundings. Three times a day, I went to the tree to meditate. Once a day, I ate steamed rice, vegetables, tubers and the occasional fruit, and drank plenty of tea. By and large, Tien Sin continued his hermit existence as if I was not there. Only on a few occasions, I sensed him watching from afar as I meditated by the tree. I knew that was all Tien Sin was interested in. When I saw him meditate, he made guttural sounds, as if he were chanting a sutra or a prayer. Those were the only sounds I ever heard him make.

As the days went by, my meditations changed. From Tzu Chan *in front* of the tree, I gradually, almost imperceptibly, began meditating *with* the tree. The tree gradually changed from being my reference point to being my companion, and eventually, as our confidence grew, my friend. More and more I found myself talking to the tree as if it were a human being, and, just like a friend, the tree slowly started talking back. As this happened, my meditations became longer and more intense. Hours on end passed in silent conversation between us.

At the end of my second week, Tien Sin approached me and signalled that I should follow him to the tree. I stopped in my usual mediation spot but Tien Sin walked all the way up to the tree, and, with a sharp flick of his hand, chipped off a piece of bark. He then picked a leaf and came up to me. He placed the bark and leaf in my hands and signalled to me to chew and eat them. I did as I was told. He then pointed to the ground, suggesting that I begin my meditation.

It was enlightening. It was one of the rare moments in life when I've felt a total, all-encompassing awakening within. I was no longer meditating in front of the tree. Nor was I meditating with the tree. I had become the tree itself and the tree had become me. As I chewed and swallowed the bark and leaf, the tree and I became one. First a reference point, then a companion, and eventually a friend: my love for that plant had grown with time. At that moment, I felt the love swelled inside me, joining me and the tree into one and imbuing me with newfound strength and faith. The protective energy the tree had given me during those weeks had become my own. The power of the tree, which had stood in that forest for hundreds of years, ran through me.

When I awoke from the meditation, Tien Sin was no longer there. I strolled back to the house and found him inside. He slowly picked up my bag and dropped it at my feet. My time with him was over; I had done what I was there to do. It was time to go.

I turned around to see whether I was still alone with Tien Sin. If my time was up, had Fu Han Tong returned? If Fu Han Tong had brought me there for a purpose, had he come back to take me home now that my purpose had been achieved? I was after all in the middle of a dense forest, a fifteen hours' walk away from civilization on a narrow path covered in leaves and branches, hardly discernible to the human eye.

Fu Han Tong was nowhere to be seen and I realized that he would not be coming back. I was on my own, but not completely: I walked back to the tree, almost without thinking, to hug my friend goodbye. But as soon as I saw it, I realized there was no goodbye needed between us. As I hugged the tree and performed my *Lai* to it, I knew he was in me, and would remain there along my journey. Enriched by the powerful wisdom of that tree, I hoisted my bag over my shoulder and left Tien Sin's hut, without looking back.

I began walking along the path I remembered, but I soon lost the trail. I had been walking for a kilometre or so when I completely lost my bearings. When I had walked to Tien Sin's hut with Fu Han Tong, I hadn't paid much attention to where we were going. I had followed my *sifu* without memorizing the way. It hadn't crossed my mind that I might be alone on the way back.

I wandered in the forest for two days and two nights. The risks I encountered over those two days were enormous. The forest was home to bears, jaguars, monkeys, snakes—including silver pitons and cobras—scorpions, poisonous spiders, and various other dangerous insects. I heard monkeys and other animals, and saw enormous spider-webs and desiccated snake-skins. I wore all the clothes I had with me in order to cover as much of my body as possible, in the event of an unfortunate encounter. I climbed up trees at dusk and slept aloft on both nights I spent in that forest, coming back down at dawn to restart my seemingly endless walk.

Fate, fortune, and the innate wisdom of the tree were on my side. I didn't get stung by any insects or attacked by any animal. On the afternoon of the second day, I came upon a farmer's house in a clearing. Relieved, I approached to ask for help. I must have been quite a sight. After having spent two days wandering the forest, and the two weeks prior to that as a hermit in meditation on one meal a day, I probably would have scared anyone off. Plus, these would likely be Chinese farmers who had never seen a white person in their lives, and they would think I was a white devil, a *Kwai Lo*. Sure enough, as soon as two women in the fields saw me, they started yelling, probably calling to their men. Three men quickly appeared and, threatening me with long pitchforks, shooed me away. Shaken by the chase but relieved to have finally found some trace of humankind, I kept walking. One kilometre or so later, I came across another farmer's house, where the same sorry scene repeated itself. I approached an elderly couple standing in front of their house. When they saw me, the man lifted his pitchfork threateningly, while the woman turned around to ask for help. When I saw four young men running towards me from the field, I made a hasty retreat.

Right at that moment, luck intervened: I tripped over an old railroad track that had been covered by overgrown grass. Even if it was no longer active, the track must have led somewhere and in a relatively straight line. The chances of accidentally stepping on a snake or dangerous insect were far lower than in the forest. After several more hours, as the night started to fall, I finally came to a small train station. There, I saw several other active train-tracks. A handful of people were waiting for a train to come in. I had no idea where I was, but I was safe.

I got on the first train that arrived at the station. It was an extremely old and rundown wooden train. It was packed with farmers, carrying all sorts of livestock, notably pigs and chicken. My fellow passengers were destitute and dirty. On their sun-burned, toothless, and jagged faces, I could read all the hardship, poverty and suffering they had been through, all the brutality of their lives. Unlike the farmers I had seen in the forest, they paid no attention to me. They stood, crammed against one another and their animals, smoking in silence. Now and then, a man turned around and urinated from the carriage. It would clearly be futile to try and gather any information from them. I stood there with them, in a silence that by then had become my companion. When the train reached what looked like a bigger station, I stepped off. I asked for help, to figure out how to reach Guangzhou. Finally a young man was able to point me to the next train headed for Canton.

I reached Canton the following morning, but I had no intention of stopping there. I felt no desire to find Fu Han Tong; it was not the time to see him. My survival instincts pushed me in the opposite direction: I longed for someone and someplace familiar, safe. What I had lived through in those two weeks and two days had been as extreme as it had been exhilarating. But at that point, I longed for its reverse: I needed safety and protection. My destination was 729 Nathan Road, Hong Kong. I needed the reassurance that only *Sifu* Chan Hon Chung could provide.

I arrived at *Sifu* Chan's *kwoon* before dusk. I recognized some familiar faces in the building, but they hardly recognized me. I had lost fourteen kilos, I was filthy, and my many layers of clothing were torn and tattered: I looked more like a war veteran than a proper martial artist. In the *kwoon* I found the comfort I was seeking; I was welcomed, nourished, and cared for. I ate, rested, and was seen by several doctors. Neither *Sifu* Chan, nor anyone else, asked me any questions. Nor was I inclined to tell my story.

It took me several days to recover my physical strength and begin to digest the enormity of the experience I had lived. After a few days of rest, I had regained my energy, and eased back into the familiar routine of the *kwoon*. I stayed there for several more weeks before I was ready to go back home.

Celebrating risk

When I returned to Genoa, Angela and the students closest to me knew that I had been through something big. More so than on previous occasions, I struggled to convey the details and, especially, the emotions I had lived. But the fact that it had been important, and that the risk I had taken brought with it unimaginable light, must have shone from every pore of my body.

The day after my arrival, I walked up the familiar staircase leading to the entrance of my *kwoon* with three-year old Shan in my arms. There was an unusual silence and tension in the air. All the lights were out. Shan wriggled; he sensed something odd and uncanny about the situation. I was puzzled too.

As we stepped through the gate, fireworks went off, the familiar rolling of the drums began, the lions lit up and a crowd of two hundred and fifty people burst into a heartfelt applause: my family and students had organized a party to celebrate my return. And what a celebration it was. With a rich banquet, martial arts demonstrations, talk and laughter, we celebrated late into the night.

Angela, my parents, and my students knew little about the risks I had experienced. But they must have sensed how close they had come to losing me. I, on the other hand, knew well all the risks I had taken. But, more importantly, I knew how much they had been worth. As I partied through the night amidst the love and affection of my Kung Fu family, the darkness of risk faded, and its light engulfed me with all its force.

Risk

Risk is part of life. No one looks for it, no one wants it, but all of us meet it along our journey. Many Kung Fu styles interpret risk, and many professions and life circumstances create it: from the choice of a medicine to a style of travelling, from the desire to save time to the sheer excitement of a game or sport. Risk can turn a positive into a negative and vice versa. Its intrinsic uncertainty draws us towards it.

Why do we take risks? We risk to preserve but also to change. Risk can edge us towards danger, defeat, or loss. At times risk chooses us, at times we consciously choose it.

I risked my life when I was caught in a landslide at fourteen. It was fate, not a conscious decision. Many other times, I have consciously chosen risk to challenge myself and grow, overcome my limits and my fears, driven by the energy to discover, see and touch, and play the game. Risk can lead to light or darkness, but when I have consciously chosen it, I have always learned to empty my mind of its demons no matter the outcome.

Risk is cold, and some people like it that way, but without a doubt it adds spice to our lives!

CHAPTER 6
Generosity

In the second half of the 1980s I was approaching my thirtieth birthday, and the balance between giving and receiving in my life began to shift decisively towards the former. During this gradual transformation into adulthood, martial arts remained the overarching context that framed and shaped my relationships with others. That fact, alongside the duality of my life between man and master, meant that giving was never straightforward for me. This complexity around giving is a characteristic of mine that I have struggled with, learned from and ultimately made peace with over the decades.

Until my late twenties, I had essentially focused on myself. The absolute conviction I'd held since childhood that martial arts were my life's path had triggered a near-break with my family. My parents' initial resistance to my choice could and would not deter me, even if it came at the steep cost of our souring relations. Our relationship improved only gradually in the 1980s, as my mother and father realized that I hadn't acted on an irresponsible childish whim, but rather made a successful life choice driven by passion, commitment, and hard work. I am especially glad that my father reconciled himself with my life choice well before his death in 1988. My time with Fu Han Tong was almost exclusively focused on me, both because he was my *sifu* and because of his inscrutable personality and troubled history. My relationship with Angela, too, revolved around me in its early years, as she was swept into my world, enthralled by the magic of Kung Fu. The scales were certainly tipped towards my own growth and development during my travels to Asia. With a few exceptions, I always travelled there alone. My desire for self-realization in the world of martial arts, even when it meant risk and sacrifice, was the light that guided me in those years.

Naturally it was not a one-way street. Since I was young, taking and giving had been intrinsically reciprocal for me; they were two sides of the same coin. I had started teaching martial arts when I was fifteen and Kung Fu at seventeen. Teaching is all about giving, but I knew that I could be a good teacher and therefore give the best to my students only if I too was growing in my Kung Fu and therefore receiving, first and foremost from my *sifu*. Thus even my travels to China and Thailand weren't only about me: they were about my school and my students, including my brother and my friends; they were about Angela and our growth as martial artists and as partners; and they were about my son Shan and his future. I could never have endured all the loneliness, hardship and darkness of those years if it had been in service of only myself. My Kung Fu was and remains the frame within which all my relationships have unfolded.

But the martial arts framing of my life has not been static. No living thing can be. The balance between giving and receiving started shifting over the years, with the former moving more to centre stage and becoming more complex as time went by. This is true for me as well as for those around me: the more I have given to my role as *sifu,* the more I have received from those who have chosen to follow me, and this is still true to this day. Angela once described me as an oak that casts a shadow on those who stand near it. At the time, her words bothered me. I have never intentionally cast a shadow over anyone, let alone over my loved ones. But there is an undeniable truth to what she said. My dual role requires a twofold generosity: my generosity in teaching and protecting, and the equally important generosity and selflessness of those who choose to live under my shadow. As I transitioned from childhood into adolescence and then adulthood, I began to understand that generosity, in all its complexity, is a foundational stone of the way of martial arts.

The kwoon

By the late 1980s my *kwoon* was over a decade old. It had developed into a somewhat large business, with thousands of students and dozens of instructors spread across the Italian peninsula, and a rather complex structure. This was due not only to its structured curricula, its practical and theoretical exams, its extra-curricular internships, its public exhibitions and its internal rules; but also to its organization and management. I had never studied management nor experienced life in a private company, and I had no idea how to run what was in practice a medium-sized business. But through instinct, trial and error, hard work, and enormous sacrifice, I established my own business model that provided a living to me, my family, and to all my instructors, who were realizing their own dreams to live and work through martial arts.

Among them was my brother Carlo. Carlo became one of the first instructors in my school after having dropped out of university to dedicate his life to martial arts. I had been uneasy about his choice at first, feeling an extra weight upon my shoulders. I shared my doubts with him, but I still felt that it was my duty to support him. To make ends meet, Carlo took a second job in the port of Genoa, while teaching and investing in his Kung Fu in parallel. As the school grew and, with it, so did its finances, he eventually dropped the second job and earned enough to support himself just by teaching in my *kwoon*. I was proud that I had given him the opportunity to work and earn through our shared passion for Kung Fu. The port job had been tough, and it was a relief for everyone when he quit. I was also happy to relieve my parents of their anxiety, which this time was not about my own future, but about my brother's.

The instructors were critical to the proper functioning of the school, both because of its expansion across the country and my regular absences during my Asian travels. To create consistency, I set up an intricate rotation schedule for myself and a group of instructors. To ensure that all our students around the country followed the exact same curricula, I felt that regular sessions with my instructors and the extra-curricular workshops open to everyone were not sufficient. I strongly believed that, as their *sifu*, each of my students deserved face time with me, and also that they should learn from as many instructors as possible. Each one had his or her strengths and weaknesses.

I developed the rotation mechanism for us. It didn't include all instructors; some of them, like those who had other jobs and families to look after, weren't available to travel non-stop across the country. Tonino Cusenza and Guido Politini, for instance, whom I had met back in Terni in 1979, were long-standing students of mine and among my first instructors. But they taught Kung Fu alongside having other jobs. They couldn't always be on the move across the country. Others could. The rotation included my brother Carlo, Claudio, Gianfranco, Giuseppe, Pier, and several other instructors; eventually I registered the *kwoon* as an association, in order to legitimize its organization and finances. I rented apartments in the various cities and towns where the branches of my *kwoon* were located, which we called *kwoon* homes. The apartments were open to all instructors, who could make use of them any time they spent a few days teaching in that particular town or city. In Rome, Milan, Genoa, Terni and several other cities, instructors were able to stay in a *kwoon* home.

This organizational structure had financial implications. Given that many of our expenses were shared and related to the operation of the school, I retained centralized control of our revenue and established a meticulous accounting system to track costs, hours worked, and compensation. Every month I collected and accounted for the revenue from every school branch, as well as all expense receipts, or at least as many as I could locate. These included fixed costs such as renting the school spaces and the *kwoon* homes, and variable ones such as the cost of travel or the public events we participated in in Italy and abroad to promote the school. Once everyone had been reimbursed, I redistributed the profits among the staff. Compensation was based on the skill level of each instructor as well as on the number of hours worked over the month. This meant that there was an overall predictability and stability to the instructors' income, and everyone felt invested in our common enterprise. The more they progressed in their personal practice and passed their own exams, the more teaching hours they would put in and the higher their income would be. The school's collective success was connected to their personal success.

This system was effective and fair, but it was extremely time consuming. This was because, in addition to its complex enough ordinary structure, there were extraordinary requests, too. Although the *kwoon* was run as a business, it remained a family above all else. Hence, if an instructor was in financial trouble for personal reasons, I always tried to help. This often meant requests for advance payments of their monthly salary. I never bit off more than I could chew: if I granted an advance payment, I did so because I was sure that it would be safely below what that instructor would eventually earn that month. Otherwise, helping one instructor would have created problems, misunderstandings and resentments among the others, damaging the overall harmony and health of the school. But each individual request—and there were many—added an extra layer of complication. Largely because of my accommodating approach, these requests increased over time. In retrospect, I see how their gradual increase became part of the degeneration and eventual poison that led to a shattering rupture within the school. But this wouldn't come until several years later. In the 1980s and early 1990s, my *kwoon* was a family, and if a family member asked for help, I would always go the extra mile for them.

This is why I organized the school in a deeply communal way. In turn, this fostered that familial feeling of belonging among us. The *kwoon* homes and the frequent travel to participate in martial arts exhibitions abroad meant that, alongside training, we often slept, ate and spent our free time together. I smile now at the memories of our Kung Fu exhibitions. For each one, I would select a team, with whom I would train intensely for several weeks prior to the exhibition. We would travel together to the event, proudly dressed in our *kwoon* uniforms to show the martial world what we were all about. Those exhibitions were incredibly intense bonding experiences for us. The emotions we lived during those moments generated a special sense of unity in our school.

There were difficult moments too, of course. The codependent structure of the *kwoon* created occasional tensions within the "family." While I rarely had arguments with my instructors, they often quarreled among themselves. Just like in a family, when certain members bond more with some than others, so it was at a larger scale within my school. Each instructor had a unique personality, history, and lifestyle, and inevitably had his or her likes and dislikes. When fights arose, all I could do was mediate, pacify, and occasionally arbitrate. When our finances were especially flush or there were no major events affecting life in the school, I could easily manage the occasional flare-up in what was otherwise a harmonious family life. At other moments, if my stress levels were unusually high, perhaps because of a particularly trying experience in China, petty arguments between instructors weighed on me.

The communal structure of the *kwoon* did entail sacrifices. For one, it meant that I could never really take a break from the school, which was ultimately work, no matter how much I loved it. This caused me incredible stress, which accumulated over the years and eventually came with a cost. It also meant that I hardly had a private life. At home in Genoa, Angela, Shan, and I were rarely alone, often hosting students and instructors from all over the country. This had its upsides, especially for little Shan, who was always surrounded by entertainment, love and affection. But here too, a cost surfaced over time, notably in my relationship with Angela.

But all in all, I felt it was all incredibly worthwhile. I had built a family woven together by a love for martial arts. I considered all my instructors to be friends and brothers in the life we had chosen and were succeeding at. I was proud of what we were building and of the results we were achieving. I was happy to have set up a company that offered great comfort and resources to its members: it represented a home for us all. There were difficult moments and sacrifices, but with generosity and an open heart, we overcame them all. The wheel was turning, and it was taking me and my growing Kung Fu family ever forward along our chosen path.

A master and a father

The balance between giving and receiving in my life changed when I became a father. Shan was born in March of 1983 and became a powerful source of love in my life. I always felt a strong sense of responsibility towards my family: I thought of Angela and Shan, first and foremost. I did everything I could to provide for all their needs. During Shan's childhood, however, our time together was interrupted by my frequent trips away from home. When he was a baby and toddler, my time with my son had to be squeezed in between my travels to Asia and the constant rotation between the branches of my school. In those precious moments with him, I tried to give him all my love; still, spending long periods away from home caused me, and no doubt my family, great pain.

Angela and Shan's pain took different forms. Angela understood me; we shared a life project. She suffered in my absences, of course, but it was a pain that she accepted because she had consciously chosen our life together. Shan was too young to truly realize what was going on. To him, it was natural for his dad to be away often, and to have to share him with all the students and instructors who constantly came over to visit. Normal as it may have been for him, I am sure he sometimes missed the intimacy of family life.

As for my pain, it took yet another form. When I was away, I felt a numb sense of emptiness, especially in the depths of my loneliness after my fights in China. It was during those moments that I missed my family the most. Paradoxically, the pain became even more acute once I returned home. When Shan and Angela came to pick me up at the airport after I'd spent two or three months abroad, the sight of how much Shan had grown would send shock waves through my body. His physical development was the living proof of my time away from home and from him. The initial shock dissolved, almost magically, as soon as I held little Shan in my arms. But the deeper numbness was ever-present over the years. When I look back, the pain resurfaces; but I have no regrets. My constant travels were part of what my path had in store for me. That pain is part of the baggage that defines me.

As time went by, martial arts came to our rescue and became

the language through which I communicated deeply with my son. Shan was raised on milk and martial arts. He began practicing Kung Fu when he was a toddler. I recall vividly his tiny *Ma Bo* stances when he was only three years old. All of our friends were somehow connected to the world of martial arts. Whether at our school, at home, or on holiday, martial arts were a foundational pillar of Shan's life, and he struggled to understand how life could be any different. He assumed that all his friends knew Kwan Kung—the famed Chinese general of the late Han dynasty period, later deified as the god of war and protector of martial arts and of the Chinese people. When he play-fought with his friends, he took for granted that rules of the game included the discipline and respect that lie at the core of martial arts; he was surprised to discover that this was usually not the case. The children who he met through the *kwoon* related to Shan's world, but many others, notably his school friends, did not understand it.

The way we raised Shan gave him a leg up in martial arts, but his talent and passion for it was as much nature as it was nurture. In this respect, I saw myself in him as a child, even as I recognized that Shan's martial arts were different from mine. As with any form of art, martial arts are a form of deep personal expression, rendered unique by the personality and life path of each practicing artist.

Shan was an incredibly sweet and sensitive boy, but he was also determined, passionate, and strong-willed. He never let Angela or I push him into doing something he didn't want to do. It was Angela and I who first introduced Shan to the world of martial arts, but he very naturally made it his own. He drew others to the practice in his own, special way. Shan's childhood passion for Kung Fu was as inward-looking as he was. In his low-key and unpretentious way, he had a magnetic power of attraction. When the opportunity arose or when he was asked to by his friends, Shan had no qualms about showing them his

Kung Fu. Some have remained his friends and martial arts brothers to this day.

Martial arts were something that Shan felt belonged to him, and there were never tensions between *Sifu* Cangelosi and Shan the martial arts student. Yes, this meant that I was his master, just as much as I was to his friends. He was expected to show the same respect and follow the same rules as everyone else. But Shan never had an issue with this. There was discipline and hierarchy in the school, and Shan's passion for martial arts meant that he understood and accepted it. Martial arts always remained the glue between me and Shan, even in our most difficult moments.

With time, martial arts came to represent even more for us. It became a tool with which we examined and overcame our misunderstandings, building our relationship over the years. Like me, Shan made martial arts his life choice. He followed in my footsteps but did so in his own way. As he got older, Shan grew within the *kwoon.* He practiced Kung Fu and Muay Thai, excelling in both. As he developed as a martial artist, he eventually began teaching, and became an instructor of both Kung Fu and Muay Thai at the school. Partly due to my growing engagements abroad and partly because of his propensity and passion, a few years after I officially opened the Muay Thai course in 1995, I delegated its coordination entirely to Shan.

Shan also became a professional Muay Thai fighter and champion. Considering how early in his life Shan had started practicing martial arts, his professional fighting career began fairly late. This was due in part to his character, which blossomed with age, but I had also never actively encouraged him to enter this world. Despite the fact that Muay Thai was even more competitive than traditional Kung Fu, I never considered it to be a sport. In fact, I had been attracted to Muay Thai precisely because I saw the art within it. Furthermore, in Shan's teenage years, traditional Muay Thai was still fairly unknown in the West. There were some professional fighting circuits; but professional referees and judges were hard to find, and most tournaments that claimed to be Muay Thai actually featured kickboxing or Savate. I was put off by the social and cultural milieu of that world, and never encouraged my students nor my son to dabble in it.

However, as Shan grew in age, ability, and self-confidence, he started feeling the need to test himself in the ring. In our *kwoon*, we organized combat tournaments every four years or so. I have always believed that it is crucially important for martial artists to have the opportunity to apply their art in combat. These moments are profoundly formative, not merely for technical reasons, but also for emotional and psychological ones. After seventeen-year-old Shan brilliantly won a combat tournament in his weight category in our school, he became hungry for more. I understood his urge and sought to fulfil it. At the same time, I was eager to keep Shan away from the commercial fighting circuits in Italy, fearing they would tear him away from martial arts.

Though I tried to avoid professional tournaments in Italy, I had many contacts in the Muay Thai world in Asia. I turned to my friends in Thailand and arranged Shan's first real fight there. I knew, and Shan did too, that one match in Bangkok was worth dozens in Italy or elsewhere in the West. Shan did not take my proposal lightly. He pondered it carefully, well aware of its implications. But he eventually accepted my offer. He understood the difficulty ahead, but he was talented, strong-willed and brave. Above all, he was passionate about his dream and determined to pursue it. Even if he had never entered a professional ring and hardly knew the specific rules of professional Muay Thai fighting, he was physically and technically ready for it. He would have his first fight at Rajadamnemm stadium, that very same stadium where I had made my first Muay Thai appearance thirteen years before.

Shan's Muay Thai was brilliant. He lost to a professional fighter who had dozens of matches under his belt, but Shan stood his ground and lost on points, not through a K.O. It was a great achievement for a novice. Imbued with newfound energy, Shan set off on his path. In the years that followed, I helped him by organizing more matches and putting him in touch with Muay Thai promoters or friends with whom he could train. Since then, my son has participated in over forty-five professional fights in Thailand and beyond, demonstrating his ability, concentration and courage each time. Whether he wins or loses, Shan always holds his head high. As a teacher, he has trained hundreds of students, some of whom have made it to professional rings too, becoming Muay Thai champions at national and European levels. With four courses a day and nonstop tournament travel on weekends, Shan continues to train himself and his students with astounding commitment and generosity. Sometimes, I think his professional choices come from the heart and not the head. But who am I to judge him for it? Shan has found his path, and that is what matters.

As a Muay Thai professional, champion, and teacher, Shan has pursued his passion for martial arts in a way that is connected to but different than mine. Shan's career in Muay Thai has also meant that martial arts remains the domain in which our deep relationship as father-son/master-student continues to develop. Our relationship has always been complex. My being Shan's father and his *sifu* at the same time wasn't easy for either of us. At times, we both felt the urge to separate these roles, so as to lighten their respective weights. But slowly our double roles have melded into one relationship, deepening our bond. Being Shan's *sifu* has made it easier, not harder, to uphold the protective, guiding, and supportive duties of a father. And being his father has allowed me to be his *sifu* in a more loving, caring and emotional way. No doubt, both Shan and I made mistakes as we played out these overlapping roles.

But we reconciled these mistakes and made our double-roles mutually reinforcing, with time. For this, major credit goes to my son. It takes incredible maturity, self-confidence, and humility to see the beauty in the fusion of a father and a *sifu*. Shan had these characteristics because he is a martial artist. Aside from the tinge of sadness at the thought that he has devoted his energy to the competitive side of our martial arts, which has drawn him away from its spiritual dimension, I am deeply proud of the person Shan has become.

A master and a partner

In my relationship with Angela, too, I had to negotiate various roles. Angela was my first wife and my work partner for life. But she was also my student and remains so to this day. Balancing these different roles was not always easy, especially when we were young. Only recently did she tell me how, amidst the pain of our separation, she felt something light, even liberating: she didn't have to be my partner anymore, and would get to be herself and no one else. But just as martial arts became the language through which I communicated with Shan, it was also the glue that held me and Angela together, despite the upheavals and transformations of our relationship over the decades.

We were brought together by martial arts. Even though she was four years older than me and already a martial arts student, Angela joined my nascent school in 1979, after trying out only one class. After a few months we became friends, and eventually lovers. Our relationship was passionate and intense. We were very different: I was a whirlwind, she was a river. But we were both on the move, seeking our paths together. I was very attracted to her, but most of all there was a great empathy between us. I instinctively felt that I could trust and open up to her. Indeed, trust has been the cornerstone of our forty-year relationship.

But the thing that gave our relationship gravity and depth from the beginning was our shared love for martial arts. We loved each other perhaps above all because we shared the same passion for Kung Fu. My love for martial arts was so intense and all-encompassing that I likely could not have fallen in love with a woman who didn't feel the same way. Despite how young we were, that shared love created a special connection between us that drove us to build our lives together. This is why we both embraced Angela's pregnancy with joy. We were in our twenties and neither of us had a fixed source of income, but we had no doubt about building our future together, and Shan would be an integral part of it.

In the project of our shared life, establishing the *kwoon* was a key milestone. I remember when Angela rushed to my house with my acupuncture set after I deliberately made myself ill to get out of my military service. She was by my side when I got discharged, we looked for a location for my *kwoon* together, and it's thanks to her that we found the old religious conservatory in Salita delle Fieschine that remains the headquarters of the school to this day. Angela has always played a pivotal role in the organization of the school, from its management and finances to the delicate dealings of human relations.

Angela also became a great martial artist. She grew within the school and eventually became an instructor, participating in endless martial arts workshops, exhibitions, and events. Her knowledge of martial arts and Eastern philosophy, history, and medicine is vast. Her practical experience is, too: from traditional Kung Fu styles to self-defence and combat, Angela is a well-rounded martial artist. Over time, she eventually specialized in the external Kung Fu style of Wing Chun and the internal styles of Pa Kua and, above all, Tai Chi.

But what is most special about Angela is her quality as a

teacher. It is here that her generosity shines through most. Angela has taught hundreds of people over the years, and each one found in her a martial mother and guide. Her passion for and commitment to Kung Fu is infectious, and she believes in each of her students, sometimes against all odds. Beyond standard classes, she has privately taught dozens of people, notably those with special needs. Seeing the wonders that Angela has worked with students who have serious physical or mental disabilities is the most tangible proof of what an incredible martial artist, teacher and human being she is.

The same generosity that she offers as a martial artist and teacher, she also displayed as a partner and mother. Angela is an extremely understanding and accommodating woman. Her empathy is often so great that it becomes a source of anxiety for her, but it is a signal of strength, not weakness. True to the nature of Tai Chi, Angela knows how to absorb and accept, rather than stubbornly resist, which makes events naturally flow her way. She does so thanks to her innate wisdom and enormous heart. She managed to support, sustain, and stand by me during those explosive years of growth. She understood my need to discover myself by exploring the world, and never resented me for it. On the contrary, she encouraged me along my path. She has been my most trusted friend, advisor, and confidante over the years.

Angela was pivotal in helping Shan and I manage our complex relationship of father/*sifu* – son/student. She always positioned herself as a neutral but caring presence, easing the tensions that occasionally arose between us. She supported and helped Shan develop his passion for martial arts but was careful not to overly influence his choices. She understood how difficult it was for Shan to endure the double hierarchical role inherent to our relationship. Between Angela and I, there was a hierarchy in our relationship as master and student, but parity and free choice in our bond as husband and wife; with

Shan, however, it was different. As a result, Angela encouraged Shan to pursue his path in Muay Thai. She believed this would help him emancipate himself from me and make him stronger and more resilient. In this respect, she was right. With time, she did come to acknowledge the risk that I had pointed out at the beginning of Shan's career. I knew the Muay Thai world and knew my son. I suspected that he would be increasingly distanced from Kung Fu and absorbed by Muay Thai. His was not a one-off professional fighting experience. Given his talent and determination, it would become his life choice. As a martial artist, Angela too became sceptical about professional combat circuits, especially in the West. As a mother, she feared the injuries that Shan might suffer. To this day, she feels great apprehension ahead of Shan's matches. But all this aside, she has always stood by Shan, prioritizing his happiness and fulfilment over her own anxiety and fear.

It has not always been easy for her. She was in her mid-twenties when Shan was born. At the height of my trips to Asia, she was often alone in taking care of our son. Shan had his grandparents too, of course. I remember when my mom Lidia used to come with us to Vitorchiano in central Italy and looked after Shan and Erica, my brother Carlo's daughter, while I led Kung Fu workshops for several days with Angela, Carlo, and almost two hundred students. But after my dad's death in 1988, my mom drifted away from us, especially after she met her current partner, Giorgio. Renata, Angela's mother, remained very close. She was of tremendous help during Shan's childhood. All this help and support notwithstanding, Angela was, in practice, a single working mother for large stretches of time. During my travels, she had to handle the *kwoon* by herself. She did so while being devoured by anxiety about my experiences in China. She was aware of the risks I was exposed to there and became terribly worried when weeks would pass without news from me. She later told me how, on one occasion, after three weeks of silence, she was on the verge of jumping on a plane to find me, nevermind that she had no idea where to look. I left on a one-way ticket every time, and she did not know when or even whether I would return. She did her utmost to keep the family united, carving out precious time for us on short family holidays in the mountains. More generally, everything she did was characterized with subtle tact, admirable dignity, and profound generosity. Angela tiptoes through life; she doesn't throw punches. So much so that in the fire of my youth, I failed to grasp the magnitude of her internal turmoil, including her pain. Being my wife in the 1980s cannot have been easy. That much I understand now.

Angela put up with a lot in those years, and I remain forever grateful to her. Eventually the fatigue, anxiety, and anger stirring inside her boiled over. In her own way, without thunder or lightening, Angela methodically erected a barrier to protect herself. I failed to see this at the time, and misunderstood the source of her rigidity and coldness. More on this later. Suffice it to say here that our marriage eventually ended. But our deep friendship and work partnership lives on to this day. Forty years later, Angela is one of the cornerstones of my *kwoon*: she remains a student, one of my most senior instructors and the Tai Chi coordinator of the school. My personal relationship with her has gone through countless ups and downs, and eventually settled into an ironclad friendship and partnership. What has remained constant throughout these forty years is our shared love for martial arts, which has framed and solidified the bond between us.

A master and a friend

As a friend, too, it was difficult to navigate my role as *sifu*. It is perhaps in this third domain, friendships, that I carry the deepest scars. This is where my dual role clouded my reason and prevented me from seeing the writing on the wall.

The structure of my *kwoon* was extremely close-knit and communal. I considered my instructors to be part of my extended family. With Gianfranco, Claudio, and Roberto in particular, I became close friends. With them, I shared my anecdotes and secrets, my thoughts and my experiences. We trained, ate, drank, and laughed together, and travelled to countless exhibitions abroad. Together with Gianfranco, I also started rally driving in the late 1980s. This never became more than a hobby for us, but we had a lot of fun in those years. I worked and spent a fair amount of my free time with these friends: we were together on our chosen path of martial arts.

On separate occasions, I took Claudio and Roberto to Hong Kong. To bring them along was a deep act of trust and faith. My travels to Hong Kong and my relationship with Fu Han Tong and Chan Hong Chung represented the most intimate side of my becoming. Since childhood, Fu Han Tong had been my treasured secret, a relationship that I had jealously hidden from my family and friends. Taking Claudio and Roberto to China meant giving them a glimpse of the most intimate part of my soul. It meant a lot to me, far more than they realized. But I trusted my friends completely. I knew I would always stand by them and was sure they would do the same for me.

Regarding Gianfranco and Claudio, I was wrong. I will return to this great pain later. In Roberto's case, there was no black-and-white outcome; it is rather a tragic story of shades of grey. I met Roberto in 1979 during my first national exhibition in Terni. In 1980 he eagerly joined my school. He was a special person: incredibly generous and extremely committed to me and to the school. He was rough, ill-mannered, and coarse in many ways, but he had a big heart and I knew that he would always be there for me. Any time I needed him, Roberto would jump to his feet, ready to follow me into all my projects and adventures. When I decided to expand my *kwoon* internationally, Roberto was my trusted sparring partner. We travelled the world for exhibitions and martial arts events and worked on dozens of educational DVDs and a few book projects. I recall our trips together to San Francisco, Los Angeles, Detroit, and New York where we exhibited, led workshops, and discovered the martial arts world in the United States. We were hosted by well-known Kung Fu schools, like Master Tat Ma Wong's well-established *kwoon* in California, Douglas Wong's, one of America's Kung Fu pioneers, and Frank Lee's Hung Gar school in New York, among others.

My most vivid memory of those trips was the 1997 world championship in California, where I had been invited to serve as judge, referee, and performer among the grand masters. As on many other occasions, Roberto came along with me. He was my sparring partner, and I was his master and babysitter. One evening in San Francisco's bustling Japantown, we gathered for an informal dinner with the organizers of the event and world-renowned celebrities like Sylvester Stallone and Whitney Houston. Faced with sushi and other dishes that were unfamiliar to him, Roberto had a sudden pang of homesickness for Mentana, his village on the outskirts of Rome. He faked a stomachache and barely touched his food. But the minute we left the restaurant and began making our way back to the hotel, Roberto's forlornness magically disappeared, and he dragged me into an Italian restaurant for a hearty plate of pasta. He was not exactly a great traveler, but he was tremendous fun. When I returned to Hong Kong from mainland China after having nearly broken my neck during the Quest of the Five Goats, Roberto lifted my spirits and helped me recover with laughter from one of the most serious physical and psychological traumas of my life. In all his simplicity, he was a great friend.

But Roberto was no angel. Travelling with him was hard; I often felt like I was looking after a child. Moreover, he was often rude to other instructors and could be extremely cheeky. In many ways he took advantage of our friendship. He certainly took liberties that other instructors would not have dreamed of. This created tension within the school; other instructors often complained to me about him. I understood why, but my emotional attachment to Roberto led me to turn a blind eye to his bad behaviour. Of course, I always maintained my role as his *sifu,* but every time I tried to teach him to change his ways, verbally or physically, he solemnly promised that he would change.

Change he did, but not for the better. As time passed, Roberto's behaviour worsened. The school had already gone through a traumatic rupture in the mid-1990s and neither I nor the *kwoon* could take another blow. I waited, and wanted to believe his crocodile tears. I always gave him another chance, despite all evidence and advice. But eventually it became obvious that he was on an irreversible collision course with all the other instructors, poisoning the atmosphere in the school. In 2005 I expelled Roberto, one of my first students, most experienced instructors and best friend. As a *sifu*, I owed it to the school, to myself, and ultimately to him too. As a master, I knew it was the only way for me to protect my school and to teach Roberto perhaps the only lesson he would truly understand. I was his *sifu* and had to behave like it until the very end. As a friend, I suffered tremendously, probably far more than he did, given the downward spiral he was already on. He had been a wonderful friend and a great colleague with whom I had shared an important part of my way. He had a special place in my heart, and he always will.

I was Roberto's *sifu* but I was also his friend, and I felt compelled to leave the door open for him in my heart and in my life. The day he left the school, as he turned away from me and headed towards the exit, I called out to him: "I may have closed the door, but I haven't locked it."

For years I waited for Roberto to walk through that door again. As a *sifu* and as a friend, I never lost faith in him completely. Perhaps he would have one day, perhaps not. I will never know.

Roberto died tragically several years later.

Generosity

Generosity is a noble virtue, a source of energy for the self and others. We can be generous towards ourselves, when we commit to our goals and dedicate the necessary time to achieve them. And we can be generous towards others, offering positivity, giving what matters to us, sharing our knowledge, and letting go of what we have gained through sacrifice.

I have given principally through my art and the knowledge I've gained through years of patient work, risk, and sacrifice. The gift of the teacher is repaid by the respect of the student, creating a beautiful synergy, a never-ending cycle of give and take.

At times the cycle breaks, and disappointment sets in. This has happened to me, too; I have seen precious pearls be squandered, without any sense of gratitude or acknowledgement. But this has not changed my approach. I still share my time and my art with my students with same passion and enthusiasm as always, because ultimately generosity is about putting the other above the self, without expectations and demands for reciprocity.

To be generous is a gift to ourselves and to others that enriches our world.

CHAPTER 7
Rupture

Up until the late 1980s, my life had been eventful, and yet the changes I lived through were the outcome of gradual transformations, not violent breaks. I had been through difficult times at home as a teenager, but even in the most acute moments of crisis, I had never cut ties with my parents. I was little more than a boy when Fu Han Tong had returned to China, leaving me behind as a young *sifu* in Genoa, but I had an address in Hong Kong and the determination to find my master. My father passed away when I was twenty-eight. I mourned his passing and regretted how little time we had had to rebuild our relationship, but his death was not sudden: I had watched him battle his illness for ten long and painful years. My joys, too, had been slow in the making: Angela and Shan, and the gradual building of our small family; my *kwoon* and its growth and expansion across Italy; and my Kung Fu, the hard work I put into every step of the path, hour after hour, day after day, year after year.

Then came a rupture.

Over the course of four years, between 1991 and 1995, I lost both of my masters, my wife and almost half of my school. Each one of these separations took place over the course of a day, and at most a few months. Fall after fall, after fall, after fall, I lost my bearings, and almost lost myself.

My Noble Hero: Losing Chan Hon Chung

In 1987, when he was seventy-eight years old, Chan Hon Chung closed his historic *kwoon* on Nathan Road. Even so, visiting *Sifu* Chan was a must every time I stopped over in Hong Kong. He had moved into a small apartment in the same neighbourhood, and never stopped practicing *Tee Taa*. It was in that small flat that *Sifu* Chan finished teaching me the legendary *Tit Sin Kune*, which is among the most powerful Hung Gar forms ever codified. My time with him was more limited, but it was no less important. *Sifu* Chan had always represented the protective and warm, while still strict and disciplined, side of the master: he was everything that Fu Han Tong was not. In sharp contrast to my risky adventures in China with Fu Han Tong, Chan Hon Chung represented the physical and emotional safety of something familiar, reliable, and comforting. *Sifu* Chan was my noble hero.

On a sunny spring morning in 1991, Angela called to tell me that a letter from my friend Sanny from Hong Kong had arrived, bearing the news that *Sifu* Chan had passed away. It was a double shock for me. I knew Chan Hon Chung was getting old, but all in all he had been rather healthy the last time I had seen him, almost a year prior. It simply had not occurred to me that Chan Hon Chung was approaching death. But the second, and in some respects, deeper, shock that day, was that no one had warned me that his health was deteriorating. I hadn't even been informed about his passing in time for me to travel to Hong Kong to attend his funeral. It was early April when I received that letter. *Sifu* Chan died on the February 23, 1991, a month and a half earlier, age eighty-four.

No sooner did I receive the letter than I instinctively jumped in a cab and headed for the airport. The letter was short and said absolutely nothing about the circumstances of his death or about those he left behind: his family and students. All I knew was that Chan Hon Chung was dead. The only thing I could do to find out more and pay homage to my master was to get myself onto the next plane to Hong Kong.

Once I landed, I went straight to see my friend Sanny. Sanny had been *Sifu* Chan's student, and I suspected that she would know more. Indeed, she did, and what I learned magnified my grief. Sanny painted a desolate picture of my *sifu*'s last years. He who had taught hundreds of students, cured thousands of patients, and been a respected figure in Hong Kong's high society, had been abandoned to himself in his old age. His son Edward had inherited his father's *Tee Taa* clinic, but neither Sanny nor I had the faintest idea where he was now. It was obvious that he hadn't cared for his father at all during his final years, despite the fact that they probably still lived in the same building. Understandably, *Sifu* Chan had always had a soft spot for Edward and treated him with velvet gloves; this annoyed others in his circle, notably *Si Bak* Cheon Yee Keung, the number two in the school and *Sifu* Chan's right-hand man. How could Edward have abandoned his father to his fate?

I needed to find out more. The only person who could help me, or so I thought, was Cheon Yee Keung himself. I was wrong. Cheon Yee Keung greeted me with a smile, but the minute I explained to him why I was there, his expression went blank. Frostily, he cut me off, and told me he didn't have any information about *Sifu* Chan's death. In fact, he had completely lost touch with him in recent years. I asked him if he knew where he was buried; I wanted to pay homage to our master. But Cheon Yee Keung said nothing. I got the impression that to him, *Sifu* Chan had been dead in the deepest sense of the word for several years already.

I couldn't believe my ears. I knew that Cheon Yee Keung had a chip on his shoulder: he had lived and worked in the *kwoon* on Nathan Road and had dedicated his life to the school and to his master. But even though Cheon Yee Keoung's title was *Si Bak*, Edward always took precedence over him in all matters concerning the *kwoon*. It was only after he got married that his resentment boiled over. Cheon Yee Keung's wife encouraged him to move out of the *kwoon* into an apartment of their own, and she didn't stop there. In 1986, she also pressed him to leave the *kwoon* altogether and open his own Kung Fu and *Tee Taa* school. I knew that he had broken off ties with Edward, and consequently with *Sifu* Chan, who had neither acknowledged his school nor agreed to sponsor it. But what astounded me most was that Cheon Yee Keung didn't seemed to care at all about his *sifu's* death. No matter what had happened between them in the past, Chan Hon Chung had been a father, a teacher, and a guide to Cheon Yee Keung; *Sifu* Chan had made him the man he was. Now that *Sifu* Chan was gone and Cheon Yee Keung had an established school and life of his own, how could he be so indifferent and cold?

From that day onwards, my relationship with Cheon Yee Keung began to fray. He had been a Kung Fu brother and a key pillar and guide in *Sifu* Chan's school for ten intense years. Our past remained alive in my heart, but the circumstances of *Sifu* Chan's death made me lose a lot of respect for Cheon Yee Keung. The unravelling of our relationship reached its climax four years later, when Cheon Yee Keung agreed to teach a group of my former students who had betrayed me. Without my name to hide behind, those students went to Hong Kong, ostensibly to learn from Cheon Yee Keung, but in reality to lend their own school greater credibility. A Chinese name leading a Kung Fu school in Italy added lustre to the enterprise. I didn't expect that Cheon Yee Keung would necessarily turn them down; he knew nothing about what had happened between me and those students and, after all, what happened at my school in Italy was my problem, not his. But Cheon Yee Keung knew me, and knew that they had been my students.

Regardless of what version of the story he heard from them when they turned up on his doorstep in Hong Kong, why didn't he reach out to me? Given our decade-long history together, at the very least he could have called me to confirm the facts and make his decision based on that. Cheon Yee Keung was free to behave as he saw fit, but just like in the case of *Sifu* Chan's death, I felt that his instinct had been that of pursuing his own self-interest while trampling over anyone in the way, or at least that's how I interpreted it.

With the death of *Sifu* Chan and the gradual unravelling of my friendship with Cheon Yee Keung, Sanny became my only remaining link to the historic *kwoon* on Nathan Road. From the very first time I had set foot in *Sifu* Chan's *kwoon*, Sanny and I had clicked. She had also bonded immediately with Angela during her first trip to Hong Kong. Sanny and I trained together over the years and became good friends. What added a special touch to our relationship was that she eventually introduced me to her family, and in particular to her father.

Sanny's dad, *Sifu* Tang Hin Kwong, was an experienced practitioner of Choy Lee Fut. But he had never opened a school of his own, nor had he ever taught his Kung Fu to his two daughters and son. It was an immense honour when I eventually became *Sifu* Tang's first and only student. I remember my encounters with him like they were yesterday. When Sanny first introduced us, *Sifu* Tang was already an old and ailing man. As soon as I mentioned Kung Fu to him, however, his eyes lit up. He asked me to demonstrate my Kung Fu to him, which I did. When I stopped, he paused for a few moments in deep thought. Then, as if his frail body regained all its youthful vigour for a moment, he looked at me intensely and, with a twinkle in his eye, proposed that he would teach me his Choy Lee Fut. I was deeply humbled.

From that day on, I often went to visit *Sifu* Tang and his

family whenever I visited Hong Kong. I took off my shoes at the entrance of the apartment and walked into the spacious living room with its old wooden floorboards. There, *Sifu* Tang sat on his armchair waiting for me. He instructed me to move the furniture around to create space for our training session. I have fond memories of those afternoons when *Sifu* Tang taught me his Choy Lee Fut, while Sanny and her sister busily cooked delicious meals for the family. On one such occasion, I glimpsed Sanny standing by the door, watching us. She stood there silently, tears welling in her eyes. I knew it was the first time she was seeing her father teach Kung Fu, and it was a moving sight given his condition. If I thought so, having only just met him, I can imagine what it must have meant for his daughter. When he taught, *Sifu* Tang's age and illness momentarily vanished, and the two of us became fully immersed in the timeless magic of Kung Fu.

That night, when I snuck back into the *kwoon* on Nathan Road way past its closing hour (the *kwoon* was still open at this time), I felt a sudden surge of joy and gratitude. I had been welcomed like a son and brother into the heart and home of a special family.

After *Sifu* Chan's death, Sanny and I kept in touch for some time. During those years, she changed home address several times, but I knew where she worked and I occasionally dropped by to see her at her office when I found myself in Hong Kong. We would go out to lunch and reminisce about the old days together. But one day, in 1994, I went to the usual address and saw her office was no longer there. Her father had died too by then, and I didn't have her or her sister's home addresses. And so, Sanny and I parted ways. We finally reconnected more than twenty years later, in 2015. It felt like two days, not two decades, had passed when we met again. All the familiarity, memories and smiles came back to us. But on that rainy afternoon in 1994, when I thought I would probably never see her again, my heart felt heavy and void: my last tie to Chan Hon Chung had been severed.

My path with Chan Hon Chung was now behind me, but he and his school have lived on. He lives on in me and in my *kwoon*: his picture is on the altar of every branch of my school, and the over thirty thousand students who have studied Kung Fu with me have learned about Chan Hon Chung, his life and the noble Hung Gar lineage he came from. The entire Hung Gar curriculum of my *kwoon* comes from *Sifu* Chan, and the very first form all my students learn—*Mui Fa Kune*—I learned from him, on Nathan Road. As for the very last form—*Tit Sin Kune*—that *Sifu* Chan finished teaching me in his small apartment only few years before his death, I felt ready only recently to teach it to a select group of my students. Such is the power of that form, and of its meaning, that it took almost thirty years before the time was ripe for me to pass it on to others.

But *Sifu* Chan left behind much more than this. It is his way of being, strict and demanding, but with an open heart and healthy principles, that I have tried to embody over time. It is his way of seeing in martial arts not simply competition, confrontation, and violence, but also exchange, love and generosity, that I have sought to teach my students over the years. Martial arts require hard work, and at times risk and danger too. There is no hiding from this. But Chan Hon Chung made me see the light and even comforting side of martial arts. He taught me through his actions, more than his words, that risk need not be lived on the edge of darkness; that martial arts need not be lonely. Chan Hon Chung showed me that martial arts are about giving, about sharing. They are a powerful form of love.

When I think of him, I see him walking down the steps of 729 Nathan Road at five in the morning, ready to take me out for breakfast. I can see him setting up his medical clinic for the day's work, painstakingly explaining to me what those dozens of herbs, oils, and ointments are for. I can recall each and every one of our one-on-one lessons, during which he patiently shared his art with me over the years. It is through these many moments together, and through all his small and big gestures, that the greatness of this man lives on in me.

Today, I have all his small presents tucked away in a drawer in my study. Not once did I leave Hong Kong without *Sifu* Chan offering me a memento of him and his school. Among the other things in that drawer, there are his watch, carefully folded away, a few photographs from his personal album, and two copies of the first edition of his master Lam Sai Wing's book, published almost a century ago. I look at these objects and rejoice that I had the honour of meeting, knowing, and earning the love and respect of this great man. My grief over his death feels a little lighter; wherever he may be now, he knows he has lived on in my school and in my heart.

My great love: losing Angela

In the early 1990s I lost not only my hero, Chan Hon Chung, but also my partner, Angela, my wife, the mother of my son, and my first love.

On the surface everything was going smoothly. Shan had settled into primary school and our small family had moved into a larger and more comfortable apartment. My travels to Asia and across Italy remained constant, as did the stress that came with them, but my routine, and consequently Angela's, was settled.

Yet there was something shifting between us, and not for the better. Imperceptibly, our relationship was becoming colder and less communicative, in sharp contrast to the passion, warmth, and empathy that had characterized our bond from the day we met. For Angela, our lifestyle was becoming increasingly intolerable. While my travels to Asia caused her great anxiety, this was not the main issue. My life in China was part of the parcel she had chosen; she understood how pivotal it was to my path.

What Angela began tolerating less and less were my travels across Italy and the communal organization of the school. As my wife, she was at the centre of the *kwoon.* Because of her deeply empathic personality, she absorbed all of the stress and problems that came with it. She felt she had to constantly mediate, filter, and absorb the tensions within the school, and especially those among certain instructors and between them and me. She shouldered much of the weight of those mounting problems. I didn't understand this at the time, and questioned on what side she was on. In those moments, I probably failed to walk the thin line between Paolo the husband and Cangelosi the *sifu.* Unable to connect deeply with my wife, I took refuge in my role as master, expecting her to act as a loyal student. The trust between Angela and I, which had always been the currency of our relationship, began to thin. In truth, neither of us knew that it was precisely during this period that the poison that eventually culminated in the rupture of our school had begun to spread. Our marriage was perhaps its first casualty.

Our respective behaviours touched the other's most fragile nerves. Angela reacted to her malaise in those years by erecting a barrier, not only vis-à-vis the school, but also towards me. In her mind she tried to separate the school from me, but in her heart she could not. She too failed to draw the line between her husband and her *sifu,* and as a result she distanced herself from both. I didn't understand what was going on. All I saw was that my wife was retreating from me. This touched me in my sorest spot: my loneliness and my deep desire to find physical and emotional refuge in my wife. Feeling rejected, I allowed myself to be wooed by a woman who seemed to offer the warmth I so needed. It was an illusion, a mistake. But I fell into the trap. It didn't cause our separation outright, but it was certainly the straw that broke our marriage's back.

Angela and I became locked in a vicious cycle in which her discomfort and distance fuelled my need and loneliness, which in turn fed her pain and encouraged her to retreat even further. Perhaps we were too immature to see that we were both rubbing salt into the deepest wounds of the other. We were definitely too young and impulsive to pause and try to find a new balance within, rather than outside of, our marriage. So it all happened very quickly. Only a few months passed between the moment the vicious cycle between us came to the fore in late 1992 and the moment when we agreed to separate in early 1993. Neither of us wanted a painful, drawn-out process. We both had strong characters, and a sharp and clean separation was in tune with who we were. Plus, there was nine-year-old Shan, whom we both wanted to shield from our pain as much as possible. We were both determined to protect our son from the violence of enduring excruciating scenes between his mom and dad. After only a handful of fights at home, the cork came off. In the course of a day, Angela and Shan moved into an apartment near Shan's grandmother's house, only a couple of kilometres away from the *kwoon*. I stayed in our family apartment that suddenly seemed horrifyingly big, empty, and silent.

The pain of the separation visited us at different times. For Angela, the hardest period was between 1991 and 1993. In those years, our relationship and its complexities became increasingly heavy, like a noose around her neck that got tighter every day. Feeling cornered, she erected a barrier; she let the passion inside her die until she had the strength to find another path.

My pain came after. Up until our separation, I was of course aware of the deterioration of our marriage, but I was so enmeshed in my own life that I failed to see the warning signs that Angela was sending me. I sensed the distance between us, and my natural reaction was to reach out to Angela to reconnect with her. I was baffled and angry to be met with her wall, instead, but never really considered the possibility of separating from her. So when we did, even though it was a fully consensual separation, I was caught completely off-guard.

On a practical level, my life continued as before. The trips to China, the rotation across Italy, the teaching, the management, the exams, and the workshops at my school persisted uninterrupted: I could not afford to stop. It was a complex machine that had to keep on running, one on which not only dozens of instructors, but also Angela, Shan, and I, depended for a living. With all its intricacies and stress, the show had to go on. It was a machine built with sweat and passion over the years; I couldn't let go.

The continued operation of the machine also helped absorb some of the shock of our separation for Shan. Given that our separation was fast and clean, and that Shan was used to my frequent absences, Angela and I tried to hide it from him. Of course, that didn't last long. When, after a few months, daddy still hadn't come home, Shan understood that something serious had happened. But the *kwoon* anchored him in that period. He kept up his Kung Fu, which meant that Shan and I saw each other regularly. The *kwoon* also provided a context in which Angela and I could interact. Though the bond between Paolo and Angela had been broken momentarily, the bond between master and student never did. Thinking back to Shan during that period, I never sensed any rancour, blame or resentment from him towards me or his mother. He kept up his studies in school, his Kung Fu, and his friendships in and out of the *kwoon*. I don't mean to suggest that Shan didn't suffer. Of course he did, and tremendously. He has always been very connected to his mom, and so he probably suffered both before and after our separation, consciously or not. But Shan's life continued more or less unaltered on the surface, thanks to our "normal" day-to-day routine, and this certainly mitigated his emotional trauma.

For me, on the other hand, the blow was powerful and immediate, so much so that I completely lost my balance. I was alone. My apartment, which had once been our family home, was spacious and comfortable, but it was empty: a perfect mirror for the solitude I felt inside. When I was in China, on rotation across Italy or conducting a workshop in the countryside with my students, I could ignore that harrowing loneliness. But when I was in Genoa, at home, I felt lost in the space and deafened by the silence of my house. There, I had nowhere to hide. Angela and Shan were gone. There was absolutely nothing and no one to help me. I had lost my anchor and I was coming unmoored.

It was during that period that, on instinct, I started sleeping in the *kwoon*. I lived there for a year and a half, even though I still kept my apartment. In the *kwoon*, I set up a mini-apartment, twenty square metres or so, with a bed, a small kitchen and a table, as well as a couple of tatami mats on the floor for my internal practice. It was far from ideal—it was small and spartan—but it became my refuge: a nook that may have been physically uncomfortable, but was exactly what I needed emotionally. I arranged my altar there, with the stern-looking Kwan Kung statuette watching over me. I stacked my books, files and notes, my photographs, magazines and letters. I crammed in most of my belongings and I felt at home, in my *kwoon*. I was in the physical space of my Kung Fu, and ultimately my martial arts were all I felt I had left.

Many people tried to get close to me, but I struggled to connect deeply with the men and women around me. My role as *sifu* did not help. When it came to the men, most failed to see my fragility. I was their *sifu* and therefore invincible: I was a superhero who, by definition, did not need help. They were present, but they remained at the edge of my personal life, never truly stepping inside. Some felt a mix of embarrassment and respect, and others felt indifference. Some must have felt that it was not their place to interfere in my personal life; it would have been inappropriate in their eyes. In truth, I never sought to confide in them and often kept to myself. I'd go out with them for a beer and a laugh. Roberto was among them. We saw each other every month and when we did, he tried to support me. I knew he was genuinely upset about my separation, and that he cared deeply about me, and about Angela, too. But Roberto wasn't part of my day-to-day life, and when I did see him, he tiptoed around my private affairs, careful to not overstep. On my part, I never fully opened up to him, even though I was desperately lonely. I appreciated the levity of our relationship and wanted to keep it that way. I didn't feel like weighing down our few moments of laughter. My life up until then had been the school, my family, and my friends. With my family in crisis and my friends either too respectful or indifferent to help, I found myself completely alone.

With women, the situation was somewhat different. In that period I had several flings, as if unconsciously seeking to untie the tangled emotional mass I hid inside. But the more I dated, the more my emotional block hardened. I was trapped in a vicious cycle in which I sought women out for comfort, but as I did, I only became more and more aware of what I was lacking, and how emotionally blocked I was. The truth was that I still loved Angela. I also failed to distinguish between women with a genuine interest in me and women who had ulterior motives. For some women, my separation represented an opportunity. The master's wife was out of the picture, and some vied to take her place. My instinct ultimately told me that these women had no genuine desire to love Paolo, but rather an aspiration to sit in a privileged spot beside *Sifu* Cangelosi.

When I realized what was going on, rather than learning to separate the good ones from the evil ones, I closed myself off to both. Only very slowly did the seeds of love and friendship eventually reawaken in me, thanks to two special women. But more on this later.

I felt trapped and desperate to untie to the knot I carried inside. I began to distract myself in a variety of ways. I trained to the point of exhaustion and continued to drive rallies to blow off steam. I'd always had a passion for cars and engines, and rally driving required a level of concentration similar to that needed in martial arts. In much the same way, the smallest distraction could result in serious injury or death. I unconsciously sought to push myself to that limit. As a momentary respite from my inner turmoil, I participated in regional rally competitions in my spare time. At that time, I exaggerated in everything I did, as though it was only by surpassing my limits that I could break through the block within. Or perhaps I was just trying to punish myself, as if the pain I felt wasn't bad enough already. Whatever the reason, it was a time of extremes, when an extreme pain was met with extreme remedies, some useful, some futile and dangerous. This behavior was certainly not wise, but perhaps it was inevitable. I had lost my balance and my centre, and was groping in the dark to find it again. Maybe it was just a torturous way of relearning the ability to discern good from evil, and of finding myself once again.

The end of the road: Losing Fu Han Tong

After my separation in 1993, my trips to China intensified. I had an irresistible attraction to extremes in that period, and in China, particularly Fu Han Tong's China, there were plenty of extremes to be found. *Sifu* Chan Hon Chung was no longer there with his serenity to balance everything out. But my life was in disarray, and order was not what I was after. Looking back, I see how I sought out Fu Han Tong not only to learn and to deepen my Kung Fu, as I had done in the past. I also looked to him for something destructive, unbalanced, perhaps slightly deranged. Through his excesses, I desperately sought to escape the tunnel I was trapped in. Unsurprisingly, it was precisely then that my relationship with Fu Han Tong came to its bitter and perhaps inevitable end.

It was the fall of 1993 when I headed off to China again. Angela and I had separated a few months before, and I needed a radical change of scenery. After three weeks of training, Fu Han Tong proposed one of the usual underground fights. In truth, these were not proposals but orders. The fight would take place in a Chinese domino—*Mah Jong*—parlour. My adversary specialized in Pak Mei, a southern style originating from the Hakka minority, which is characterized by short and rapid movements, and whose power is magnified by the repeated emissions of wave-like *Fah Jing* energy. That was all I knew. Fu Han Tong was never generous with the details. He had never been a talkative man, but the longer he spent in China, especially on the mainland, the more closed off he became with me. At the time he lived primarily in the People's Republic, and his interest in Hong Kong seemed mainly connected to the organization of my fights.

It was late morning when we arrived at the *Mah Jong* parlour. A few men were busily folding the play tables and stacking them to one side to create space for the fight. On the other side, they lined up the small stools for the audience that would presumably turn up to watch the fight, which was scheduled to begin in two hours. To kill time, we went downstairs where there was a *Yam Cha Dim Sum*, a Chinese teahouse. In a slightly surreal atmosphere, or so it felt to me, we sat down to drink tea and nibble on a few snacks. As the men around me ate and drank, I sat tense and silent, knowing that at some point the jovial atmosphere would come to an end and those very same people would be watching a potentially deadly fight.

A stern looking man sat at our table. He had the distinct air of a *sifu,* but it would be strange if he were my adversary's *sifu.* I was partly right: he was a Kung Fu master who specialized in the style of the white crane—Bak Hok Pai. His name was Ngao Da Yuk and, apparently, he was a good friend of Fu Han Tong. When Fu Han Tong mentioned his style, I realized Ngao Da Yuk could not have been my opponent's *sifu*, since he was a Pak Mei fighter. I figured that he must have been the promoter or the organizer of the fight. Because by then I had started admitting the truth to myself. There was money, a veritable business, behind those fights. Bets were made and the victor's *sifu* cashed in on a jackpot. I had never seen the bets taking place, nor had I received a single Yuan or Hong Kong dollar from them. But after twelve years of fighting in China, I could no longer deny what was really going on.

Once the meal was over, Ngao Da Yuk stood up and the rest followed suit. Silently, the group climbed up two flights of stairs and entered the *Mah Jong* parlour. Several others were there already, perched on the stools along the wall. Only two men were standing. One was short and stout, wearing a smart shirt and a pair of dark trousers. He was talking in a coarse voice to the other man, who was younger and had very dark skin but eastern features, wearing jeans, a denim shirt and sneakers. Even though he was not dressed for a fight, I immediately understood that the young man was my adversary and the older one, his master.

A few moments later, Fu Han Tong, Ngao Da Yuk, and Fong Po, my adversary's *sifu*, consulted one another briefly and Ngao Da Yuk introduced the fight to the twenty-odd people sitting in the room. Nothing was said about the rules of engagement and there was no velvet cushion with a ring. I sensed that it was either a gold or a jade ring fight; in other words, one of the least regulated and therefore most dangerous fights. I was escorted to one side of the room, about six metres away from the man with the jeans and shirt. I saw him roll up his sleeves above his elbow on the other side of the room. Instinctively, I took off my sweatshirt, ready to fight in my tracksuit. The fight was about to start.

Ngao Da Yuk walked to the centre of the room, acting as a referee of sorts. Fu Han Tong came up behind me and whispered furtively in my ear: "*Keng lek*"—"Hit hard," in Cantonese. He repeated those words several times, as he always did when he wanted to make sure I got the point. Then he backed away. *Keng lek, keng lek, keng lek*: those words rang in my head as Ngao Da Yuk signalled the beginning of the fight.

As soon as we were in the centre of the room, my adversary aggressively made the first move. This rarely happened. Normally a fight begins with the fighters studying and testing one another's moves, but it seemed my rival was in no mood for a playful start. In a split second, he closed the distance between us with a powerful low-kick on my left knee. My leg bent, turning my body with it. That involuntary twist was good luck, as his ensuing punch aimed straight at my face only managed to graze my jaw. In this full-on attack that partly missed its target, my adversary lost his balance, enabling me to regain my distance and guard. But he didn't back off. Undeterred, he threw himself on me again, with even greater force than before. But by then I had fully awoken from my stupor; his attempt to end the fight with a K.O. wouldn't catch me by surprise again. Sticking to the same tactic was a fatal mistake for him. Not only did I now know his game, but I was intent in giving him a taste of his own medicine. As he flung himself toward me, I back-kicked him on the side of his stomach. My foot slid to the side of his body, and, as my body turned naturally, I hit him in the face with the back of my hand. I didn't stop there. As his face swung to one side, I put his neck in a lock and kneed him twice. After the second, I felt his body collapse in my arms. It was a K.O.

Fu Han Tong, Ngao Da Yuk, and Fong Po rushed up to us, and while Fong Po kneeled down to assist my opponent, Ngao Da Yuk pushed me to the side to prevent me from finishing him off. I had no intention of doing so; the fight was over as far as I was concerned. But stopping was not a foregone conclusion. A jade ring fight, if uninterrupted, could and sometimes did end with death. Voluntarily killing my adversary never crossed my mind, but Ngao Da Yuk couldn't have known this. My adversary had fainted and lay motionless on the floor. Ngao Da Yuk and Fang Po lifted him up by his feet and armpits and carried him to another room. As the adrenaline wore off, my mind focused on what had just happened. Both the back-kick and the kneeings had fully hit their target; I worried about the damage I had done. But worry was the last thing on Fu Han Tong's mind and his adrenaline was still sky-high as he stood beside me repeating excitedly, "Thirty seconds, thirty seconds." It had taken me thirty seconds to take down my rival. I didn't care; my only concern was whether that man was alive and well. I asked Fu Han Tong, but he dismissed me distractedly, replying in Cantonese: "*Mhou man thai.*" Whether "No problem," meant that my adversary was fine or that his wellbeing was not our problem, he did not say.

All this happened on a Monday afternoon. Two days later, Fu Han Tong picked me up at my guesthouse and proposed that we spend the day together. This rarely happened. Normally when we met it was either to train or to fight. Training or fighting would often be preceded and followed by meals or travel, but at the core of our encounters was always Kung Fu. Not that Wednesday. Fu Han Tong and I went to visit a secluded temple up on a hill on the outskirts of Hong

Kong. It was a magical place, only a few kilometres away from the hustle and bustle of the city. Hidden in the midst of a thick rainforest, the tiny temple had a timeless greatness to it. We spent a few hours there in silence. As I sat cross-legged in the temple, for the first time I felt the inklings of an inner peace that had eluded me for so long. It was then that I felt my emotional knot start to slowly loosen inside.

On our way back into town, we stopped by a cemetery. Fu Han Tong wanted to light some incense for a deceased relative of his friend *Sifu* Ngao Da Yuk. As we approached Kowloon, his mood changed. He was no longer feeling introspective; Fu Han Tong wanted to party. We had lunch in a crowded seafood restaurant, washing down the prawns, squid, and fish with plenty of beer and cognac. I didn't quite know why, but Fu Han Tong was in the mood to celebrate. It was only towards the end of the meal that he told me that we would meet the following day to "talk." I had no idea what he had in store. Normally, our "talks" boiled down to his announcement of an imminent fight. But since I had fought only two days ago, it had to be about something else.

I was wrong. The following day, Fu Han Tong announced that he had organized another fight for me that coming Saturday. My adversary was known to be extremely strong, but he did not mention in what style. All I was told was that he was nicknamed Hak Ying: Black Eagle. My spirits sank. I felt physically fine; that wasn't the problem. My fight the previous Monday had lasted thirty seconds, as I had been reminded repeatedly, and apart from a bruised knee, it had left me physically unscarred. But emotionally, it had been tough. I could still picture that man with his jeans and rolled up sleeves collapse before my eyes. I knew I had hurt him, but I didn't know how badly, and I would never find out. The thought of reliving a similar experience made me shudder. But I couldn't confess this to my *sifu*; I knew well that it was one of the unspoken rules between us. All we talked about was my bruised knee, and Fu Han Tong was quick to fetch me a concoction of herbs from a traditional clinic to wrap around it and speed up healing. When it came to my bruised soul, however, no word was uttered.

That Saturday afternoon, I again found myself in the dirty atmosphere that had become so tediously familiar to me: an empty room, several shady looking characters standing to one side, and the acrid smell of adrenaline in the air. Among the group, I immediately spotted my man. This happened often: no matter his build or clothing, I had an eagle's eye for my adversary. Black Eagle stood there in front of me, slim, with almost unusually long and narrow eyes and a thick, jet-black bob. His distinct look was probably the origin of his nickname: a Black Eagle was exactly what he looked like.

For the first time in my twelve years of fighting, Hak Ying and I were given a clear set of rules. We were not meant to seek a K.O., but rather to fight by demonstrating as many techniques as possible. Floor fighting was not allowed. It was not only the rules that were uncharacteristically soft; the atmosphere was, too. As the rules were announced, I felt the tension in the air dissolve. The mood became calmer, almost serene. I felt a mix of relief and confusion. I had come to detest the tension that built up before a fight. It was so strong that it was almost palpable, and created an intolerable weight in the room. As that tension evaporated, the room suddenly looked brighter, lighter. I breathed in relief. At the same time, I was completely confused. The heaviness of those situations was excruciatingly familiar: I had developed a Stockholm syndrome-like attachment to them. Among that lightness, I lost my bearings, unsure of where I was and what I was there for.

We were given ten minutes to warm up. As Black Eagle stretched his legs, making me immediately suspect that he was a kicker, I was struck by his calmness and composure. I stretched, too, and warmed up my muscles as I studied him and thought about what strategy to pursue.

It was an incredible fight. Hak Ying was an elegant fighter. He was extremely powerful and skilful, but there was grace in his every move. We immediately struck the same chord. Through the language of martial arts, we began communicating through a vast array of techniques. Each move exuded energy, but the precision and care with which we executed them communicated a deep respect for the art and for one another. There was no aggression or violence between us, despite the speed, strength, and power of our exchange. I was ready to up the ante if he had made the first move, and I knew he would have if I had done so, too. But neither of us did, and instead we revelled in the beauty of our communication.

At a certain point they called for a pause in the fight, as if signalling the end of a round in a competitive match. A few minutes later, we started again in exactly the same style and mood. The more Hak Ying and I sparred, the less we sought to prevail over one another, and the fight became increasingly elegant and controlled. We were interrupted again, and this time we had a longer break. The fight was gradually losing its competitive spirit as our adrenaline decreased, but it became more and more physically demanding, precisely because it was so technically rich. As we rested, a few men conversed animatedly to one side, as if consulting one another on what to do next. Fu Han Tong was not among them. He stood alone in a corner of the room, waiting for the men to signal the beginning of the third round.

We picked up the fight again with the same tone and tempo. But this time, we were quickly interrupted. As if awoken from a dream, I stood there, perplexed. I had entered the spirit of the fight, forgetting all about the underground fighting scene and its darkness, aggression and violence. Those fights were all about winning over the adversary, who in fact became an enemy, not a fellow martial artist, let alone a companion. It was all about prevailing as quickly, decisively and irreversibly as possible. If the price to be paid was that the fight was mean and dirty, then so be it. This fight had been profoundly different; it had been about harmony, respect and generosity. Prevailing or even winning had gradually slipped my mind as our exchange took place. Now I stood there, in front of a martial artist with whom I had had an intense, almost sublime, encounter. As we bowed in our martial salute, I wondered what was in store for us. To my surprise, after a few moments of private talk, the group of men came up to us. They didn't announce a winner, but rather congratulated us for the art we had performed.

It had been a beautiful experience. I was physically exhausted but, unusually, full inside. Unlike the sense of dark emptiness that always came after my fights, this time I felt an energized happiness. It was a new feeling, one whose beauty I wanted to latch on to, making me realize fully for the first time just how much I hated the spirit of the underground fights I had been through over the years. Perhaps it was this realization, or perhaps it was because Fu Han Tong went a step too far, but when he and I met again, after two fights in one week, something inside me changed.

On that Monday morning, Fu Han Tong informed me that we were going to Shenzhen, only eighty kilometres or so away from Hong Kong, but on the mainland. I had to get a visa and prepare for the trip. In Shenzhen, I was scheduled to fight against Black Eagle again. It felt like getting hit in the face with cold water. All of a sudden, it dawned on me that instead of wanting to immerse us in the beauty of martial exchange, Hak Ying and I had been encouraged to fight that way so as to give the onlookers the opportunity to observe us, place their bets and set the rules of the real fight. I understood that we were at the top of the pyramid of the gambling business, and there was probably serious money involved. In Shenzhen, the real fight would take place, with all the tension and violence I knew so well. I was speechless. I knew that something had irreversibly transformed within me. But I had to digest it, understand fully what it meant. I asked Fu Han Tong to meet me at my hotel the next day; I needed to sleep on it.

But I had already decided. I would not travel to Shenzhen; I would not fight against Black Eagle again. What I needed to understand was not whether I would go, but why I would not. It was partly a question of quantity: three fights in little over a week was hard to swallow. I felt saturated, nauseated; it was simply too much. It was partly a question of quality, too. The beauty of the fight with Hak Ying had made me see the ugliness of those underground fights more clearly. The thought of experiencing that ugliness again was revolting; and to do so with, or rather against, the man with whom I had had such a beautiful exchange was intolerable. On top of all this was the money. I felt used and exploited. Without even knowing, I had climbed up a betting ladder, each time risking my life, each time with a higher price tag on my head. Perhaps it had started off as a game for Fu Han Tong, but as I went up the pyramid, I had become a business for him, perhaps even his main source of income. Regarding his earnings, he never said one word to me, nor did he offer me any, if only to cover my expenses in China. Where had the generosity of Kung Fu gone? Where was the spontaneity of a fugitive Chinese Kung Fu master teaching an eleven-year old Italian boy for free? Nothing stays the same, of course. But I still searched for an echo of the generosity that Fu Han Tong had showed me in the past. To no avail. All I saw was greed and avidity in its stead.

The most important reason I didn't want to go to Shenzhen was not a reason at all; it was an instinct. What ultimately gave me the strength to say no was a strong pull that I felt, which had become stronger and stronger: to return home. My family was broken, and I lived in a crammed corner of my *kwoon*. But I loved Angela and Shan and they loved me; I knew this for sure, and it was all that mattered. I had my school, my students and a life that revolved around it. That was where I belonged, that was home. Never again would I voluntarily put my life in danger and risk throwing it all away, no matter what the purpose was. Nothing was worth as much as what I had at home. Under a hot shower that evening, the knot I had felt inside for so long melted away. As my heart opened and I surrendered to a warm wave of nostalgia, I knew I had to leave.

That was a turning point in my life. Fu Han Tong and I met in the hotel lobby. He went straight to the point, asking me if I was ready for the trip. Up until that moment, I wondered whether I would summon the courage to speak, to confront him, to say no. I knew what I wanted, but I still didn't know whether I was strong enough to tell my *Sifu.*

I was. It all happened over the course of a few seconds. Fu Han Tong looked me straight in the eye, as if to discern the true meaning behind my words. He asked me to repeat my decision again, to say "no" twice. Just like when he repeated an important message to me to make sure I fully understood it, this time he asked me to repeat myself to him, to make sure that he, and perhaps more importantly I, truly understood what I meant. I knew what I wanted, and I was strong enough to say it. Twice.

Fu Han Tong didn't have a negative reaction. In fact, he didn't react much at all. He told me that I was a grown man and in control of my life. He would pay a price for my decision with his community, but that was his problem, not mine. He respected my choice; I was free to go my way. He then added that he was moving, and I would no longer be able find him at his usual address. In reality what he was saying was that I shouldn't look for him again, but I didn't understand this at the time. It was all happening so fast and my head was spinning. I had spent the previous twenty-four hours figuring out what I wanted to do and why. I hadn't even started coming to grips with the consequences. Whatever they were, they were secondary. But those consequences were now hitting me with full force, and I felt disoriented. I asked him somewhat naively how I could get in touch with him in future. In his usual fashion, he said it twice: we had come to the end of our road.

I fell silent. There was nothing left to say; I was sure about my choice. As I stood there, my yearning to go back home felt stronger than ever. And trying to persuade Fu Han Tong of anything, let alone something as big as this, was futile. I didn't even want to try. There was no point: Fu Han Tong was right. We had reached the end of our road. Hurriedly, we shook hands, and then he turned around and left. After twenty-two years together, Fu Han Tong, master carpenter, man of extremes who had influenced me so profoundly, walked out of my life, forever.

That night I went to my local pub in Hong Kong, a familiar place where I often took refuge after my Chinese adventures, to let it all sink in. But I just couldn't focus. My mind flitted from the gravity of what had just happened to the mundane details of my travel home. I booked a ticket on a Garuda airlines flight, which had only one flight back to Italy a week. In my state of panicked confusion, sorting out my return seemed as significant as my separation from my life-long master. Getting myself onto that flight meant getting home. Returning to the boundedness of home was ultimately the reason I had broken from the boundlessness of Fu Han Tong. The Garuda flight and the rupture with Fu Han Tong were intimately connected.

When I walked into my apartment in Genoa, the enormity of what happened finally dawned on me. Up until then, my heart and mind had focused on home, on hugging Shan, seeing

Angela, and teaching my students. I still felt all of that, but the emptiness of my apartment and the loneliness it represented roused me to the truth that I was now alone in my Kung Fu. Chan Hon Chung was dead, and Fu Han Tong had left me. As Fu Han Tong had said, I was on my own.

I braced myself as a bottomless sadness possessed me. I felt a desperate need to talk, to share, to feel the warmth of my loved ones. But I couldn't call Angela, and Shan was only a boy. Roberto was in Rome and I lacked the confidence to speak so openly with my other friends or students. So, I picked up the phone and rang Carlo, my brother. Despite all our differences, my elder brother had known me since birth and was a part of my life and school. While I never shared the details of my experiences in China with anyone, Carlo knew who Fu Han Tong was and what he represented to me. Carlo was surprised to receive my call. He knew I'd been in Hong Kong, and when he heard my voice, he assumed I was still there. Usually my trips lasted a few months, but this time, I had returned after only five weeks. I told my brother that I was home, that I needed to talk, and that I was not well. He rushed over to my place. As soon as he saw the state I was in, he insisted on taking me to the hospital. I was physically, psychologically, and emotionally devastated, and it showed. I refused. I just needed to talk. I knew I would find the strength to recover; I no longer felt emotionally blocked. But at that moment, I just wanted a hand, a voice, and someone to listen. I talked: I talked about Chan Hon Chung, about Cheon Yee Keung, and about the end of an era in Hong Kong; I talked about Angela, about Shan, and about the emotional knot that had entangled me, making me unable to feel or discern for a long while; I talked about Fu Han Tong, about what he had been and what he had become for me, and about the end of our road. Carlo listened. He did not say much, but we connected. He made his presence felt and that was all I needed. I was profoundly grateful to him.

Something became clear in my mind during those first days after my return and continued to be a source of constant reflection over the months that followed. I didn't try to repress those emotions, but rather tried to embody them using every organ in my body.

I felt anger and resentment towards Fu Han Tong, Hong Kong, and China in general. The violence, the loneliness, the greed, and the tedious repetition of the situations I had experienced manifested themselves with full force. I had fought thirty-nine times in those illegal betting environments. I had lost once, and that one time, not only did I lay on the threshold between life and death, but I had been cruelly abandoned to my fate by those around me. I had won thirty-eight times. On some occasions, I was confident that my rivals would be fine, but on others I was not, and the uncertainty of their fate had devoured me. The power of that darkness took hold of me and temporarily obscured everything else, all the beauty and light I had experienced in China during those years too.

I hated myself for not having said no before, for not having drawn the line when I started to see, but not admitting to myself, what lay behind all that. At first, I had genuinely believed that it was all about love and respect for Kung Fu and my *sifu*. It was about demonstrating gratitude to him in the most generous way—entrusting him with my life—for the generosity he had demonstrated to me since I was a boy, for the teachings, the training and the three hundred and sixty degree exposure to the universe of martial arts. Everything I knew and had become was primarily thanks to Fu Han Tong, and those fights were my way of paying him back. But with time, I started to see the risk they entailed, began to question their meaning, and, above all, I slowly awoke to the dark side of that underground scene, of Fu Han Tong and of myself. I started to understand this long before I stopped fighting, and I waited too long before I found the strength to say, enough. The more time passed, the more I found myself on one side of an equation that had allowed my relationship with Fu Han Tong to transition from selfless generosity to a game, and then to a greedy and inhumane business. We had reached the end of our road.

To protect myself from the pain, anger, and hatred, at first I closed myself off. I didn't want to see Fu Han Tong or return to Hong Kong or China ever again. I didn't care about having new experiences there, with different masters or in different schools. It was a form of total rejection of my *Sifu*. In that first period after our break, he came to symbolize everything that was wrong with me, my life, and the experiences I'd had with and because of him. He became a mirror in which I could see all the darkness I felt inside. But mine was also a rejection of China more broadly. China had been my childhood dream. It had given me the most enlightening and enriching experiences of my life. But all that faded temporarily. I felt nauseated by China. All of a sudden, the country was reduced in my mind to images of men burping and spitting on the floor, to run-down warehouses and smelly restaurants, and to linguistic and cultural barriers that made everything there such a slog. From the most delightful to the grimmest of my experiences, all those differences that had once enthralled me became dirty and despicable.

It did not last long. I returned to China less than a year later, in 1994. It was a completely different trip. I wasn't there to find Fu Han Tong, nor was it my intention to search for other schools, masters, or new Kung Fu experiences. I went to China with one of my closest students, Claudio, to prepare for a second trip with a screenwriter, Lorenzo de Luca, who had taken an interest in my life. He wanted to work on a movie with film director Enzo Castellari and executive producer Franco Nero. On one level, that trip to Bangkok and Hong Kong had a specific focus. It was about making contact and showing Lorenzo the places and people that might inspire his writing. On another, deeper, level, I was driven to organize that trip so I could relive Hong Kong with a different outlook and spirit. It was about closing a chapter of my life, about letting go of the anger and hatred that I felt, and about searching for a new beginning.

The film project reenergized me and the school, and the instructors and students were excited to work on it with me. It was a dream that I latched onto to refocus on my life and my practice, to rise again after my falls.

But it was not yet the right time.

The following year came the last, and in some ways the most damaging, rupture.

Betrayal: Secession in the kwoon

It was late 1994, and I finally felt that I was picking up the pieces of my broken life. After that trip to Hong Kong, I was sizzling with new ideas. I was excited about the film project—*Seasons of the Dragon*—and, above all, I was enthusiastic about involving my students in the endeavour. It would have been a powerful new bond between us all that could catapult the school to new heights.

Back then, the *kwoon* was doing extremely well. It was one of the first traditional Kung Fu schools in Italy, and certainly the largest one in those years. At each of our main branches in Genoa, Milan, and Rome, we had over two hundred students; at the smaller ones, there were around one hundred. In total, the school had over two thousand students. By the mid-1990s, there was also a solid group of instructors and several advanced students who aspired to join them. Their aspirations generated some tension, as not everyone's expectations could be met. We were registered as a non-profit, not as a company, and sharing the profits between us meant that we could only have a dozen or so instructors if we were to remain financially sustainable. Adding staff would have led to self-destruction. The strength of the school had to translate into a decent living for the instructors that had made Kung Fu their profession.

By late 1994, I began to realize that tension was mounting not only between the instructors and certain advanced students, but also within the group of instructors themselves. Sympathies and antipathies had always existed, as is often the case in any social or professional milieu, but something deeper and more poisonous was spreading, too. The instructors were arguing among themselves far more often than before. As head of the school, I was often dragged into these discussions and tried to mediate. But it took me a while until I realized, or admitted to myself, that it wasn't just a passing phase; there was something else going on. In the past, after our collective meetings, even if there had been heated discussions, we always patched things up with a laugh and a few glasses of wine. We were work partners, but we were a family above all, and that brotherly warmth was tangible between us. As fall tipped into winter at the end of 1994, it was not just the weather that cooled. The atmosphere in school became frostier, too. Every meeting devolved into an argument, with even the most meaningless detail becoming the perfect excuse to pick a fight. There was something rotten under the surface, something that no one would tell me about.

Some of the instructors closest to me had started complaining behind my back. They were nursing secret ambitions that did not align with our collective endeavour. No one ever complained to my face, but rumors continued to spread behind the scenes; when the instructors who remained loyal to me became aware of them, the conflict between the two factions escalated. During our meetings, we never openly discussed what was going on. The instructors picked fights over the smallest things, as proxies for the real issues. For a long time, those who were loyal to me tried to gently open my eyes, but they were reluctant to trigger an enormous crisis at the school. They only hinted at the problem. As for me, I didn't want to acknowledge the magnitude of what was going on. In all honesty, if they had come right out and told me that a group of my most senior instructors was scheming behind my back, I would have been annoyed or simply laughed. I certainly wouldn't have believed that the students and friends to whom I had given so much were betraying me. So, my students had to blow off steam with those petty fights. Their frequency and venom sowed seeds of negativity throughout the entire school.

I guess those who planned to betray me were not all driven by the same motivations. For some, it was about new horizons. Perhaps they felt that I was an obstacle to their growth, rather than a vehicle for further development. I was the head of the school and I was *sifu.* While this did not mean they would never become masters themselves, it did mean they had a long way to go. If a title was what they were after, they certainly wouldn't get it anytime soon. If it was growth in Kung Fu that they desired, that was a completely different matter, but I guess the two are easily confused once ego gets in the way. For others, it was mainly a question of money. The instructors earned good money in those days, but it's easy to fall into the trap of wanting more. Perhaps they thought that great riches were in store for them if they went it alone. For others still, it may have been plain jealousy, envy. This I will never know.

Their motivations were diverse, but there was one thing those people had in common: cowardice. Rather than having the courage to confront me individually with their lists of grievances, they ganged up on me behind my back. Had they approached me, I may have agreed with some and disagreed with others, but we could have settled matters as adults, friends and work partners. But this is not what they were after: they had no intention of settling anything. They had teamed up to leave the school together, poisoning their students against me. Their goal, in fact, was not simply to exit the school, but to bring along with them as many students as possible. They plotted and planned, but they didn't have the courage to stand up to me face-to-face or make the first move.

When I could no longer deny that something big and bad was brewing, I convened two meetings, one in Genoa, the other in Rome. At that point, I didn't fully understand the magnitude of what was going on, nor did I expect that my school was about to fall apart. When I openly confronted those instructors, they stuttered, failing to come up with a single cogent argument about what was wrong with the school or with me. When I asked them why they hadn't spoken with me, only one person spoke up to say, meekly, that he was afraid of how I might react. The rest kept silent. For a brief moment, I didn't know what to do. Here they were, a group of the students closest to me, who claimed to be unhappy but were unable to articulate why. I tried to unpack the problems, to explore solutions, but it was like hitting my head on a brick wall. None of them wanted to solve anything. They had already found their solution, without me. Practically speaking, I didn't quite know what to do, but the emotional impact was crystal clear to me. The energy was bad, far worse than I'd feared. My school simply couldn't survive the poison that spreading throughout it like wildfire. I had to cut off the head of the snake before it was too late; I had to throw out the rotten apples before they spoiled the whole bunch. I loved those people, and each and every one of them held a special place in my heart, but they had to go. Ultimately, I gave them what they wanted but didn't have the courage to do themselves: I threw them out of my *kwoon.*

After the showdown, I understood the full depth of their traitorousness. For months, the instructors had been weaving threads of betrayal, persuading a large group of advanced students and beginners to leave with them after they split from the school. Just a few weeks after our meeting, my *kwoon* had shrunk to half its former size. I had completely lost the two main locations, in Rome and Milan. In those two branches alone, there had been approximately five hundred students enrolled. In Rome, the damage was more limited. Some advanced students, like Maurizio, Enrico, Fabio, Laura and others, refused to follow the secessionists. They rolled up their sleeves and opened a new branch of the *kwoon*, giving the students who didn't want to leave the option of continuing to practice with me. In Milan, the results were devastating, because there were no instructors in a position to establish a new branch. In the second largest and in many ways most vibrant city in the country, we lost each and every student.

The group of secessionist instructors from Milan did not stop there. On the September 2nd, 1995, as the academic year was about to begin and parents were busy enrolling their children in after-school activities, I found hundreds of flyers and posters in my neighbourhood advertising the opening of a Kung Fu school only two kilometres away from Salita delle Fieschine, where my *kwoon* was based. The flyer advertised a Hung Gar course, in the lineage of Gran Master Chan Hon Chung; the head of the school, according to the flyer, was none other than Cheon Yee Keung.

Those instructors had been smart enough to know that their credibility would be at rock bottom if they had gone it alone. They needed legitimacy; what better way to find it than referring to highly respected Chinese martial names? They stole the curricula from my school in four Kung Fu styles: Hung Gar, Wing Chun, Tang Lang and Tai Chi, and each instructor picked one style to teach. They then went off to China to look for Chinese masters whom they could latch on to, paying them and claiming to have studied with them directly. They knew most of those Chinese personalities from my stories or because I had introduced them in person when we had travelled to China together. As for Cheon Yee Keung, they knew him because I had invited him to Italy, and we had met him in France several times.

I was not surprised that the Chinese masters agreed to teach them. Kung Fu in China in 1995 was very different from what it had been in 1981, when I first visited Hong Kong. It was a China in which Deng Xiaoping's gradual opening to the world had reached all corners of Chinese life, including martial arts. As China opened to the world and Kung Fu became well-known in the West, scores of Westerners flocked to China to study Kung Fu. Seeing a profitable business opportunity, Chinese martial artists designed expensive packages for them. Foreigners could buy weekly or monthly courses, or the teaching of a specific form from a set menu. As with all forms of modernization, this created great gains, both by providing better financial sustainability to traditional Kung Fu and encouraging its cultural diffusion beyond China; but the commercialization of Chinese martial arts also deprived it of much of its mystique and magic.

What I was surprised about, and what hurt me deeply, was that of all the Chinese masters they could have turned to, they went straight to my Kung Fu brother, Cheon Yee Keung, who in turn agreed teach them and lend his name to their rival school. Who knows what those people told him about me, but whatever it was, Cheon Yee Keung could have at least contacted me, instead of casting me to the side just as he had done so definitively with our shared master, Chan Hon Chung. Was Cheon Yee Keung's behaviour motivated by his personality and history, by the materialism of Chinese culture, or by the commercialization of Kung Fu? It was probably a mix of all three, but rational explanations made little difference to my grief.

When the seeds are rotten, the flowers are unlikely to bloom, or certainly not for very long. Only five years after this schism, the project of the secessionist students fell apart. First they split among themselves. Their cowardice to face me had been the glue holding them together. With that bond gone, the bricks they had laid started to break, one by one.

This was of little consolation to me, however. I never felt, not even in those first dramatic days after they stabbed me in the back, the faintest desire for revenge. Some of the instructors and students that remained loyal to me were livid with rage and encouraged me to declare an all-out war. But I knew it was the wrong thing to do, and two wrongs would never make a right. Those people had made their choice and had taken their path. They would eventually reap what they had sowed, and we would, too. That was all that mattered to me: the seeds I had sowed, and what we would continue to build as a school. Hatred and revenge had no place in our thoughts and deeds. If there was only one thing worth repeating to myself and teaching others, it was this.

But my pain was deep. I had been betrayed by some of the people I loved the most, some of my closest friends, with whom I had shared the most formative period of my life: Claudio, Gianfranco, Giuseppe, Pier, and others. Among them was the person whom I'd known since the day I was born, and who had been with me through thick and thin: Carlo. My brother Carlo, who had seen my curiosity and passion for martial arts bloom; Carlo, who had been infected by my enthusiasm and started studying martial arts with me in 1977; Carlo, whom I had supported during his illness and who had subsequently decided to dedicate his own life to Kung Fu; Carlo, who was one of my best instructors and was making a successful living through his passion; Carlo, who had stood by my side during my separation from Chan Hon Chung, Angela, and Fu Han Tong. Carlo had betrayed me, as I saw it.

Carlo has always been a special person. He is a prima donna, with character and charisma, who has always strived to win. He relishes leadership and basks in the limelight. Plus, Carlo is my elder brother. I always knew that it wasn't easy for him to play that role. Accepting his place in a hierarchy that his younger brother was the head of, and not him, must have been hard to swallow. But never, ever, did it cross my mind that my brother would leave me.

And yet he did. Carlo joined the group of Milanese instructors and continued to teach in what had been my school in Milan. To my mother's grief, he moved out of town. He did have the decency, however, to not participate in an attempt to open a rival school in Genoa, and he never knocked on the door of any of the Chinese masters I introduced him to or spoke to him about. His was an all-out attempt to emancipate himself from me, for better and worse. He established his own school in Piacenza, where he still teaches Wing Chun and Tai Chi today. He found other Chinese masters on his own from whom he could learn. It was not long before he broke away from the group of Milanese instructors. Perhaps his intention was always to go his own way. Perhaps he just didn't have the courage to do so alone, and temporarily put his lot in with them to take the first step towards independence. Maybe he even encouraged them to break from me, since he felt he needed to break away himself, but was incapable of doing so on his own. One thing I am sure of: in Carlo's case it wasn't about money or a useless title. For my brother, it had to do with something much deeper, with his autonomy and independence. It was about defining his own identity; sadly, he felt that he could only define himself in contrast to me. And so I became my brother's "other."

* * *

It all happened so quickly. In only four years, I lost two masters, my wife, half my school, my brother, and some of my closest friends.

Or maybe it had not happened so quickly after all. In each case, the break was sudden because either I or others had repressed certain things for too long. When Chan Hon Chung's health was deteriorating, no one had bothered to tell me about it, which meant the belated news of his death hit me in all its tragedy. Edward was probably busy with his business, and to Cheon Yee Keung, *Sifu* Chan had been dead for a while.

When Angela and I separated, she had been swallowing her pain for many months; rather than let it out, she allowed it to mute her passion within. I, for my part, was too insensitive to see what was happening to her, and to us. Caught up in my own loneliness, I fell into the arms of a woman who seemed to give me the attention and affection I yearned for. Angela's jealously came out in Angela's way, by creating an even thicker barrier between us. For too long, I failed to see this for what it was, mistakenly reading it as Angela's distancing herself further from me. Each of us blinded to the reality of our predicament, we allowed the trust at the heart of our relationship to erode, pushing our marriage to a breaking point.

With Fu Han Tong, it was I who silently stewed; for too long I had lacked the clarity and courage to confront my *sifu* and tell him I had had enough. If I had managed to do so earlier, perhaps this separation would have been less painful.

With my students too, I had waited too long, not wanting to see the writing on the wall. Had we talked before the poison began to spread, perhaps we could have cleared things up and avoided the end of a precious brotherly and professional bond. Or, if I had expelled them earlier, I could have avoided some of the damage they brought upon my school.

But, things happen the way they are supposed to, and maybe this was the only way possible.

Either way, it was time for me to rebound and rebuild. I would start by diving into the mistakes I had made and unpacking the lessons they carried for me.

My fall was the greatest opportunity that life had presented me thus far. I was determined to seize it.

Rupture

The rupture of human relations, either professional or emotional, spring from the interplay between the internal and external. It can be driven by external pressures, which create internal fragilities, or vice versa, combining to trigger a break. The rupture of the relationship becomes part of a defense strategy, a conscious or unconscious survival instinct, which can and often does result in acute pain.

The separation within my school generated great pain and sadness. I had invested time and money in my students, and had transmitted my art to them. But I had to protect myself, and I felt that separating from them was the only cure for the illness that was spreading within my school. A rupture, like any change, requires the strength and courage to embrace risk. We can lose what we built, or choose to renew it. But avoiding a necessary rupture presents a risk, too: remaining chained to negativity and condemning ourselves to a never-ending uphill battle. Through the spirit of the warrior we can face this acute pain, aware that it will eventually give way to renewed peace; breaking those chains is, at times, the only way to ensure a better tomorrow.

CHAPTER 8
Resilience

It was time for a new start. But I couldn't simply return to where and who I had been. The past was past, and it had profoundly changed who I was.

For the second half of the 1990s, resilience would guide my way.

As suggested by the etymology of the word itself—from the Latin *resilere*—I felt ready to bounce back, absorb, adapt and recover from my crises. This did not imply a mere return to the state I'd been in prior to them. Springing back from a human trauma does not mean a return to the *status quo ante*: Resilience is about reorganizing and renewing, not about returning. It is about bouncing forwards, not backwards, using the force of the fall itself to rise to new heights. Building resilience did require regaining my baseline balance, but I did so by learning from my crises and expanding my capacity to prevent, adjust, and restore after stress or trauma.

As a result of those difficult times, I learned to live Asia as a master and not just as a martial arts student, with freedom and humility as my guiding lights. At my school, I learned to be a *sifu* in a more detached yet more well-rounded way, rebuilding its foundations on far more solid ground. And in my private life, I learned to open my heart once again, building bonds that have warmed my days ever since.

Freedom and humility in Asia

During the first two decades of my martial arts practice, I had grown into a teacher and a mentor to my students in Italy. I had thousands of followers, and while many were my age or older, I felt confident about what I taught them. I shared with them the teachings of my masters, Fu Han Tong and Chan Hon Chung, which I had fully made my own. As a result, over the course of those fifteen years, there were two sides to my martial life: I was a *sifu* in Italy and a student in China. Both countries represented the different ways in which I had developed as a martial artist.

But that period was over. I had lost my masters; I could no longer place my life in someone else's hands. Entrusting myself completely to them had exposed me to thrilling experiences. As a Westerner, I could have never dreamt of gaining access to the mysterious world of traditional martial arts in 1980s China without their introductions, suggestions and recommendations. In dramatically different ways, Fu Han Tong and Chan Hon Chung had carefully guided me; they had been my compasses, navigating me across the ocean of traditional martial arts. They had pointed me towards what they believed was best for me and I had fully entrusted myself to their wise hands. In all its beauty and its pain, I owed everything to them.

Without Fu Han Tong and Chan Hon Chung, I was as much a *sifu* in China as I was in Italy. The duality of my life as a martial artist had disappeared. Location still mattered, of course: I could not be a master in Italy and in China in the same way. In Italy, I taught others, while in Asia, I learned to teach myself. From the mid-1990s onwards, I mastered how to become a *sifu* in Asia, seeking new experiences that could enrich my way.

Becoming a martial arts orphan was deeply liberating. It gave me an empowering sense of freedom. I was the only master of my destiny, the only arbiter of what was right and what was wrong for my personal development as a martial artist. I was free to experiment, to step into new adventures and to refuse others. I was the only architect of my successes and my failures. As Fu Han Tong had told me the day he left, the time had come for me to stand on my own feet.

This led me to think more deeply about myself, about my strengths and my weaknesses, and thus about what I needed to become a more well-rounded martial artist. Whether I was in Hong Kong or, less frequently, in mainland China, I let instinct guide me when approaching other martial artists, often without a set agenda but with a light heart and an open mind, soaking up the good they offered. I would roam misty parks at the at the crack of dawn, joining other martial artists as they practiced their Kung Fu. I stopped by traditional schools, more interested in understanding how their martial arts were a part of popular culture than learning about their curriculum. The freedom of my seemingly aimless wandering bestowed a calmness and serenity upon me that I'd never known in China. It wasn't all rosy. I still encountered the hurdles I was well-accustomed to China, but the loneliness I had so often felt there magically vanished, paradoxically, now that I was truly on my own.

Humility was the flip side of freedom. I felt liberated and empowered by freedom to be my own master, and at the same time I was deeply humbled by everyone and everything that came my way. I emptied myself of all preconceptions and prejudices, embracing new experiences with a clean slate. By presenting myself with the humility of a beginner, I learned to be accepted. I could face any new situation without a protective shield, allowing myself to be surprised and taking in whatever was in store for me as a gift.

In those years, my instinct did not draw me towards the exploration of new styles, forms, or techniques. This was because the masters and schools I encountered were very different from those I had known in the 1980s and early 1990s. My two monumental masters were gone and I had no intention of replacing them. But besides Fu Han Tong and Chan Hon Chung, I had met several other real and true *sifus* in my first fifteen years of travel across China. Imprinted in my mind is *Sifu* Ho Tang Sing, heir of the lineage of the eight immortals of the drunken man style—Tsui Pa Hsien. Ho Tang Sing was a proud, powerful, and strong-willed man, strict in his teachings and with a hermetically closed-door policy in his school. I suspect I may have been the only foreigner ever admitted to his *kwoon.* I also remember *Sifu* Hau Chau, who specialized in the internal styles of Tai Chi, Pa Kua, and Hsing I. He was a man of few words, and extremely meticulous in his method of work. Or *Sifu* Hong Tak Hung, a great expert in the monkey style and in southern Kung Fu styles, as well as the official trainer of the national team of Guangdong, who, despite his greater openness compared to other masters, was highly selective about admission to his *kwoon.* Only one decade had passed since I had met them, but masters like these had become increasingly difficult to come by.

By the second half of the 1990s, China was changing at the speed of light. As the People's Republic embraced capitalism, martial arts underwent a genetic mutation. It had become much easier and cheaper to travel to China. As a result, hordes of Western tourists, especially from the United States and Australia, began flocking into the land of dragons. A fair share of them were fascinated by martial arts, particularly in light of the Chinese government's commercialization of Wu Shu and its active promotion of it in China and abroad. This generated unprecedented pressure on traditional Kung Fu schools, particularly those in Hong Kong, Macao as well as in Singapore, to either open up or be swept away altogether. Especially in Hong Kong, *kwoon*, and martial arts associations started opening their doors to foreigners to become more financially viable and to spread traditional Kung Fu culture: golden pebbles in a desert of government-sponsored Wu Shu.

I fully understood but only partly appreciated these traditional schools' heroic efforts. They were in a battle for survival; but I couldn't help but notice that even the traditional Kung Fu *kwoon* I encountered in the late 1990s were far more superficial, commercial, and easily accessible than those I had known only a few years before. Attending these schools to learn a new style or form lost its lustre in my eyes. It wasn't just because I had been studying martial arts for almost thirty years by then, nor because I wasn't looking for a new master to guide my way. My instinct turned me away from these *kwoon* because the world of traditional Kung Fu was fading, and I didn't want my memories of it to vanish, too. Keeping my distance from the current permutations of traditional Kung Fu was my way of protecting the purity of my memories.

Instead, I became very drawn to learning more about the ancient practices and disciplines that surrounded martial arts, as well as new methodologies to revisit and apply them, particularly for medical purposes. In those years, I picked up my studies of traditional Chinese medicine and significantly deepened my knowledge of Chi Kung. I explored how medical research was experimenting with and adapting ancient practices to cure different pathologies and illnesses, and I deepened my understanding of diverse traditional practices and therapies. I enrolled in courses when they were available, and when they were not, energy, humility, respect, and sympathy usually opened the doors I knocked at.

I remember an enlightening course I took in the late 1990s, in Nanjing. It was not my first experience with traditional Chinese medicine. Fu Han Tong had always stressed the importance of medical knowledge and practice in the way of Kung Fu. The true martial artist, he tirelessly repeated to me, can call herself such only if she deepens her knowledge of at least one branch of traditional medicine. After my studies with him and with Dr. Su Yang in Italy, where I was introduced to the basics of acupuncture, digital pressure, moxibustion, and therapeutic massage, Fu Han Tong had encouraged me to pursue further studies in China. Through those courses, notably in Hong Kong in 1986 and Canton in the early 1990s, I delved into diverse aspects of traditional medicine as well as therapeutic Chi Kung. With Chan Hon Chung, on the other hand, I was drawn into the world of traditional Chinese orthopedics—*Tee Taa*. But the more I studied these medical disciplines and practices, the more I realized how little I knew and how much I still yearned to learn.

Those experiences whet my appetite for more knowledge and connected me to doctors and medical practitioners with whom I continued to exchange views, insights, and information over the years. Through one of them, Peter Chang, I discovered a well-known course in Nanjing in the late 1990s, considered amongst the best graduate courses in mainland China and the only one open to Western students at the time. I did some research into the course and applied to join. Thanks to my previous experiences and Peter's recommendation, I was accepted into the intermediate level, which was certainly challenging and also deeply enriching. What helped me make the most of that experience was that, unlike the somewhat erratic pedagogy of traditional Kung Fu masters, the course in Nanjing was organized, taught, and structured well. This helped me connect the dots of the scattered knowledge I already had, and build upon it with fascinating new details.

The experience in Nanjing was precious in my professional life in at least two ways. As far as publicity was concerned, it allowed me to showcase both martial arts and traditional medicine in my documentary *The Journey*, which I worked on assiduously in the early 2000s. While making the documentary I relied heavily on my contacts with traditional doctors in hospitals and clinics in Hong Kong and mainland China. As far as my own practice was concerned, I found myself helping some of my students and their relatives suffering from diverse pathologies, with some success both in the diagnoses as well as the prognoses and subsequent therapies. Let me be clear: I am not and do not pretend to be a doctor. I am a traditional martial artist, and as such I have cultivated a keen interest in and passion for traditional medical disciplines and practices. I have put my interest and passion to use in service of others when I have felt that I could be of help, however small, to people I love and to their loved ones. In particular, teaching and transmitting Chi Kung comes naturally to me, not only for the prevention of illnesses and for general wellness, but for therapeutic purposes too. In my courses, workshops, and one-on-one lessons, Chi Kung is the area of internal practice I have concentrated the most on over the years.

Back to Asia. Starting in the mid-1990s, I never set foot again in the underground fighting environments I had been so nauseated by. I never again felt the anxiety, the pressure, and the physical and emotional violence those situations had created in me for fifteen years. This did not mean that I closed myself off to the martial dimension of the art; quite the contrary. I wanted to learn more about the evolution of Kung Fu fighting outside of the illegal world I had known, and in a more rule-bound, competitive, and protected space. Kung Fu fighting was becoming more like a sport in those years, and as much as it was losing its secrecy and mystique, it was also becoming cleaner, lighter, and just plain fun.

A key component of this was the deepening of my Muay Thai skills and experience. For over a decade, I visited Thailand as often, and sometimes more, than I did China, and it was there that I assiduously trained, fought and studied Muay Thai. The matches I competed in were completely different from the fights I was accustomed to. This made things easier and harder at the same time. It was naturally easier to fight in a safe and regulated professional environment where the aim was beating an adversary, but there was no ugliness nor violence involved. When we'd make full contact, there was certainly pain, but there is a categorical difference between pain and violence, and there was none of the latter. In other ways, it was harder for me. I had fought countless times in very different environments. When there were no rules, I was used to using all the techniques in my martial arts toolkit. But in Thailand, there were clear rules of the game, and they were strictly limited to Muay Thai's codified regulations. While fighting is a human activity in which instinct reigns supreme, I could not let my instinct loose, but instead had to rein it in and limit myself to Muay Thai. This more constrained form of combat was a learning experience precisely because of its fundamentally different nature. When I fought in Thailand, I never felt anxiety, sadness, or fear. There, I fully grasped the joy of fighting.

In Thailand, I also established life-long professional contacts and friendships. Particularly close to my heart are Master Alfred Skuntalak, Vice President of the International Martial Art Promotion of Bangkok, and his close friend, who eventually became mine too, Petchyindee Sakat. I trained and exchanged martial arts tips and insights with them and taught in their organizations. I exhibited my martial arts, held regular classes and participated in public conferences and private exam sessions. This enabled me to open my Muay Thai course in Genoa that, in Shan's hands now, remains an integral part of my school. Perhaps most important of all, I had a deep human exchange and great fun with my Thai friends, through which I immersed myself deeply in Thai culture and tradition. Compared to China, I learned the far more joyful, sociable and fun ways of the Thais. In my bouncing back to a new start, that lightness was just what I needed.

The man and the master: opening my heart again

It took time before I found my emotional bearings again. My relationship with Angela was settling into a new normal; given that Shan and the *kwoon* bound us together, we never stopped seeing one another, even in our most difficult moments. Still, several years passed before we managed to rebuild our relationship on a new and more solid foundation. Her transition from being my wife to becoming a friend and sister took time. While several women crossed my path in those years, I struggled to let anyone into my heart. Confusion and chaos prevailed in my private life and there were moments when the emptiness I felt almost choked me. Particularly when I rally-raced in the mid-1990s, I knew that I was consciously pushing myself to the limit, and unconsciously toying with the risk of falling over the edge. Had it not been for my *kwoon* and the responsibility I felt towards it, I might have fallen prey to the temptation of breaking rather bending.

Still, in those years of emotional darkness, two women tip-toed into my life, helping me slowly rediscover the beauty of friendship and love.

Barbara Macciocu was my student. She had enrolled in the *kwoon* back in 1988 and had always been very present at the school and diligent in her practice. Barbara was not an extro-vert; it took time before I opened my eyes to her. But she had always struck me as an intelligent and sensitive woman, and above all, one with a kind heart. In those years of darkness, Barbara and I became closer almost imperceptibly. This was rare for me. At the time, I was suspicious of everything and everyone. After the schism at the school, I became extremely cautious about opening up to my students. I had been badly burnt by some of them; I told myself that if I hadn't allowed myself to get so close to them, I may have had the lucidity to see them for who they really were.

But Barbara was different. I knew she understood my troubles and felt my pain. I knew that I could confide in her as a friend and that she would always respect me as her *sifu*. She would never use her personal advantage as my friend to make headway as a student. Barbara was simply there for me; she wasn't after anything, she had no hidden agenda. I could rely on her. From her, I slowly learned to receive once again, without fear of ulterior motives or betrayals. With her exquisite warmth and lightness, she showed me there was good for goodness' sake.

When I think of Barbara and the warm lightness of her giving, one tragicomic incident comes to mind. It was 1997, and at a martial arts gala in the United States, I had met a woman. She was famous and highly respected by the actors, film directors and producers in her entourage. I happened to sit next to her at dinner, and she began enquiring about my life. I was parsimonious with the details, but she seemed spellbound by my stories all the same. She proposed that she come visit me in Genoa, where I could tell her more about myself so she could write a screenplay based on my life. In the moment, I played along, but I barely took her seriously. She was intelligent and interesting, and I enjoyed her company. I had spent a fun evening with her and assumed it would all end there.

It did not. A few months later, she landed in Genoa on a one-way ticket. As the days dragged by, I realized the screenplay was only half the reason for her journey. The other, far more relevant reason was that she had a huge crush on me, and was determined to get what she wanted. I kept her at a healthy distance and she gradually started losing it. She would oscillate between desperation and rage, aggression and suicidal instincts. On more than one occasion, I genuinely feared for her life. She was clearly unbalanced, and I felt I had a ticking bomb on my hands. My aim was to get her, alive, onto a plane back across the Atlantic as quickly as possible. To do so, I had to walk the fine line between tact and distance, caring and firmness.

Barbara came to the rescue. For forty excruciatingly long days, the woman stayed in Genoa and Barbara was at my side. The whole affair would have been tragic were it not for the fun that Barbara brought to it. My friend helped me disentangle myself from that awful mess. She sprinkled a touch of comedy on top of the drama and saw me through it. When I finally drove the woman to the airport and saw her safely walk through customs, I sighed with relief. Barbara was there waiting for me with a drink and a smile.

With Barbara I found true friendship. With Minou, I rediscovered love. Minou was the owner of a pub that I occasionally visited for a beer. The pub was in Genoa Quinto, ways away from my neighbourhood, but it was renowned for its excellent beers. Minou was not a student of mine, although she did have a passion for the martial arts. She was a blackbelt in Taekwondo and had practiced Jeet Kune *Do* as well. Thus, while she was completely out of the orbit of my *kwoon*, where most of my relationships grew, Minou and I still had a martial arts connection. But that was only one aspect of our connection. In truth, we talked about countless things, from beer, to cars, to travel. She was fascinated by my travels to China and intrigued by someone who was obviously an alien compared to the average client in her pub. I loved when she brandished her vast knowledge of beer and filled me in on the details of her latest trip across Europe to discover new artisan ales. She occasionally offered me a few bottles and asked me to bring them to China with me.

She would often stop by me for a brief chat in between attending to her other customers. I enjoyed those moments tremendously and I sensed she did too. Light as our conversation was during those evenings at the pub, I quickly figured out that Minou was a strong, kind, sensitive, and intelligent woman. She could be extremely serious and at the same time she was great fun. Plus, she was beautiful.

With Minou, I could relax and be totally myself. I felt none of the responsibility or expectations that weighed on me in my relationships that revolved around the school. At times, I felt tired of being a *sifu*. In all of the most important relationships of my life—my ex-wife, my son, my brother, and my friends—I was *sifu*, not Paolo. I didn't regret it. The school was such a foundational element of my life that that was the only way it could have been for me. But sometimes all I wanted was to shrug off the weight of being *sifu* and just be Paolo. With Minou, that was exactly who I got to be. She was intrigued and fascinated by the master and she was always extremely respectful of that role, but she knew very little about my professional life and past. She was interested in me for who I was, not just what I did. She was respectful of the master, but she fell in love with the man.

It took me ages to figure it out, however. When, many years later, she finally confessed that she'd had a crush on me since the day we met, it felt totally out of the blue. She was eighteen when we first met. She was little more than a girl, with her whole life ahead of her, and I was in love with Angela and fully immersed in my Kung Fu. Hers was a girlish fantasy, which remained hidden for many years. She was physically attracted to me and drawn to someone who was so out of the ordinary in her eyes. But for years, her desire remained unexpressed, while I didn't have the faintest clue about her feelings for me. It wasn't until a decade later—after a marriage, separation and son for me, and a first marriage for her, too—that something between us changed.

It happened one night, in my sleep. I woke up startled, with an image of Minou fixed in my mind. It had been a powerful dream, one of those dreams that is so vivid that for a few moments of utter confusion you cannot believe that it was a mere figment of the imagination. Her image stuck with me all day long. When I showed up at the pub the following evening, I just knew I had to tell her about it. I didn't have a clear game plan, and had no idea how she would react, but I summoned my courage and told her. Minou's eyes twinkled with a touch of spice, as she continued to pour, seemingly unmoved, a pint of draft beer. As if I had blurted out something obvious, she smiled and said: "Listen, listen to what the man of my dreams is saying! You dreamt about me once? I've been dreaming about you for the last ten years!" This caught me completely off guard and my nerves calmed down. I asked her, amused, "The man of your dreams? Tell me more!" Smugly, she replied, "Oh, it's a long story. I'm sure I'll tell you about it some day . . ."

The seed of something special was planted that evening. But several months passed before it blossomed. One evening at the pub, Minou and I ended up talking about martial arts. Knowing that she practiced Taekwondo, I proposed that she sign up for a training session at my *kwoon.* She accepted the challenge and showed up the following morning with a colleague, Francesco, who trained in her same gym. At the end of the lesson, she was as exhilarated as she was exhausted. She was enthusiastic about the class, its teachings, exercises, and methods. It was the first time she had trained in that way and she was beaming. She was also exhausted and strangely amused by the fact that her black belt had dwindled in value to her. For Minou it was a new challenge and she dove headfirst into it: both she and Francesco enrolled in my school that very day.

Around that time, I was working on a big new project: *The Journey*. It was a documentary, written, filmed and produced by me. Over the course of seven, forty-five minute long episodes, I aimed to cover a wide range of topics, from Kung Fu to Muay Thai, as well as the cultural, medical, religious, and spiritual dimensions of traditional martial arts. Through the documentary, I hoped to spread basic information about traditional martial arts and its underlying values to the wider public, ideally through television. For the personal defence episode, I had written several scenes, shot in a bar or a club, in which a female bartender successfully defended herself from harassment by a group of rowdy men. Minou's pub was the ideal shooting location for the scene, and given her martial experience, I thought to myself, why not cast her as the bartender?

She accepted, and that gave us the opportunity to see each other far more regularly. Our relationship deepened as a result. Up until then she had been a friend, and, more recently, a student, but I still only saw her occasionally. In the weeks shooting the documentary, however, we spent a lot more time together and became much closer: first, when we were filming the personal defence scenes in her pub, and later when we shot another episode on the Kung Fu style of the "drunken man." For that scene, I had to recreate the ambience of a traditional Chinese tavern. The scene would be filmed in my *kwoon* but I needed to fill the place up with old wooden stools and tables. Minou came to the rescue, bringing over as many pieces of old furniture from her pub as I needed. The more time I spent with her, the better I felt. At lunch one day, I looked her in the eye and the memory of my dream came flooding back. Without thinking twice, I blurted out, "What was that story about the man of your dreams?" That day, I realized that Minou was not just my friend and student. In her simple and direct way, she was becoming an important part of my life; I was falling in love again.

I had been pushed off-balance emotionally by the end of a relationship with a woman. Thanks to two new women, I was finding my emotional bearings once again. In truth, I have opened up and shared who I truly am only to women, and I give thanks to all of them. In the opposite sex, I have found unconditional generosity and a readiness to listen without judgment. Instinctively, I have entrusted them with my most intimate thoughts and feelings. I don't mean to say that the men I have come across in my life have been insensitive or untrustworthy. Yes, the betrayals I suffered have all been by men. My friends, my brother, Cheon Yee Keung or, ultimately Fu Han Tong himself: it has always been men who have let me down. But many other men have stood loyally by my side and do so to this day. To them, I will turn later. From Graziella, my first teenage love, to Angela, my first wife, mother of my son and life-long work partner, to my faithful friend Barbara, to Minou, my current partner and mother of my daughter Mei, I have always and only allowed women to reach me deep inside.

New horizons for my kwoon

Following the dark years of the early 1990s, I was ready to rebuild my school on a stronger foundation. It was partly out of need. My *kwoon* was my job and Angela's too. It was our and our son's only source of material sustenance. Making it soar again was a necessity. But money was only one thing that encouraged me to roll up my sleeves and bounce back. I was also driven by a sense of appreciation and gratitude. I owed it to the instructors and students who had remained loyal to me; I owed it to my family; and above all, I owed it to myself, to prove there was genuine value in what we had built together over the years.

What had happened could not simply be erased, however. I could not go back in time and rebuild the school exactly how it had been. For my *kwoon* to remain resilient, by definition, there needed to be a change. There must have been a reason for the secession in the school. And even if the majority of that reason had to do with those who had left, with their personal ambitions, motivations, and complexes, I had to address the part I played in that dynamic, too.

The changes had to do both with the organization of the school and with me as its *sifu.* After the secession in the school, I became more distanced from my students. Initially, it was a question of trust. I had been hurt so badly and so unexpectedly that I began doubting everything and everyone. Minou recalls how when we first met, she was struck by my doubts and suspicions, which were seemingly at odds with the stories of strength and courage she heard about my past. Most importantly, for a while, I questioned my own ability to discern who was trustworthy and who was not. I took a step back from all my students. Rationally, I knew that those who had remained loyal to me were more than trustworthy. They had been with me through thick and thin and I could count on them one hundred percent. But emotionally, I had to rebuild my ability to trust others—it had to do with me more than with them—and to do so, I had to put some distance between myself and my students.

While those scars will never fully heal, I did gradually regain my ability to trust, but I still retained a more detached attitude. It was partly a generational difference. The new generation of instructors were not just younger than me age-wise; they were also much younger than me, martially speaking. I did not share with them my twenty-odd years of martial arts experience as I had done with the first group of instructors. I had developed as a martial artist and teacher alongside that first cohort, and I had lived some of the most formative moments of my life with them. It was that shared professional path that created our closeness, and it could not be replicated in the same way with the newer instructors. It was simply a different moment in my life.

Learning from my past also meant changing the organization of the *kwoon.* I dissolved the non-profit that had bound my instructors and me so closely together, both physically and financially. The method of constant rotation across all branches of the school and of the collective sharing of our revenues and costs could not continue. It had been a wonderful adventure while it lasted, and I cherish fond memories of those years. But that time had passed, and the school had to become more decentralized, both administratively and financially. The new instructors had to become more independent and assume full responsibility for the management of their respective branches. There would still be centralized dimensions of the *kwoon*, of course, namely our common curricula, exams and stages. These would be strengthened further. But I couldn't continue zigzagging non-stop across the country, nor could I be held responsible for the administrative and financial performance of each instructor. The constant demands by some instructors for advance payments, the complaints by others about their monthly income, and, above all, the frequent tensions between them often driven by our shared finances had to stop. The only way to do this was to make them fully responsible for themselves. If any of them ran into administrative or financial trouble, I would of course do my best to help; I continued to do my best to ensure that each instructor built a promising future for him or herself. However, I could no longer live with an organizational structure that gave each individual the power to bring down the whole company on a whim. If a particular branch is struggling, it shouldn't endanger the life of the entire tree. Changing the school's organizational structure was a recipe for a healthier and more mature relationship between myself and the instructors, as well as for a more sustainable future for the *kwoon* as a whole.

The resilience of the school also required a redesign of its technical curricula. I wanted to revamp them to differentiate my school from the schools of my former instructors, who had no qualms about teaching what they had learned from me. I also wanted to enrich my program with the new insights I was gaining through my ongoing travels to Asia. As I continued to grow as a martial artist, no longer under the guidance of my masters but free to roam my own way, I was keen to transmit that development to my students. In some cases, I added greater specialization and detail. I significantly deepened the Muay Thai, combat and internal practice courses. In other cases, I removed some Kung Fu forms that I felt were no longer essential to the didactic method I was developing, while replacing them with new ones that were more in line with the messages I was hoping to convey.

More specifically, I introduced changes to the exams, grading and levels for all students, as well as systematized the learning and training paths of the instructors. I established three levels for the instructors based on their experience, seniority and knowledge. I had been let down by a group of instructors, and so I felt I had to insert as many structural supports as possible to avoid something similar from happening again. Introducing specific exams, apprenticeships, certificates and diplomas was not a guarantee that the instructors would be serious, passionate, and professional, and it could certainly not replace a human touch to discern who was trustworthy and who was not. But standardizing the rules, requirements and structure to the instructor career path would add clarity, ensure greater commitment, and reduce misinterpretations and misunderstandings. It also allowed for a clearer organization of the school and provided an insurance policy against the risk of fragmentation.

The *kwoon* bounced back in no time. Thanks to a clearer organizational structure and a team of second-generation instructors with the energy, passion, ability and determination to succeed, the *kwoon* rose to new heights. There was no need for trial and error; I was now well aware of what worked and what did not. While the atmosphere of seriousness and commitment remained the same, the school's pace became more consistent and I was no longer inclined to subject my students to extreme martial practices and experiences. Both the *kwoon* and I had matured. The odd problem surfaced now and then, but the school was fully equipped to deal with them. Like me, the *kwoon* had become more resilient.

The school's relaunch wasn't only a domestic one. In the second half of the 1990s, I was determined to expand the *kwoon* internationally, too. I was proud of what I had built and rebuilt on stronger ground, and I began feeling confined by staying within Italy alone. Of course, my professional path had certainly not been restricted to my home country. Much of my development as a martial artist had taken place in Asia. On a few occasions, I had taken one of my students on a trip with me, beginning with Angela and Roberto. On other occasions, I had invited fellow martial artists to Italy to conduct seminars and workshops for my students. But these instances had been the exception, not the rule. Asia, and particularly China, had been about my growth as a martial artist and only in that way were they related to my *kwoon*. Through those trips, I brought Asia to my school, but I had not brought my school to Asia or into the wider world. Now, I started feeling the urge to promote my school internationally and, through it, help spread the culture of traditional martial arts.

We began performing far more often in martial arts championships and halls of fame across Europe and the United States. One of the most exhilarating experiences of that period was in June 1997, in San Francisco. I had been invited by *Sifu* Tat Ma Wong, a world-renowned Choy Lee Fut grand master and martial arts event promoter, to the Kung Fu World Championship. Tat Ma Wong asked me to be a judge and referee in the championship, as well as to perform at the masters' evening, during which thirty-six Kung Fu masters chosen from around the world would close the event with their exhibitions. It was a huge gathering and I was honoured by the invitation and accepted. On a warm summer day, I set off for California with my sparring partner, Roberto. We had scheduled our flight ten days before the event to have plenty of time to acclimatize, train, contact the masters flocking into town, and relax and explore San Francisco together. Tat Ma Wong had set up a stellar organization. Roberto and I were pampered in a five-star hotel and assisted by the organizers in all our needs. I recall our morning trainings in the park nearby our hotel, where Roberto and I meticulously revised our exhibition. Even more vivid in my mind are our meanderings across town.

Travelling with Roberto was absolutely hilarious. My friend was not exactly a good traveller. Whereas I had travelled far and wide, he was provincial, to put it mildly. It wasn't just his sheer terror of flying, a fear that was abated only by copious amounts of alcohol on the flight. Nor was it his refusal to speak a word of English or Chinese, stubbornly speaking not only in Italian, but in his strong Monterotondo dialect, convinced that he'd be understood if only he repeated the same sentence often and loudly enough. In every respect, Roberto was truly lost the minute he set foot outside his hometown. Sometimes this made traveling with him complicated, to say the least, but on most occasions it was a real laugh.

The championship itself was a memorable experience. During the three days of the event, I was busy refereeing several of the matches as well as judging the traditional Kung Fu form competition. On Saturday evening, Roberto and I, alongside thirty-five other masters, performed. The exhibition was a huge success and we were unanimously judged as the best performance. This led to great publicity for our school, notably in the United States, as newspapers and TV shows reported generously about the championship and our role in it. The exhibition also brought me new connections and allowed me to make contact with the VIPs of the martial world who were present at the event. The seeds that were sown in San Francisco continued to blossom for many years thereafter.

In those years, I also started conducting seminars and workshops across Asia, America, and various European countries; as a result, my students were no longer based only in Italy, but they were in Germany, France, Spain, and Portugal, too. I was determined to reach out to even greater numbers using different communication channels. The more my trips to China confirmed the sad truth of a thinning traditional Kung Fu culture there, the more determined I became to share far and wide what had been my lifelong passion. Initially I looked into the possibilities that television had to offer. In 1993, I started working on a TV show in New York about traditional Kung Fu, but it turned out to be a great deal of work for an extremely niche market, which ran counter to the purpose of mass dissemination I had in mind. It took a while before I found the right opportunity to spread the message of traditional Kung Fu to a wider public.

Finally, in late 1996 I found the key. In Spain at the time, there was a highly popular martial arts magazine, *Cinturón Negro*, which also produced a successful series of training videos. *Cinturón Negro* was published in Madrid, but it was well distributed across the martial world. I set off for Madrid and sought out the magazine's director, José Fraguas Maria, proposing a collaboration in the production of his videos. I sensed that this was both a great opportunity and a huge risk. If the production was successful, it would have certainly served my purpose of spreading knowledge of traditional Kung Fu to far greater numbers than I could reach through in-person lessons, workshops, or exhibitions. *Cinturón Negro* boasted impressive sales that could propel me. By the same token, if the video was a failure, my *kwoon* risked a dreadful blowback effect. Finding the right style to teach Kung Fu both to specialists and to amateurs was not easy, but I was up for the challenge.

I remember feeling awed when I stepped into *Cinturón Negro*'s offices. The whole set up was highly professional, with large pristine offices packed with professional employees working in the editorial, graphic, interview and administrative departments of a business entirely dedicated to martial arts. I had never seen anything like it, and I was enthralled. Fraguas bombarded me with questions, trying to gauge who I really was and what my credentials were as a martial artist. Having had a rather eclectic martial upbringing, he probably struggled to locate me in the martial arts world and only partially believed the explanations I provided. Alas, there are so many charlatans in my field, and, being fully immersed in it, Fraguas knew this well. But I must have tickled his curiosity, so he asked me to perform a short sketch of what I had in mind. Enthusiastic about what he saw, Fraguas took a gamble on me.

Back in Italy, Roberto and I spent two months meticulously preparing the material for the first two videos: one on freestyle combat and the other on the internal style of Pa Kua. We returned to Madrid in early 1997 to film, over an intense week of work. *Cinturón Negro*'s team was ecstatic about it. The magazine, which collaborated with an impressive roster of martial arts masters across different disciplines, published a grading of its products based on an assessment of the feature artists' presentations, didactic skills and performance. A jury of masters assigned a grade to each video, ranging from one to five belts. Both the combat and the Pa Kua videos received the full five belts and were distributed worldwide.

That was only the beginning. Only a few months after my return to Genoa, Fraguas rang me up and proposed that I film a new video for them. I accepted and began preparing it, focusing on the Hung Gar style. He also invited me to direct a workshop in Madrid and participate in the International Budo Gala. I could film the third video during my visit.

Both the workshop and the exhibition at Budo Gala were

huge successes and bolstered the *kwoon*'s reputation in the international martial arts circuit, and especially in Spain. 1997 was the beginning of an extremely fruitful collaboration with *Cinturón Negro*, which was eventually renamed Budo International when Fraguas emigrated to the United States and the company came under the leadership of its current director, Alfredo Tucci. Under Tucci, Budo International reached new international heights, becoming the most well-respected and famous martial arts magazine worldwide, translated into six languages and with tens of thousands of copies sold. With Afredo, I established a solid working partnership and friendship that exists to this day. Alfredo Tucci is a wonderful person: sensitive, intelligent, and a strong believer in martial arts. A Spaniard of Italian and Argentine origins, he is a man of wide horizons who has greatly contributed to our world. He has been a tremendous communicator of the art, history, philosophy, and spirituality of martial arts. He is a father figure and a just referee who has diffused tensions between styles, disciplines, and masters, while always remaining above the politics of sport. Alfredo Tucci, who was honoured with the well-deserved title of *Shidoshi*, has my unconditional friendship and fullest respect.

I have penned over sixty articles for and been featured on eighteen covers of Budo International, which is published in ten languages. In collaboration with the magazine, I have produced twenty-three training DVDs and four books in six languages, of which tens of thousands of copies were sold. I have participated regularly in Budo's halls of fame and galas, significantly widening my network of contacts. Thanks to Budo International and its director Tucci, I met Grand Master Soke Santiago Sanchis, a Marine General and expert in dozens of martial methods and styles, who organizes and presides over one of the most famous martial arts halls of fame in the world. I have been inducted into many halls of fame over the years, receiving awards that I cherish in my heart and in my home. On those occasions, I met many martial artists and actors, some of whom became good friends with whom I exchanged martial knowledge and experience. Thanks to Soke Sanchis, I participated in workshops with security specialists and special forces, receiving an instructor diploma from the International Alliance of Security Forces in 2007. I have enormous appreciation and respect for my friend General Sanchis: thanks to his virtues and experience, he's a man who inspires strength and confidence, reawakening the warrior's spirit and opening the way to wisdom. It wasn't the praise or fame that was most important to me. Of course, I was happy and humbled by the appreciation that my school and I received from martial arts masters, film directors, actors and producers around the world. But what really mattered was that, through this international expansion, I was working to slow the erosion of traditional martial arts.

* * *

Resilience is not about going back, but rather about moving forward and seeking a new equilibrium after a shock or a fall. In different spheres of life, my resilience has offered me a more well-rounded way of being.

My resilience has meant becoming a *sifu* in Asia just like I was in Italy, albeit in a different way. I stopped feeling lonely in Asia precisely when I started standing on my own two feet there. On my own, I relished my newfound freedom, but that sense of empowerment humbled me, too, as I appreciated the world of learning that still lay ahead of me. Casting aside all my baggage, I absorbed the beauty that came my way with levity and surprise.

My resilience has meant reconciling the man with the master. The duality at the core of my life, which had been the silver thread running through my most important bonds—with

Angela, Shan, Carlo, Roberto—became less distinct, and at times dissolved altogether. As I rediscovered friendship through Barbara and love through Minou, and as I learned to trust again, the man and the master began to join into one.

Finally, my resilience saw me become both more detached and more caring towards my students, with distance helping me see with greater clarity the opportunities and the challenges that lay ahead, while a newfound maturity helped me become a more well-rounded master. Gone were the days of extremes and I began thinking more deeply about what was right for my *kwoon*, beyond what had been right for me.

Resilience is, by definition, dynamic. It is something that must be fought for and earned every day. After my fall, I did not acquire resilience once and for all; I simply embarked upon a journey of resilience that continues to this day.

Resilience

Resilience is essential for personal transformation. Just like metal bends without breaking, human resilience is the ability to bounce back after a fall, returning not to our previous reality but to a new and stronger one that enables us to better withstand stress and pain in future. We can learn from our falls, drawing positive lessons from seemingly negative experiences, thus imbuing them with new meaning and value.

My resilience surfaced in the dark period of my fall. Over the course of four painful years, the death of *Sifu* Chan Hon Chung, the distancing from Fu Han Tong, the separation from my wife Angela and the secession in my school drove me to the brink of a breakdown. But rather than break, I rolled up my sleeves and changed. I rebuilt my school on stronger ground and cherished the treasures I'd received from my masters. My separations generated a new maturity, a new internal balance that eventually enabled Angela and I to find renewed harmony in our unconditional friendship.

My resilience helped me to stand with my head held high and not give up, persevering in my drive to live and share positive energy with those around me. So, just like metal, you must bend, adapt and constantly change in order to pursue the essence of your way.

CHAPTER 9
Rebuilding

I was on the cusp of my forties and had set the foundation for a new start as a man and as a master. I had learned how to blend the two roles into one.

My first thirty years had been an exhilarating whirlwind of adventures. I had seized every risk and every opportunity, at times for the better, at times for the worst, but either way, I had lived my life to the fullest without any regrets. I had made mistakes and been wronged, but every step was full of meaning, and explained and guided the next.

There had been plenty of pain, too, crystallized in the solitude of my dual identity as a man and as a master. It was a loneliness that I had known since childhood, as Paolo the martial artist grew amid the secrecy of the relationship with his Chinese master, alongside but separate from the light-heartedness of his peers. Family and friends knew about my passion, but had no idea where, how and above all with whom I was blossoming as a the martial artist. It was in the isolation of a special relationship between a Genoese boy and a Chinese traditional Kung Fu master that the seeds of my duality were sown.

To bounce back, I had to reconcile that duality. I learned to fully claim the mantle of master, not just in Italy but in Asia, too. By charting my own way in the martial arts world, I discovered comfort. The harrowing loneliness that had haunted me in China for many years evaporated magically into thin air. At the same time, I learned to strip myself completely of the *sifu*'s title in my personal life, as I fell in love with a woman who loved the man over the master. And I rebuilt my school on more solid ground, learning to give more to my students without entangling myself in a web of inauthentic friendships. It was a painful journey that sprung from the ashes of my ruptures, but I knew that the foundations of my existence were now much stronger.

Having bounced back, I could now rebuild.

Rebuilding a family

We didn't plan it. When Minou and I fell in love, rebuilding a family did not cross my mind. I enjoyed spending time with her and felt no inclination to meet other women. We had great fun together and I relished the fact that I could be totally myself with her. She had fallen in love with me, Paolo, and this filled me with a warmth and lightness the likes of which I had never experienced.

For a good three years, our relationship was rather erratic, however. When we saw each other in Genoa, it was magical for both of us. Minou believed in love, respect and friendship: she is steadfast about her values. At the same time, she has an exquisite lightness in living by them, and through her delicate warmth, I opened up to her as she conquered, cell by cell, every corner of my heart. But those moments came and went. In those years, I travelled frequently to Asia, the United States, and Europe, so Minou and I spent long periods apart. Meanwhile, her marriage had come to an end, but she was fully immersed in her professional life and totally committed to making her pub a success.

It was only in the early 2000s that our relationship took a more serious turn. As our love blossomed, I realized that she was filling the emotional void that I had felt for many years. On one trip to China, I found myself thinking intensely about her and our relationship, and for the first time I questioned the block I had unconsciously erected against building a new family. As I chiselled away at it, the desire to build something new with Minou swelled in my heart. Upon my return, I summoned the courage to tell her.

She was surprised, but not shocked, by my words. She had this wonderful way of being totally committed to our relationship, without harbouring specific plans for our life together. As soon as I told her I wanted to build a new life with her, her eyes brightened, conveying at once surprise and reassurance: she was both taken aback by my suggestion and deeply aware that this was our destiny. Looking at me intensely, she whispered: "I feel the same way." Right at that time, Alfredo Tucci, Budo International's director, proposed that I join a new company he was establishing to promote the magazine's distribution worldwide, notably in the United States. I took two gambles: I accepted Alfredo's offer and proposed to Minou that she enter the business with me. She eagerly accepted, and that was the beginning of a work partnership between us that has lasted to this day. After a trip we took to Hong Kong, we started living together: we were becoming a new family.

Several years had passed when, one evening, Minou looked pensive as she busily tidied up the kitchen sink. She was rarely in this mood and I sensed something was bothering her. But hiding her feelings is just not her, and before I could ask, she asked me to sit down and talk. In her warm but firm voice, Minou talked about her deep desire to have a child with me and to become a mother. I was taken aback; I hadn't thought about it before. On the one hand, there was something wonderfully enticing about the idea: I loved Minou and had no doubt whatsoever that I wanted to be with her. Adding a child to our life together was a beautiful thought. I also understood and respected her desire to be a mother. Minou had been married once before but didn't have children. She was in her late thirties, and it was only natural for her to be interested motherhood. On the other hand, I knew how intense raising a child can be, and was conscious of the hectic rhythm of my life. I was terrified at the thought of falling into the same habits again, and subjecting my son or daughter to my frequent absences. Amid all these mixed feelings, there was one person I knew I should talk to.

I decided to discuss the matter with Angela. Angela had become my greatest friend and gave me the best advice. Angela was a woman, and she deeply respected and empathized with Minou. I had a long talk with her about Minou's wish to become a mother, and subsequently spoke to my son, Shan, too. Angela and Shan both met the idea with incredible warmth, understanding and encouragement, creating space for my enthusiasm to spread. My family could now enlarge in harmony.

Xiao Mei was born on December 27th, 2007, my late father's birthday. After twenty-four years, I became father again, this time of a beautiful baby girl. I was besotted with her from the moment she came into being. As a man in his late forties, rather than a boy in his mid-twenties, my second paternity was a completely different experience. It was not always easy. The emotions Mei stirred in me propelled me back into memories of my past, as I meticulously unpacked what was different and what had remained unchanged in my experience of fatherhood. Be it because of age or gender, I had seen myself in Shan, my successor and my right-hand man. Martial arts are the glue that had bound us together, blending with the love between father and son. But becoming a father again was also sublime. I felt strongly that Mei represented the completion of my Tao, a baby girl born twenty-four years after my baby boy. I imagined Mei as a beautiful and intelligent woman, with a passion for Kung Fu, I hoped, and with an energy that emanated beyond martial arts. Mei and Minou gave me unprecedented courage and energy: I would do everything I could to make them happy and build a solid nest for my new family.

With Mei's arrival, my life changed—or, perhaps more accurately, I was ready to commit to a change in my life that had been brewing for some time. I was still driven by the same curiosity to explore, to discover, to study and to know. My life remained full and engaged both through my work and my hobbies, in some respects even more so than in the past. But my search became more orderly, sedentary, and generally less hectic than in previous years. I became more present at home and at school. The choice was entirely my own. I never felt any pressure whatsoever from Minou. On the contrary: Minou has always demonstrated utmost sensitivity and intelligence in not intruding or imposing her wishes on me, and I have tried to do the same with her.

Minou sold her pub. Mei must have been no more than a week old when Minou went back to work, serving beers while Mei was in her cot. As the pub's owner, she was fully responsible for it. It had been her baby, and she couldn't imagine working there without giving it total and unconditional commitment. Her job, however, was simply irreconcilable with maternity leave, and all the help I could give her would not change this simple fact. I remember those first months when Minou would come home from work at four in the morning. While she was away, I looked after Mei, but during the day, I worked too, which meant that both Minou and I ended up with a couple of hours' sleep at most. She was exhausted and soon came to terms with the fact that the pub and Mei were incompatible. Selling the pub was painful, but she was determined to move on. She had desired motherhood so much that she wanted to enjoy it to the fullest.

This did not mean that Minou stopped working. While dedicating herself to her family, she immediately ramped up her work in the *kwoon*. She initially started helping me with publicity for the school as well as writing and editing books and articles. Over time, she started working on the tatami mat itself. In 2012 we moved back to my childhood village of Casella and opened a branch of my school there three years later. In Casella, I personally taught every lesson in every course, and Minou was by my side the whole way. This allowed her to develop a solid approach to teaching, particularly children, but also combat and Tai Chi. Alongside her, I asked Giovanni Sciaccaluga, a young and talented instructor, to work with us in Casella. Together, the three of us have created a great team, dedicated to the diffusion of Kung Fu in this valley.

What is so special about Minou, however, is that while being fully in the *kwoon* and completely respectful of it, she has always followed her own path in martial arts. She trains and teaches Kung Fu daily, but prides herself on being a transparent belt and has never taken an exam. As a result, her Kung Fu is "eclectic": at times she mixes and mashes styles and forms so much that I cry tears of laughter. At the same time, she has a wonderful way of teaching, especially children, and I know I can rely on her no matter what. In her inimitable way, at once highly respectful and totally undisciplined, the overall cocktail of Minou's Kung Fu simply works.

Ultimately, if I were to put a finger on the fundamental similarities and differences between the two sides of my family, Angela and Shan on the one side and Minou and Mei on the other, it all boils down to the constantly shifting role of martial arts in my life. Minou and I, just like with Angela, are bound together by trust and respect. We work side-by-side in the school and support one another unconditionally. Minou and Angela have also developed a wonderful friendship over the years. I was touched when Minou invited Angela for a weekend together in Madrid to celebrate Angela's birthday. Mei, for her part, adores auntie Angie and calls Angela's mother Renata her "granny." In our first years back in Casella, before I opened the children's course in the village, Mei was thrilled to go down to Genoa twice a week to attend Angela's children's course at the *kwoon*. Like her brother Shan, Mei was born and raised fully immersed in the martial arts world. She started practicing Kung Fu when she was five and continues to do so today. She now loves helping her mom with the children's course, while continuing to practice and spend time with her friends in the village.

At the same time, the differences at the heart of the two sides of my family also stem from martial arts. Angela struggled to reconcile my roles as man and master, not least because of the primacy of martial arts in her own life. For Minou, I am the man well beyond being a master. She never feels she must show or prove anything to me, and at home, after a full day's work, she avoids asking me about Kung Fu, sensing my need to unplug.

Likewise, whereas for Shan I am both father and *sifu,* for Mei I am just daddy. In some ways, I share more with Shan than I do with Mei. My son, like Angela and me, has always fully believed in martial arts. His commitment, like mine, has been complete. Furthermore, he was born and grew up in a time when there was no real line separating the *kwoon* from home, as students came and went from our house in the years when the school was more akin to a commune. Hence, for Shan, I was always both his father and his *sifu*; rare were the moments when I was the former without also being the latter. Mei has fun practicing Kung Fu, but also enjoys messing around with her friends. She certainly lacks the unconditional dedication to and passion for martial arts that her father and brother share.

Mei and I had similar childhoods. Mei, like me, is growing up in the simplicity and solidarity of village life. Her friends know about our martial arts, and several of them attend our classes, too, but most know nothing about Kung Fu, just like my own family and friends when I was a boy. I don't deny that I hope Mei will become more serious about her Kung Fu one day, but it is only a fleeting thought and I certainly avoid projecting my expectations onto her, like I did with her brother. I spend more time with Mei than I ever did with Shan, and my daughter and I argue more. But Mei has a unique ability to make me melt like a chocolate bar in the sun and open my eyes to how important it is for her mother and I to just let her be.

My life has changed tremendously over the last decade. Unlike in my twenties and thirties, when all my family, friends and acquaintances revolved around martial arts, the tightly knit social fabric of Casella has driven us as a family, and me in particular, to develop relationships that have nothing to do with Kung Fu. As my new friends came to learn about my professional background, some started calling me *Sifu*, or sometimes just "*Si*," instead of Paolo. But to Mei, who grew up in a world in which most people call me *Sifu*, "*Si*" or Paolo, it is only natural that I be simply dad.

Rebuilding the school

The last two decades have also brought the rebuilding of what has become a completely new school, enshrined upon the unchanging ethics of traditional Kung Fu. A new generation of students has grown within the *kwoon* and has done so with a master—me—who has become more detached but also more present and caring. My students have grown in an organization that is certainly less familial, but undoubtedly better structured and organized, aided also by the reduced impact of distance in the digital age. This has given the new generation of instructors greater freedom and responsibility in their own development as martial arts teachers and entrepreneurs. With time, my own diffidence towards them, a consequence of the scars from my past, has faded. As they have proven their ability, knowledge and passion, and, most of all, their unwavering commitment to the *kwoon* and its values, my trust in them has deepened. Together, we have carried the school to new international heights; with them, I have created a new and more sustainable definition of a Kung Fu family.

The hierarchy within the school is much clearer today than it was under the first generation, which has had the effect of erasing misunderstandings and focusing expectations and aspirations within the *kwoon*. Instructors, all of whom have passed the black belt exam as well as the specific instructors' exam and apprenticeship, have different levels of certified seniority, which are recognized by all. Some are also the heads of their branches. Most are supported by assistant instructors and advanced students, some of whom also aspire to become instructors one day. Today the school is growing at a slower pace than it did in the whirlwind years of the 1980s. But its growth is far more sustainable than in the past: I now know that I have rebuilt a school that is here to stay.

As in all families, there are a select few at the head. In any traditional *kwoon*, including mine, these people are entrusted with great responsibility. Our school is almost half a century old and rests on a thousand-year-old history following the lineages of the styles and disciplines we study. Those who stand by my side are responsible for upholding the name and the values of our school before our thousands of students and the outside world.

Hierarchy in traditional Kung Fu schools is crucial. It is not a matter of the colour of one's belt or the number of forms and techniques that one knows. Moving up the hierarchy certainly requires ability, passion and hard work. But most importantly, it is a matter of loyalty and trust. It is a reflection of commitment, perseverance, and humility. It is about the protection and the promotion of the school and its underlying values.

There are three main pillars of our *kwoon*: two *si bak* (male) and one *si mo* (female), who are next in line after the master, as dictated by Chinese tradition. There is Angela Podeschi, who enrolled in the school over forty years ago, in 1979. She oversees our headquarters in Genoa, teaches Kung Fu and Tai Chi, and is responsible for the latter at national level too. Angela has stood by my side through thick and thin, and despite the rollercoaster of our personal relationship, she has never let me down as a trusted work partner in over four decades. The mutual trust and respect between us are ironclad. Today, Angela is my family; she is the sister I never had. Without her, the *kwoon* would not be what it is today.

By Angela's side are Nicola and Fabio. Nicola Pastorino enrolled back in 1986. He began studying Kung Fu with me in Genoa prior to the split, and had almost a decade of experience when it took place. Back then, he used to help the instructors, but I had little direct contact with him, since our interactions were generally mediated by the first line of instructors. When the rupture happened, I reached out to Nicola, amongst others, and he unequivocally stood by my side. After the trauma of the secession, it took me a while to open to him and others on a personal level. But our martial relationship immediately intensified: I wanted to develop a new generation of instructors, of which Nicola, I hoped, would be part. Indeed, after having passed his black belt exam in 1995, he opened a branch of our school in Florence. For several years, he divided his time between Genoa and Florence, until 2002, when he moved to Tuscany for good, and his school has flourished since. With almost thirty-five years of experience, Nicola now teaches Kung Fu, Tai Chi, and combat, oversees the branch in Florence, and is responsible for everything we do in Tuscany.

Fabio Tozzi signed up in 1988. As an advanced student with seven years of practice when the secession took place, Fabio played an instrumental role in ensuring that our *kwoon* survived in Rome, unlike, alas, in Milan. At that time, Fabio was a teaching assistant in a branch led by some of the instructors who betrayed me. Just like in Milan, the traitors had not informed their students of their plans, hoping to siphon off as many as possible from the school. Most students had no idea about the separation that was taking place. In the meantime, I was going back and forth to Rome, and Fabio, alongside others, was always present. When a group of advanced students, including him, found out what had happened, they were indignant and determined to help. They offered to look for an alternative location where those who wanted to remain at the school could move. Thanks to this effort, we didn't lose all of our students. Maurizio and Enrico found a run-down but large space where we could continue working, and Fabio opened another branch soon thereafter, enabling us to retain a greater number of students in what is ultimately a large metropolis. Thanks to their work and my ongoing trips, the school lived on in Rome. In the summer of 1996, Fabio Tozzi passed his sixth exam and in fall of that same year opened his own branch, which is active to this day. Fabio teaches Kung Fu, Tai Chi, and combat, and is responsible for all our branches in the Lazio region.

As *si mo* and *si bak*, Angela, Nicola and Fabio are at the highest level of authority in the school and work with me directly in the organization and planning of the *kwoon*. True to tradition, they are next in line to become *sifu* on the fiftieth anniversary of my Kung Fu practice in 2021, when I will become the master of the masters, or the grandfather of the school: *Si Gong*. Sticking to tradition is rare. Alas, the world is rife with improvised and self-appointed masters, who seek a title and belt regardless of their actual accomplishments. I have seen many masters appear out of nowhere throughout my career, beginning with my former students who left the school because of their egos, hungry for status and recognition. It has happened around me, just like it happens everywhere else within and beyond the martial world: inflated egos, careerism, and insecurity are widespread. Hierarchy, hard work, and the sheer time that it takes to move up our school's ladder are the key ingredients for humility, the principal value that I seek to transmit, as dictated by the wisdom of traditional Kung Fu.

Angela, Nicola, and Fabio have demonstrated their worth. But they are not alone. Below them are dozens of instructors and advanced students, many of whom have been practicing Kung Fu in the school for over three decades. Some were children when they started and are now grown men and women with families of their own. They continue to study and practice devotedly, and on some occasions their children have joined the school with enthusiasm, too. Some are elderly, men and women over eighty years old, who are steadfast in their practice of Kung Fu, demonstrating how it is an art for all ages and all times.

Several of these students have decided to dedicate their own careers to Kung Fu, which is certainly not an easy choice to make these days. Gone are the days in which martial arts was a fad and money was easy to come by. Today, much more so than in the past, choosing martial arts as a profession is a challenge, and it requires even more work, courage and perseverance than it did back in its heyday in the 1980s. The instructors who have made that choice have all my respect and support. It is thanks to each and every one of them that we can collectively continue to deepen and spread this art and its values. It is with immense gratitude that I want to thank Flaviano Muzio, Shan Cangelosi, Pierluigi Bellini, Barbara Macciocu, Massimiliano Perez, Valter Marini, Andrea Pesce, Fabrizio Scelfo, Gianluca Longo, Massimiliano Menei, Leandro Bocchicchio, Alfred Koennen, Luca Cammarano, Erika Lotti, Barbara Maltagliati, Giovanni Sciaccaluga, Roberto Imperi, Maurizio Iorio, Claudio Conti, Giuseppe Lippi, Andrea Lombardi, Daniel Dos Santos, and Letitia Dos Santos. I want to thank them all for their tireless work, their professionalism, and their unwavering loyalty and commitment to the *kwoon* over the decades. They are the columns of my Kung Fu family.

Beyond the instructors are of course my students, all of them, in Italy and abroad, within and outside of Europe. Some have been studying and practicing Kung Fu for years, often for decades, every week of every month, throughout all seasons. I am proud of them, of their perseverance and of their achievements. It is largely for them that I decided to organize a major event on the thirtieth anniversary of our school, an event that would repeat itself at five-year intervals. I wanted to celebrate our *kwoon* with its students, friends and guests across the martial arts world, and remember its history, sacrifices, and achievements. Of the over thirty thousand students who have practiced in the school, I wanted to reward those who have been studying Kung Fu with me for twenty years or more, the top performers of the eight thousand exams we've given and those who have distinguished themselves in professional fighting. Above all, I wanted to pay tribute to our shared journey in the way of martial arts.

So, on our thirtieth anniversary, I put on a play about the history of Kung Fu. By representing the most salient legends and facts, heroes and masters, texts, and practices, I wanted to pay homage to the art of Kung Fu through our school. The entire project was developed by us at the *kwoon*, from the direction to the sets, the music, costumes and texts, and of course all the martial demonstrations we performed to recount this majestic story. On stage, over sixty students starred in the show, and another twenty were hard at work behind the scenes. The show took place in a major theatre in Genova, the Teatro della Corte, and the following evening we had organized a gala dinner during which we would be announcing prizes. It was to be a great gathering with masters, champions, and martial arts movie stars who were joining us from across Europe, the Americas, and Asia in celebration.

Then disaster struck. I had hired a production company to film the show, the gala, and to interview several of our international guests. The following Monday morning, I went straight to the agency to pick up the film, but I realized that while video had been captured, there was no sound: the gala had been muted. I couldn't believe it. Eighteen months of hard work alongside close to a hundred people led to a major success, and we had nothing, absolutely nothing, to show for it. All that effort had exhausted itself in two wonderful evenings, which would remain in the hearts and minds of those who participated, but nowhere else. And all this because of a cameraman's stupid mistake.

My heart sank. I was speechless. I was furious. The manager of the production company was devastated, or so it seemed initially. But when push came to shove, he simply handed me the invoice, unaltered, demanding the full amount he was due, and conveniently forgot the moral and financial damage he had caused us. I was shocked, refused to pay and went straight to a lawyer to sue. The case was crystal clear to me and it should have been an obvious win.

But things went in a dramatically different direction. Eleven years after the event, I lost the lawsuit and thirty-five thousand euros. I was encouraged by my lawyers to appeal but I lost that too, both against the agency and the cameraman, and had to pay another twenty thousand euros. I still cannot get my head around how this happened. Whether it was incompetence or bad luck, the facts remain the facts, and this ugly affair clouded an otherwise beautiful story of rebuilding.

But despite this injustice, I have not allowed this to deter me from celebrating our school and rejoicing when I see all my students gathered, demonstrating their steadfast presence and passion. Ultimately, this is what gives me joy. Individually, I know many of their life stories, their ups and downs, their traumas and their joys. Through each one of them, I have learned how martial arts can be lived in a million different ways, accompanying different lifestyles, social backgrounds, professions, personalities, and aspirations. There are so many students whom I would like to cite here, but the list would be endless. Tens of thousands have passed through the *kwoon*, many of them have contributed in their own special way, and each one has left his or her mark. Collectively, they convey to me that unique sense of togetherness, family, and belonging.

At the same time, I know what fuels their passion and their commitment. I have seen how martial arts have enriched their lives in a myriad of different ways. I have watched our martial arts support students with different physical and mental conditions, pathologies, and disabilities, and sustain them through difficult and even traumatic moments of their lives. I have observed martial arts accompany children as they grow and the elderly in their old age, adapting itself to every stage of life. Our school has always embraced everyone, making no distinction between the young and the old, the healthy and the sick, the strong and weak; we have always sought to prove how the art is inherently for everyone. Particularly when it comes to martial arts, this essence is often lost on the outside observer. Martial arts are often seen as exclusionary, a discipline for the young, the strong, and the healthy. Far from it. Martial arts are for and can be adapted to everyone and every circumstance. Its magic is precisely this. Just like in China, where Kung Fu is practiced in everyday clothing and contexts. As with any art, it is universal, a universe in which unity embraces diversity in all its might. We accept everyone without prejudice, in the same way that we celebrate different styles, disciplines, and methods, because it is precisely in the beauty of this diversity that each one of us can find the uniqueness of his or her way.

Paolo, the martial artist

My martial arts have changed significantly over the decades. In some ways, I am the same martial artist as I have always been: I am still driven by the same curiosity, perseverance and passion, that same fire that burned in me as a child. In other ways, I am decidedly different today; my martial arts have become "full" in a way that I could have never imagined as a boy or even a young man.

Until my thirties, most of my attention was devoted to physical exercise, technique, and aesthetics. I used to train my body intensely to cultivate strength, power, explosiveness, and speed. I used to study the training methods of great athletes, boxers, and martial artists and apply them to my needs. Much of it was through trial and error. To seek and find the right information in the 1980s and 1990s was no small feat, and I see now the mistakes I made, often training my body to the point of exhaustion unnecessarily. I remember the thousands of kicks I made every day, of every month, of every year, which no doubt made me a remarkable kicker, but certainly didn't do any favors for my hips, pelvis or groin. But it was because I trained so much that I got to know every inch of my body and eventually developed the correct methods, which I continue to enjoy to this day.

Back then, the precision and aesthetics of my technique were of the essence, too. True to the teachings of my masters, Fu Han Tong and Chan Hon Chung, a millimetre here or there made a world of difference, be it to the effectiveness of a technique or its pure aesthetic value. In those years, I did work on my internal practices, especially mediation and Chi Kung, but they came second to the exterior dimension of the art, which reigned supreme for me. I meditated because I wanted to become a stronger and more powerful martial artist.

Today, the internal aspect of my practice shines a light of its own. While retaining a strong sense of aesthetics, I now know how to save energy, including in my dynamic practice, to concentrate and apply my intention—*I*—to every move. By feeling and directing my energy, my practice has changed, and moves that were once empty have acquired new meaning. In many ways, it's like love. When we're young, we often expend our energy carelessly, constantly seeking a new flame and moving on to the next when it burns out, leaving us exhausted, disillusioned, or hurt. As we mature, we learn to keep that fire alive. My Kung Fu is the same.

I now see beauty when a move is full, not empty, and thus when it does not begin and end externally, regardless of its strength or precision, but rather when it exudes energy from within. I have started appreciating the value of small things, enjoying the million different ways in which I can perform the same form, technique, or breathing, while remaining true to its essence. I have practiced all of my martial arts tools endless times, but rather than letting the comfort of repetition dull my experience, I have sought to go one step deeper each time, discovering gems that I had carried with me for years without knowing it. I have been practicing internal exercises such as the Taoist *Ba Duang Jin*—the "Eight pieces of brocade"—since the early 1970s, for instance. For many years, I experienced this soft exercise through its purely physical dimension, enjoying the stretching of my muscles, the mobility of my joints, and the flexing and twisting of my body. As time passed, the physical structure of my *Ba Duang Jin* remained the same but my experience of changed radically. By entering the depths of each move and moving beyond its physical border, I have begun listening to my organs and feeling the flow of my energy through my meridians. Like magic, I have felt the blending of my vital energy—*Ch'i*—with that of the universe that I am part of—*Ch'i Yu*. Change is an essential part of life. In the same way, my practice has adapted to the physical changes in my body and the maturity of my mind and soul.

In my development as a martial artist, I have also often found myself using my knowledge of traditional Chinese medicine, most often related to accidents in the *kwoon*, which led to less serious injuries to my students. I have fixed dozens of broken noses, dislocated shoulders and other joints; more rarely, I have intervened in more dangerous situations, including cardiac arrests, haemorrhages, and fractures. Kung Fu is, ultimately, a "martial" art, making the risk of physical injury inevitably higher than in other artistic activity. It only takes one wrong move, bad timing, insufficient preparation, or plain bad luck for an accident to occur.

I recall one afternoon, when a boy fell to the ground right before my eyes in the middle of a lesson. He looked petrified and was as white as chalk, covered in a cold sweat, his throat stiff and gasping for air. I leaned over and immediately recognized that he was in cardiac and respiratory arrest. I had no time to think. I performed some manipulation techniques that unblocked his diaphragm allowed his breathing to return, while preventing his tongue from falling back into his throat and choking him. A few moments after he began breathing again, the boy's heartbeat normalized too, and his cold cheeks started to regain color. This was one of many occasions when I had to act fast; one right move and the problem would be resolved, while a wrong step could prove lethal. I remember each of those moments clearly, as if they had happened yesterday.

In other cases, I have stepped into situations that were not accidental, but rather structural, developing long-term therapeutic programs that weren't intended to substitute medical therapy, but to complement it. These cases included relatively simple ones such as hernias, disc trouble, and muscular contractions, as well as more serious pathologies caused by the malfunction of vital organs. In certain cases, I performed massage techniques, acupuncture, or acupressure; in more serious cases, I focused on therapeutic Chi Kung instead. I have also worked with students who lost faith in western therapies, which often address symptoms but not the root causes of an illness. While I never seek to direct any student away from Western medical therapies, I do believe that even in the most serious and desperate cases, trying to work on a deeper energetic level is always a good idea. It upsets me tremendously to observe the persistent scepticism of Western medicine towards alternative Eastern approaches that have existed and been proven effective for thousands of years. It is a close-mindedness I just don't understand, given that these approaches work on different and not mutually exclusive aspects of our wellbeing and health.

One evening, a student knocked on the door of the *kwoon*. I invited him in and, with a long face, he asked if we could talk in private. He blinked back tears as he asked if I could help him, or more specifically, help his wife. She was in bed, semi-paralysed from her lower-back down, unable to work, go out or even stand. Moreover, she had been experiencing unbearable pain for months, and no one had been able to alleviate her suffering. She had tried different therapies, a long list of painkillers, and had seen a plethora of different doctors. Nothing seemed to work. The woman was suffering from a very serious herniated disc with two sharp protrusions at her lumbar vertebrae. I was unsure whether I could full resolve her problem but confident I could help. It took us seven intense sessions of massage and acupuncture before she could stand up and regain partial mobility. Once she could slowly walk, we continued our work through different internal practices that helped her reduce inflammation, regain full mobility and compensate for the muscular imbalances she had developed from the injury. The results were far better than I had anticipated. It gave me great joy to see her and her husband smile again.

The memories that remain closest to my heart, however, concern students or their relatives with diagnosed cancers whom I tried to help. It is well known in China that Chi Kung is not only good for general wellness purposes, but also that medical Chi Kung can be an important part of therapy, including for severe illnesses such as cancer. That the Beijing regime recognized this fact was not a foregone conclusion. While 21st century China is far more open to re-appropriating its past, beginning with martial arts and its related philosophies, disciplines, practices and medicine, it continues to handle traditional Kung Fu with great caution. China is ultimately an authoritarian state, and continues to show it in its attitude towards any uncontrolled and uncontrollable traditional martial arts. However, medical Chi Kung is one of the areas where there has been greater openness, and this is because of the statistically relevant certified results that it has yielded.

Having studied and practiced Chi Kung deeply for over four decades, I believe strongly in its power, given that it works at the cellular level. Our cells, in fact, are fed not just by blood and oxygen, but can also be stimulated by light, sound, temperature, and vibrations. By stimulating their protective membrane, Chi Kung, with its visualizations, breathing, sounds, and vibrations, influences the functioning and thus the health of our cells. I am not claiming that Chi Kung works miracles. However, it can prove an extremely effective complement to Western therapies such as chemo and other radiation therapies, for instance, by supporting their attack on cancerous cells and fighting against the destruction of healthy ones. In other words, Chi Kung amplifies the positive effects of western therapies, while mitigating against their more nefarious consequences.

And so, as the years and decades have passed, my Kung Fu has transformed with me. My training methods have changed, adapting to the changed rhythm of my life and my many professional and personal commitments. My free time has reduced significantly, as my hours spent teaching have increased, and my weekends are filled with workshops, instructors' meetings, exams, or international engagements. But my fifty years of practice come to the rescue. I know how to keep my body fit, my mind alert and my soul at peace. I know how to do so in the little time I have available and I no longer need the endless hours of repetitive training of my youth. At times, in a split second, perhaps through a movement without prior warm-up or in the sudden switch from one lesson to another, I feel the flow of my *Chi* pervading my entire being, that vital breath that moves us along our path. And it only takes that one moment for all the weight, stress, and fatigue to disappear, as I rediscover with greater wisdom the lightness of a new beginning.

Rebuilding

Rebuilding means starting anew, while making sure that what was broken is not lost nor forgotten. It is about retaining the essence of what has been deteriorated or destroyed to give it new life. When we face the debris, be it material or immaterial, we must learn from it, recalling the origin of our journey to continue moving forward.

I was faced with the rebuilding of my school, its organizational structure, rules and professional relations. Above all, I had to rebuild myself by meditating on my fragilities, weaknesses and mistakes. It is only through deep meditation that we can rebuild a more solid future in pursuit of our goals. It is a meditation that ties our past to our present, enabling us to face the future. As a master, I had to rebuild, constantly seeking to improve and expand my horizons. It is a responsibility that I have felt towards myself as much as others. Like a flower releasing its pollen, this rebuilding can generate new forms of life, energy, and meaning. By rebuilding, our Yin and Yang achieve a new balance.

CHAPTER 10
Becoming

Half a century has passed since a village priest announced the opening of a *Jiu Jitsu* course in the village of Casella, and I, a boy of nine, enthusiastically signed up. Fifty years during which, driven by curiosity and passion, I devoted my life unconditionally to the magical world of martial arts. Over the decades, my Kung Fu practice has changed, alongside the ups and downs of my life and as an integral part of it. While the core of my origin story has remained intact, my successes and satisfactions as much as my failures and crises have transformed me as a man and as a master.

Humility is the key. By casting off my baggage, shedding the protective shell of my experience and rediscovering the lightness of the beginner, I live in the present moment with an open heart and mind. Only through humility can I fully seize the value of my becoming.

Starting all over

Over the course of almost four decades, I had travelled countless times to the East. I travelled to discover, to learn and to enrich my Kung Fu. I travelled to meet risk, seizing both the darkness and the light that came with it. I travelled to dive into the depths of my solitude, as well as to find new company in myself, thus building my resilience. In the years that followed, I travelled to discover myself as a master in Asia as much as in Italy, reconciling the two geographical dimensions of my life and practice. As a *sifu* in Asia, I met many peers, and had the opportunity to give and to receive in an equal exchange between me and other martial artists.

Then, suddenly, I felt an ancient call. It was a calling me to my roots, calling me to start all over again. It was a call to shed myself of my titles, experience and knowledge. It was a call to get back into the game, to challenge myself again. I had been a master for too long; I had given so much to my students and received respect and devotion from them in return. I now felt the urge to be in their shoes again and rediscover the awe of the eleven-year-old boy who watched, spellbound, as a Chinese carpenter demonstrated a few basic techniques of his magic art.

I did not have a plan. There was no specific place or person that I was after. I felt an intuitive need to travel once more to China, but to do so in a radically different way: as a student, as an amateur in search for adventure.

I knew it would not be easy. How can we set aside who we are in the present and pretend we have no past? Especially when confronted with inevitable hardships and uncertainties, or when we face the scorn, rejection and humiliation reserved for those who are seemingly weak? It would not be easy, I knew, but that was the point. This was the quest that I was magnetically drawn to. This would be a source of newfound energy for me, for my Kung Fu, and for my school.

I kept this project to myself. I felt my students may not have understood, but mainly it was a deeply personal endeavour, and sharing it within the *kwoon* at that moment just didn't feel right.

I discussed it with Minou, of course. As always, she was unwaveringly supportive. I knew she would miss me; by 2010 my life had become far more settled, orderly and predictable. She and my daughter, Mei, were not used to my being absent for long. But setting aside her worry and sadness, Minou immediately grasped the essence of that ancient call. She sensed how important it was for me, and she knew this was a mission that I could simply not shy away from.

It all happened rather quickly. There were no plans to make, no complex itinerary to follow. I just had to book myself a one-way ticket and take off. And so, in 2015, I found myself on a flight headed for Hong Kong once again. At thirty-five thousand feet, I experienced that same mix of excitement, joy, anxiety, and fear that I had felt thirty-four years earlier, when I had boarded a plane headed East for the first time, with a crumpled note with an address scribbled on it in my pocket. When I landed, I was immediately intoxicated by the same sweet-sour smell of a city that was both my second home and the gateway to what had always been and will always be my mysterious world of the East. In the rumble of a city that never sleeps, I was lulled by the rhythm and blinded by the colours of my Hong Kong.

Once there, I was tempted to abandon my idea. I felt the urge to visit old friends, to drop by and train in familiar schools, to pay visits to fellow masters. I felt the impulse to remain in my comfort zone of places and people I knew. My Cantonese was a bit rusty, but my Mandarin and English were fine. Not only would it have been easy to slip back into the martial arts life of the city that I knew so well; it would have brought me great contentment and peace, too.

But that was not what I was there for. There had been many occasions in the past and there would certainly be more in the future when I could seek comfort and the reassurance of the familiar in Hong Kong. But this was not one of those occasions. I was there to start all over, to zero-out my knowledge, to become a student and a beginner once again. Stripped of my cultural and practical baggage, I was there to experience the exhilaration and humiliation of a new start.

Harnessing this spirit, I dove into Hong Kong's frantic rhythm, mingling with the locals. I knew how to avoid the many tourist traps in town and instead lived to the fullest the sounds and smells, colours and customs that were true to tradition. I relished sunrise in the parks, practicing popular exercises with old women and men. I walked past familiar *kwoon*, but did not step into any. I was not there to be greeted as *Sifu* Cangelosi. I was in Hong Kong as Paolo, a forever student in the ancient wisdom of martial arts.

After several days of seemingly aimless wandering, it suddenly dawned on me. Decades had passed, and traditional schools and masters had become increasingly rare. Among them, there was one master I had never met and about whom I had heard great things. He was a master of the Southern Mantis style—Chow Gar—developed by the Hakka people, an ethnic minority.

I knew a little about Chow Gar. Many years before, I had met someone by chance in Hong Kong who had introduced to me to the basics of the style in our joint training sessions. But like all other styles deriving from the Hakka minority, the spread of Chow Gar has always been highly constrained. In fact, for much of its history, the style had remained within the strict confines of the community itself. An instinct drew me powerfully in this direction. After all, I was a beginner in Chow Gar, I did not know this master, and presumably he did not know me: this could be my new beginning.

The problem was how to find him. My wandering now had a purpose, but I was not quite sure how to pursue it. First I tried technology. True, I was after a traditional school and master, but it was 2015, not 1985. Globalization must have reached the depths of traditional Kung Fu, too, or so I hoped. But the digital route was a failure.

The days passed as I popped into different unknown Kung Fu schools in town. I was curious to see how Hong Kong's martial arts scene had changed. I presented myself as a beginner in each *kwoon*, and in an odd way, I enjoyed the act. I trained in Wing Chun and other styles, and the time passed pleasantly along as I was enveloped in the energy of a city that will never get old.

Then, magically, it happened. One afternoon, I found myself walking in a neighbourhood I hardly knew. I was there without a clear purpose. I stopped by a Thai restaurant, which wooed me with its delicious smells. The meal lived up to expectations. It was a cuisine I knew well after all my years of travel in Thailand, and that restaurant was truly top-notch. Replenished physically, but with a restless soul, I walked out for a stroll and to phone home. While talking to Minou, I lifted my gaze, and there, lazily fluttering in the warm wind, was a yellow flag with a praying mantis waving from a window. Hypnotized, I began walking towards it, while explaining what I had seen to my wife. My eyes were glued to that flag: it signalled that there was a Kung Fu school in the building. I was so completely focused on the flag that, having crossed the street, I walked face-first into a billboard in front of the building. I stood back, rubbing my bruised nose, and finally saw his name in large printed letters: I was standing in front of Grand Master Ip Chee Keong's Chow Gar school.

I ran up the stairs two at a time. The door was shut and the *kwoon* closed. But on the sign hanging on the front door, there was a telephone number. I jotted it down and immediately called. After three or four rings, a deep voice answered the line. I was speaking to *Sifu* Ip Chee Keong himself.

I quickly explained that I was an Italian Kung Fu student on a study visit to Hong Kong. I told him that I had heard great things about him and his school and was extremely interested in learning his Chow Gar. To my delight, the master, while curt and rather cold in his replies, gave me an appointment that same afternoon at the school.

I wandered around the neighbourhood for the next few hours, killing time and processing what had just happened. I thought about how I should behave. Had I told him that I was a complete novice in Kung Fu, he would have shown me the door. A grand master wouldn't deign to teach a beginner from the West who contacted him out of the blue. Still, I was determined not to reveal my true colours.

Ip Chee Keong turned up right on time. He looked just like the photos I had seen of him: small and extremely thin, a bundle of nerves ready to spring at any moment. He had a piercing look, seemingly intent on x-raying whomever he set his eyes on. True to his style, this grand master looked like a mantis: his appearance, build and rapid movements reminded me of the killer insect. I had met many traditional Kung Fu masters before and I could always sense their seriousness, depth and value right away. I knew almost nothing about this man, but I was sure of one thing: I was standing before a great *sifu*.

He tested the waters, asking me several questions that were both general and very specific about me and my Kung Fu. I was humble in my replies, seeking to express my deep desire to learn his Chow Gar. In the most respectful way possible, I disclosed some of my Kung Fu knowledge. I scantily mentioned the styles I practiced and some of the masters I had learned from to give him a vague sense of where I was coming from. In other words, I wanted him to know that I had not popped up at his doorstep randomly: I knew enough about Kung Fu to appreciate how special he and his school were. At the same time, I presented myself as a student without any title, stripped of any protection.

Naked as I was, he doused me with ice-cold water. Ip Chee Keong rejected me flat out. His words were harsh and his tone uncompromising. "I no longer teach the public," he replied. "I reserve my art for a few select martial artists around the world."

His reply barely concealed his disdain: I was a nobody, one of an indistinguishable mass of unworthy amateurs. How could I, a mere speck in the ocean, even dare to ask for his teachings? He began insulting my Kung Fu and the styles and masters I had mentioned.

He did, however, leave his door open just a crack by introducing me to his brother, Ip Bak Wing, who was also a martial artist and had fifty years of Chow Gar practice under his belt. Theirs was one of the best-known living martial arts families, custodians of a style introduced at the turn of the eighteenth century by the monk Chow Ah Nam and which had remained exclusive to a few select families within the Hakka minority since then. Their father, Grand Master Ip Shui, had raised his children in the tradition, culture and practice of Chow Gar. Both Ip Chee Keong and his brother were living legends of that style.

Ip Bak Wing turned out to be just as scornful as his brother. Full of himself and dreadfully rude, he agreed to teach me but at an exorbitant cost. It wasn't just the prohibitively high rates that took me aback, but also the fact that they were clearly meant to humiliate me even further. I was unworthy of their teachings, and the only way I could make up for my lack of personal value was by filling up their pockets. Quite clearly, this was the message.

I hesitated, unsure what to do. Were these brothers, so pompous, rude and disdainful, not worthy of their reputation? Or was it my own wounded pride that clouded my view of them? Was this part of the game, part of the teachings of these great artists? And was it not precisely this humiliation that I was after? Once upon a time, I would have never tolerated such disrespect. I would have reacted, and the situation might have resolved itself with a physical showdown between us. But I was there now in a different spirit, to push past my own boundaries. I had crossed the ocean in search of a new beginning. I had found this school thanks to something that seemed like an indecipherable message from the heavens. I was there to delve in uncertainty in all its forms. It was there to start all over. I nodded in agreement: I would stay.

The next morning, the training and study program began. The work was hard, and not just physically. Each lesson ended with a metaphorical slap in the face. Ip Bak Wing constantly sought to humiliate me, flaunting the superiority of his martial system. Ip Chee Keong was always present. True to his word, he refused to teach me directly. But I saw him watch me with curiosity as the days flew by. He intervened in our lessons only sporadically to give me a few scattered pieces of advice, which I jealously guarded.

Two weeks later, the brothers announced that I was done: the teaching was over. Expecting nothing but an insult in response, I asked *Sifu* Ip Chee Keong whether I could see him again and continue learning in his school. By that stage, I had been on the receiving end of so much contempt and vilification that I was fully resilient to it. I had seen past their insolence and fully grasped the value of their art. I had nothing to lose by testing my luck one last time.

To my utter bewilderment, not only did Ip Chee Keong agree, but he curtly gave me an address and what seemed to be a specific appointment. He would be traveling to Europe in a few months' time to visit one of his closest students in Hungary. The address he gave me was in Budapest, but the appointment was not: it was at my home. I was utterly confused as I sought to decipher the man who stood in front of me. I had spent two weeks learning and appreciating his art but had been smeared with a good dose of daily humiliation. Other than his silent observation, there had been nothing, absolutely nothing, to suggest he had the faintest amount of respect for me. And now, suddenly, not only was *Sifu* Ip Chee Keong telling me we would see each other again soon, but that we would do so at my home. This great master would make a house call for me, Mr. Nobody.

Minou and Mei sprang to mind. I felt that I should consult them. An old and spiteful Chinese master wanted to invade the intimacy of our home; the least I could do was to ask their permission. But how? Ip Chee Keong had not asked me whether he could be my guest—he had told me he would be. If I had shown even the slightest hint of hesitation, it would have ended our brief encounter, and I knew that this man was special. His school had already taught me a lot. I had not only started to learn his style, but my mind and soul had been tempered in a way that it can only be by a true master. His daily humiliations were an integral part of his teaching. It could not simply end there.

Without a trace of uncertainty in my voice, I accepted.

Lo and behold, a few months later, *Sifu* Ip Chee Keong and his best student, the Hungarian Vitarius Balint, landed at the Milan airport. I picked them up and we drove to Casella, where I hosted them at my home, together with my wife and daughter. We began an intense program of daily training. In some ways, the nature of Ip Chee Keong's teachings remained unchanged. Just like in Hong Kong, the work was physically demanding and the *sifu* never missed an opportunity to insult my Kung Fu. He remained just as strict and closed-off as he had been in Hong Kong. At the same time, something between us began to change imperceptibly. I sensed that he gradually started to look at me with greater respect and affection. I, too, began opening up to him, perhaps because we were getting to know each other better or because he was staying at my home. I gradually revealed more about my own history, my experiences and my background in the world of martial arts. He wasn't surprised at all by anything I told him, as if he had known all along—if not the factual details, then at least the essence of what I was sharing.

Our time in Casella ended with a third appointment, this time in Hungary, at Vitarius' place. Unlike his master, Balint was immediately kind and courteous. He was a highly skilled Chow Gar master, but he was immensely humble. I eagerly accepted the invitation to Budapest. There, we trained intensely once again, this time together with a group of Balint's advanced students.

I remember one day towards the end of a tough lesson, Grand Master Ip Chee Keong interrupted the group and began praising me and my Kung Fu despite the lack of any apparent connection to the flow of his teaching. He then put me on the spot, asking me to exhibit my Kung Fu, and more specifically my Hung Gar. Up until that very moment, he had reserved only insults for any style besides his own, and now he was asking me, a student, to demonstrate another style to the class? I stepped up without hesitation, performing the *Sap Ying Kune*, one of the most advanced Hung Gar forms. As soon as I finished, one person began to applaud, and the others joined in. Ip Chee Keong had kicked off a hearty round of applause for me.

When the clapping finally quieted down, the grand master spoke. For the first time, he praised my Kung Fu profusely, telling everyone that while it was very rare for him to accept new students, it was an honour to have met me and become my master. As he spoke, I fully understood what I had sensed from the first moment he pierced me with his mantis-like gaze. I had had the incredible fortune of meeting a true grand master, great in his art and pure in his spirit, a traditional *sifu* in the deepest sense of the word. He had put me to the test and challenged my curiosity, my perseverance and my resilience, precisely in order to demonstrate the generosity of his heart. I had passed the test and felt immensely grateful to this man who had blessed me with the greatest gift of all: by pushing me to empty myself completely, Ip Chee Keung had filled me up with the true value of humility. Thanks to his teachings, I had completed the next step on my way to becoming.

Returning to my roots

At the end my 2015 trip, something else happened. The teachings I'd learned at Ip Chee Keung's school and the daily humiliations they had exposed me to made something click into place for me. The exercise of questioning of myself, which was the real gift my last *sifu* gave me, awakened within me a deep desire.

I would pay a visit to Cheon Yee Keung. My Kung Fu brother and I first began to grow apart in 1991 with the death of our shared *sifu*, Chan Hon Chung. I had been shocked by his seeming indifference. Four years later, I was deeply hurt by his agreeing to teach my former students without reaching out to me. I met him once again in 2000 on a trip to Hong Kong to film my documentary *The Journey*. But our encounter had felt cold and distant, and I decided that our relationship had simply run its course.

Fifteen years had passed since I lost touch with Cheon Yee Keung. But something new stirred in me. It was not a rational thought: there was no real reason why I decided to step back into my past. As at other pivotal moments in my life, I was driven by instinct. Putting my biases aside, I decided to visit Cheon Yee Keung's Kung Fu school and *Tee Taa* clinic.

When I arrived, I nervously circled the block a few times, trying to collect my thoughts and calm my spirit. I eventually walked up the steps but stopped at the door, doubts assailing me once again. Yes, we had been great friends in the past. Bonded by the teachings of our shared master, we had gone through formative experiences together, within and beyond 729 Nathan Road. But there had also been a great deal of ugliness that passed between us. I had felt betrayed, humiliated and misunderstood by my Kung Fu brother. Then there was nothing but a gaping void between us. These and many other thoughts and feelings weighed on my heart and clouded my mind. Then, all of a sudden, my doubts vanished: this was my opportunity to revisit the past and fill that void. I had no idea whether it would work or who I'd find on the other side of that door. But I had to try.

I summoned my courage and tiptoed along the corridor up to a glass door at the clinic's entrance. I peeked through it and there he was. At his desk, intent on curing a patient with a traditional treatment, sat Cheon Yee Keung. My stomach tightened; my heart skipped a beat. He still had his jet-black hair and compact build, the contours of which I could make out underneath his tracksuit. Only his glasses and a few scattered wrinkles around his eyes and mouth betrayed the years that had gone by. As if sensing my gaze, he looked up and our eyes met. He stared at me in disbelief, stood up, walked over to me, and without uttering one word, embraced me. It was a long and quiet hug, one which instantly dissolved all the disappointment and the pain I had harbored for so many years. With that hug we said all there was to say, settled all our misunderstandings, asking and receiving forgiveness for the past.

Still without saying a word, but with an inimitable sparkle in his eye, he reached for his mobile phone and dialed a number. I heard her voice on the other side of the line: twenty-one years had passed since I had last heard it, but it could have been no one else but her. It was Sanny, our dear friend Sanny Tang. Sanny who had stood by my side in Chan Hon Chung's school; Sanny who had taken Angela under her wing during my ex-wife's trip to Hong Kong; Sanny, whose late father, Grand Master Tang Hin Kwong, had blessed me with the pearls of his Choy Lee Fut Kung Fu in his old age.

Cheon Yee Keung handed me the phone. I stuttered a few

words, gripped with emotion. Both Sanny and I faltered, stammering a mix of broken Cantonese and English, like two adolescents on their first date. Having broken the ice, we arranged for the three of us to meet in person.

Two days later, Sanny Tang, Cheon Yee Keung, and I met at a lively restaurant in Prince Edward. It was an evening filled with laughter and tears, dense with powerful emotions and vivid memories. It was a dinner glowing with the magic of brotherhood and love, and warmed by the deep awareness that our bond had stood the test of time.

Revisiting the past

During that dinner, Cheon Yee Keung, Sanny, and I reminisced about our intense years at 729 Nathan Road. The memories of our *Sifu* Chan Hon Chung came flooding back, as they often do at home when I practice his art and convey it to my students. Like in a movie playing on the screen of my mind, I watch us stroll in silence in the stillness of Hong Kong's alleys before dawn. I sense his firm and steady pace as we walk back to the *kwoon* after breakfast through a city that slowly awakens. I recall his working method, always careful and meticulous, but never pedantic, able to fully capture the greatness of his art. Over the years, I have sought to blend his technical repertoire into my school's Hung Gar program, which also draws from the teachings of Fu Han Tong and other masters. But technique aside, Chan Hon Chung has always been a model master and human being for me. His noble spirit, generosity and humility have warmed my heart and enlightened me over the decades. In so many moments of my life, at so many crossroads, I have stopped and asked myself: "What would *Sifu* Chan say?" And when I hear his answer echoing in my head, my heart swells with joy and I feel at peace.

Sifu Chan Hon Chung is a foundational pillar of my life and practice. In my fifty years in the world of martial arts, however, there were many masters who shaped me into who I am. I feel indebted to each one of them. Describing them one by one would be futile, but looking back, a few deserve special mention. In particular, I am deeply grateful to those who encouraged my curiosity and passion for martial arts when I was a child. It is thanks to the emotions and the enthusiasm they instilled in me that I walked through the portal to this magic world. Nicolino Rosa, my very first teacher in the Japanese art of Jiu Jitsu, was a superhero in my eyes. I remember staring at him, wide-eyed, as he brought his student and sparring partner Stelvio Sciutto down to the tatami mat, who later became a famed Jiu Jitsu master in Italy himself. I can still picture his spectacular scissor technique, when he jumped in the air and wrapped his powerful legs around his opponent's neck. As I watched in awe, I clenched my fists and was determined that one day I would exude such power.

Also from my childhood, I pay tribute to my Karate masters Simone Dominici and the incredible Oreste Nagliati. Simone, with his eastern features and small but powerful build, introduced me to the basics of the Japanese art of Karate. Oreste, a great champion and sportsman, was certainly one of the best *karateka* of his generation. But beyond his indisputable technical skills, he was a role model for all his students, and especially for me.

But, of course, the greatest tribute goes to the single most important guide of my life, to the man and the master who shone a light on the mysteries of Kung Fu. I pay homage to the man who led me through the depths of darkness and dazzling light. I bow to my *sifu*, who earned this title in the fullest possible way, from the day he performed the martial salute among the wood chips of a Genovese carpenter's shop, to the day he shook my hand in a Hong Kong hotel and told me we had reached the end of our road. I will forever be indebted to Fu Han Tong.

Fu Han Tong represented hard work, sacrifice, hardship, and unmitigated dedication. Fu Han Tong stood for destruction and rebirth, resistance and resilience. Fu Han Tong showed me risk in all its cruelty, and also all the love that can blossom from it. When rupture came, the emptiness it generated unleashed extreme emotions that settled in me only after many years. At first, there was hatred, anger, and pain. I felt hatred toward the man who had put my life at risk time and time again. I felt anger toward the money he had made on my back. I felt pain for the soiling of the pure bond between the boy and his master.

But slowly the hatred, anger, and pain subsided, opening my soul to gratitude and love towards my *sifu.* As the years went by, I realized that just as Fu Han Tong had been a radically free man, our bond had been unconditionally free as well, and this was precisely its beauty. He may have opened the doors, but it was I who chose to walk through them. For better or worse, with an unspoken balance of give and take, Fu Han Tong showed me the way, but it was up to me to take it. And if my way has brought me to where I am today, in all my strengths and my fragilities, I can only applaud or reproach myself. I now feel only immense gratitude to Fu Han Tong.

As I have reconciled our past and as my love for him has grown, I have found myself wondering time and time again where my *sifu* might be. On some occasions, I have been gripped by an irresistible urge to see him. Once I even tried to track him down, but I didn't succeed. I have no idea whether Fu Han Tong is dead or alive. If he is still alive he'd be ninety-five years old, and who knows where he lives or what his life is like. But one thing I do know: Fu Han Tong lives on in me, and always will. He lives on in my family and in my school, in my stories and my teachings.

Fu Han Tong is simply the cornerstone of my way.

Looking forward

I am forever on my path to becoming. I have built a solid, tight-knit family that is respected internationally. Confident in the shared path we have embarked upon, I look ahead with hope.

My work is not over. I am constantly seeking new sources of energy to bring to my practice and teaching. I launch new initiatives, some of which take off while others do not, but which are always driven by the deep desire to make progress on our path. Every year, I add to my school's activities, hoping to inspire a curiosity and light a fire in my students. And every day, I pursue my own studies to deepen my knowledge and convey it with greater clarity and detail to those around me.

I still feel that I have a lot to learn and teach, but I also know that I won't be around forever. I think about my legacy, and especially about my responsibility to ensure that what I have built with the help of many others will outlive me. As in all traditional schools, where the master passes on his legacy to his offspring, I have placed my highest hopes for continuity on my son and daughter.

In many Kung Fu families teachings were passed down for generations, but in others, the legacy of the family name was eventually interrupted, giving way to others. But this does not always mean that the legacy of a master ends. Beyond the form of the name is the substance of the art, and thus the legacy of its values, which must be cherished with care and transmitted with love by those who follow it.

I know I can rely on a wonderful group of instructors. I know I will continue to give to and receive from a community of students, and most importantly to children, who have not simply carved out a space for Kung Fu in their routines, but have imbued all aspects of their lives with the ethics of our art.

Living by these values is not so easy nowadays. Times have changed and the unspoken rules of our society often distract us from the essence of our way. In the comfort of material wealth, it is harder to discover passion, combat sloth and foster the perseverance to pursue our innermost goals. Our curiosity is dimmer, our determination flabbier, and our lives are impoverished as a result. While the flattening of hierarchies has created the possibility of greater equality, it has also fueled disrespect towards our past and towards one another. From behind the safety of a screen, it is easier to bully and to insult, protected as we are by our laminated hearts. In the frantic and compartmentalized lives that we lead, we often forget the simplest and most important things that nature has taught us. And in the certainty of our high-tech world, in which technology can seemingly solve all problems, we have lost our humility when it comes to the mysteries of life itself. We risk sleepwalking in a world where machines know our inner journeys better than we do. And so, when life in all its wisdom presents us with risks and challenges, we lack the resilience to learn, to rebuild and to continue walking, stronger than before.

Yet I remain hopeful. I rejoice when I see children and grandparents, women and men, and people from all social backgrounds and walks of life practicing together in full respect and gratitude for our shared art. Within the context of our *kwoon*, our roles and titles, our power and our wealth, are all cast aside, and we stand as equals enjoying our art through constant give and take. We learn the beauty of physical touch, in full respect for one another. We learn to be grateful for the teachings of our master and those who came before him, who have contributed to this ancient art. But perhaps the greatest joy of all is to know that our Kung Fu is not confined to a few hours of practice within the four walls of our school. It is an integral part of our lives, shaping our daily habits, igniting our passions, and making us rediscover the warmth of generosity and human touch.

My wish is to see this beauty expand beyond our small world. The world of martial arts is often misunderstood by the public at large. It is a world that has partly failed to communicate what its true essence is, and which has been pigeon-holed by prejudices and misconceptions over the years. Martial arts are often equated with physical exercise, or self-defense at best. These are certainly valuable, but as this book has sought to show, martial arts, and Kung Fu in particular, are much more. Kung Fu is philosophy and it is medicine, it is physical well-being and spiritual development. Kung Fu helps us keep our bodies healthy and our minds alert. Like life itself, Kung Fu is as much hard work as it is fun.

Kung Fu is art.

I have dedicated my life to the art of Kung Fu. In sharing this journey with you, it would be an honor to have made even the smallest impact on your own unique way to becoming.

Becoming

Becoming, changing, and transforming. All living things experience these stages. Becoming is about living the present while looking ahead to the future, and also drawing on the lessons from our past.

Consciously, we are driven by our dreams and our goals, envisioning what we want to achieve and who we want to become, building on the groundwork of where we come from. Our goals can be external as much as internal; in both cases, we direct our energy and give meaning to our lives.

When I was young, I dreamt about becoming a martial artist and teacher. It is a dream I have pursued for over fifty years now, and it remains as much my goal today as it was back then. Because becoming does not have a fixed destination. Every milestone we reach points the way to the next in our journey. As we reach a goal and get to know ourselves better, we refine our search, revise our assumptions and pursue our objectives with greater awareness. At times, we may insist in our efforts; more often, we understand that we can achieve our goals only by letting go and dropping our resistance. Like the *Tao,* my becoming today is about celebrating the moment, blending the present into the future by immersing myself in the void from which life itself is born.

Cities and regions of China where
Sifu Paolo Cangelosi lived and practiced

Sifu Paolo Cangelosi (2020)

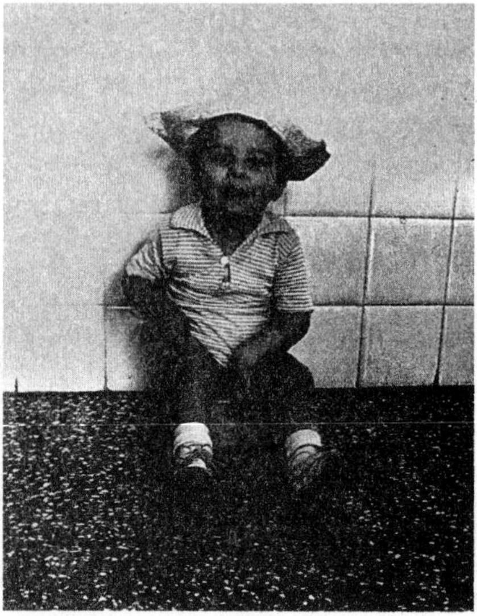

Paolo at three years old (1963)

In elementary school (1966)

With mom, Lidia, and dad, Piero (1974)

A flying kick
with his student Claudio (1975)

With a group of students
in his first Karate gym (1976)

Exhibition in Lavagna
with Cosimo (1977)

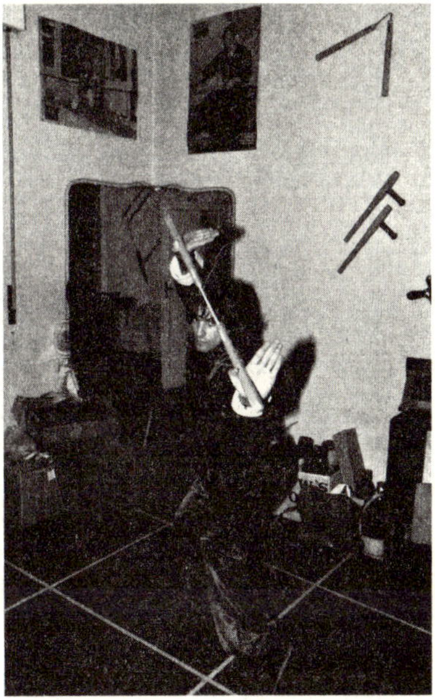

Training in his bedroom (1978)

Flying kick (1982, Viterbo)

The Hung Gar form of the ten styles (Sap Ying Kune)
(1985, in *Sifu* Chan Hon Chung's school in Hong Kong)

In *Sifu* Tang Hin Kwong's home training in
Choy Lee Fut (1985, Hong Kong)

With *Sifu* Chan Hon Chung the day *Sifu* Paolo Cangelosi was recognized as a Hung Gar master (1986)

With his Italian team at an international Kung Fu event (1988, Paris)

In *Sifu* Fu Han Tong's home (1989)

Training the lion dance in Canton (1989)

Training in a Guangdong school (1989)

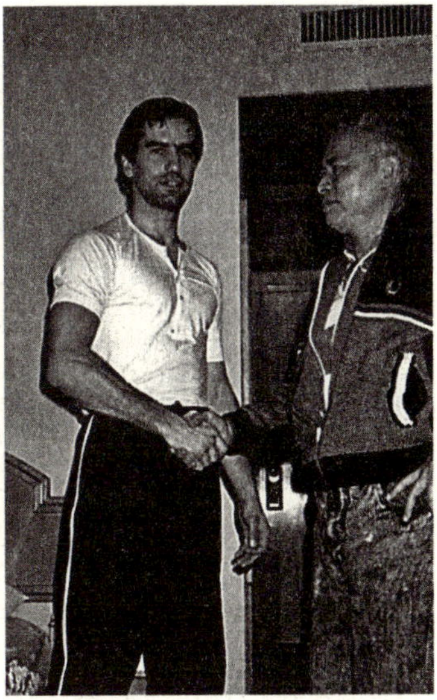

With Grand Master
Fu Han Tong (1989)

On guard in his school in Genova (1990)

Training in a park in Nanjing (1990)

With Roberto and the actor Carter Wong
at the Kung Fu World Championship in San Francisco (1997)

Exhibition with Roberto (1997, Madrid)

With his children Mei and Shan (2013, Rome)

Fan workshop (2016, Rome)

With Angela and Minou at the 50th anniversary of his martial arts practice (2019, Florence)

With Nathalie Tocci (2020, Casella)

Martial Arts Glossary

Aikido: Japanese martial art, the way of the union of energy

Ba Duang Jin: "eight pieces of brocade," eight ancient Taoist exercises aimed at physical wellbeing (also known as Pa Tuan Chin)

Bak Hok Pai: style of the white crane, with its southern and northern variants (also known as Bai He Pai)

Biu Ji: spear-shaped hand technique

Buddhism: religious doctrine of Indian origin

Ch'i: vital energy, whose ideogram includes a symbol representing matter, namely rice from which we derive our nutrition, and another representing steam, breath and more broadly everything that is immaterial. It is from the union of these two elements that human energy is formed.

Chi Kung: the power of energy, the art of controlling the vital breath, developed through wellness exercises and used in martial arts and traditional Chinese medicine (also known as Qi Gong)

Chi Yu: universal energy, the energy of the cosmos

Chow Gar: Kung Fu style of the southern mantis, deriving from the Hakka ethnic minority (also known as Zhou Jia Tang Lang Quan)

Choy Lee Fut: southern Chinese Kung Fu style (also known as Cai Li Fo)

Chull Tek: circular kick

Hap Gar: southern Chinese Kung Fu style originating from Tibetan techniques

Hsing I: internal Kung Fu style focused on action and will (also known as Xing Yi Quan)

Huang Di: the legendary Yellow Emperor (2697-2597 B.C.), known as the father of Chinese civilization

Hung Gar: southern Chinese Kung Fu style developed from the Shaolin tradition (also known as Hon Jia Quan)

I: intention, will, capacity to focus the mind on a technique

I Ching: ancient philosophical text based on the theory of the eight trigrams and their combinations
into sixty-four hexagrams

Jeet Kune Do: the art of intercepting the punch, a combat system created by Bruce Lee

Jiu Jitsu: the art of compliance, an ancient Japanese martial art

Judo: the way of compliance, a Japanese martial art derived from the ancient techniques of Ju Jitsu

Karate: the empty hand, a martial art originating from Okinawa and deriving from ancient Chinese techniques, which was later developed in Japan

Kata: the Japanese term for a martial art form

Kendo: a Japanese martial art using bamboo sticks that represent swords, enabling fighting without the risk of serious injury

Kune: translated as punch, but also used to refer to martial art forms, also known as Lu (Chinese for an ensemble of movements) and Tao (Cantonese for the way of the style). A martial art form is a codified sequence of techniques, often dating back centuries, aimed at preserving and transmitting the program of a martial art style from one generation to the next. Forms represent the cultural and technical history of a style, as well as its symbolic and philosophical message.

Kung Fu: Chinese martial art literally meaning great ability obtained through hard work (also known as Gong Fu)

Kwan: generic term referring to a martial art staff. In Kung Fu there are many types of staffs, including the single and double headed ones (respectively Yat Tour Kwan and Seon Tour Kwan), amongst many others (also known as Gun)

Kwoon: traditional Kung Fu school (also known as Guan)

Lai: traditional salute conveying respect and gratitude in Chinese culture

Lau Gar: southern Chinese Kung Fu style belonging to the Siu Lam school

Loon Yin: southern Chinese Kung Fu style of the dragon, deriving from the Hakka ethnic minority

Lop Sao: a controlled way of fighting in which each sparring partner takes turns with attack and defense techniques

Ma Bo/Sei Pi Ma (Cantonese): horseman stance (also known as Ma Bu)

Makiwara: a Japanese wooden board used to train techniques

Mou Si: traditional lion dance

Muay Thai: Thai combat art that developed into a national sport

Muk Yang Chon: wooden man, used by different styles to train techniques

Nam Siu Lam: southern Shaolin, southern Chinese Kung Fu tradition (Nam Shaolin), distinct from Pak Siu Lam, heeding from the north

Nei Chia: soft or internal Kung Fu schools and styles (also known as Nei Jia)

Pa Kua: an internal Kung Fu style known as the style of the eight trigrams (also known as Ba Gua Zhang)

Pak Mei: Kung Fu style of the "white brow," a method derived from one of the five ancestors of the Siu Lam Monastery of the south (also known as Bai Mei Quan)

Pang Tek: side-kick

Pao: kicking pads

Sap Fu: "ten tigers," ten heroes, inscribed in the history of Kung Fu of the south, heeding from different styles

Savasana: typical Hatha Yoga position, a lying position facing up, also known as the dead man

Savate: French boxing utilizing punches and kicks

Shaolin: Chinese temple where monks developed martial arts and Chan Buddhism

Shidoshi: priest, master, expert of the art who communicates with primordial forces and ancestors' spirits

Si Bak (Si Mo): Kung Fu level, representing the uncle (or aunt) in the family hierarchy of a school

Sifu: Kung Fu level, representing the ability of a master and responsibility of a father (also known as Shifu)

Si Gong: Kung Fu level of grand master, representing the family head of a school (also known as Si Gung)

Si Sook: Kung Fu level, representing the elder brother/sister in the family hierarchy of a school (also known as Si Suk)

Siu Lam: monastery of the south, literally "small forest," the Cantonese term for Shaolin

Taekwondo: modern Korean martial art, which eventually developed into an Olympic sport

Tai Chi: an internal Kung Fu style aimed at the balance between Yin and Yang energies to foster a long life (also known as Tai Ji Quan)

Tai Sifu: title awarded to amplify the title of master into grand master

Tang Lang: Praying mantis style, a Kung Fu style that imitates the movements and strategies of this lethal fighting insect

Tao: the "way," indicating the essence and soul of infinity (also known as Dao)

Tao Yin: soft gymnastics and postural exercises aimed at stretching the meridians and improving breathing (also known as Dao Yin)

Taoism: philosophical and religious Chinese doctrine based on the equilibria of nature

Tee Taa: southern Chinese orthopedic method, using manipulation techniques, traditional herbs and ointments

Tsui Pa Hsien: Kung Fu style of the eight immortals, also known as the style of the drunken man (also known as Zui Ba Xian Quan)

Tzu Chan: meditation techniques

Wai Chia: external or hard Kung Fu schools and styles (also known as Wai Jia)

Wing Chun: literally meaning "beautiful spring," a popular Kung Fu style codified by two women (also known as Yun Chun)

Wu Shu: modern Chinese martial art adapted from traditional Kung Fu

Yang & Yin: philosophical concept of the law of opposites and the dualism that governs the equilibrium of the universe and its components

Yishang: typical uniform used to practice Kung Fu

My Martial Arts Masters

My most important masters are marked in italics, both because of their contribution to my technical toolkit and the human relationship I established with them.

All others contributed to my martial arts education and experience.

I have not listed others with whom I had only limited exchanges.

BEYOND KUNG FU

Nicolino Rosa—Jiu Jitsu

Simone Dominici—Karate

Oreste Nagliati—Karate

Yoshitaka Kuota—Karate

Senanan Yodtong—Muay Thai

Petchyindee Sakat—Muay Thai

Payakaroon Samart—Muay Thai

Hiroshi Shirai—Karate

Taiji Kase—Karate

Massimo Bondi—Karate

Toyofuku Tomonori—Kendo

Miyazaki Kentaro—Kenjitsu; Iai do

Alfonso Speranza—Boxing

Beya Mueho—Boxing

Marsano—Boxing

Alex Sing—Muay Thai
Rainbow Saiphanmay—Muay Thai

KUNG FU

Fu Han Tong—Kung Fu, multiple styles
Chan Hon Chun—Hung Gar
Ip Chee Keong—Chow Gar
Tang Hin Kwong—Choy Lee Fut
Hong Tak Hung—Nan Chuan; *Chang Chuan*; *Hou Chuan*; *Hap Gar*
Cheon Yee Keung—Hung Gar
Tien Sin - Chan
Su Chang—Tai Chi; M.T.C.
Ho Tang Sin—Tsui Pa Hisien
Hao Chan—Pa Kua; Hsing I
Tsui Seon Tin—Wing Chun
Lee Kong Hung—Choy Lee Fut
Chan Wan Lee - Choy Lee Fut
Kwook Cheon—Loong Yin
Wong Kwook—Loong Yin
Chen Chan Feng—Tang Lang
Lee Kam Wing—Tang Lang
Chan Fai Chen—Wing Chun
Kuo Feng Chi—Tai Chi; Pa Kua; Hsing I
Chen De Wu—Tai Chi
So Chi Lan—Tai Chi
So Wai Chin—M.T.C.

Officially Recognized Instructors
1971-2020

(Instructors listed in italics are currently practicing at the school. The dates refer to when they first enrolled, not when they graduated.)

1971
Fu Han Tong—*Paolo Cangelosi*

1977
Luciano Mura—Carlo Cangelosi

1978
Giuseppe Turturo

1979
Angela Podeschi—Gianfranco Galluccio—Vinicio Pelaco

1980
Tonino Cusenza—Guido Politini—Roberto Macaluso

1981
Pierluigi Barbieri

1982
Claudio Mingarini—Angelo Riolo

1983
Lorenzo Redoano—Tinino Macaluso

1984
Enrico Iovine—Sergio Marzicchi—Paolo Barontini

1985
Claudio Tassone

1986
Nicola Pastorino—*Flaviano Muzio*—Enrico Mori—Maurizio Di Bonifacio—Maurizio Pellini

1987
Shan Cangelosi—*Pierluigi Bellini*

1988
Fabio Tozzi—Barbara Macciocu

1989
Monica Pino

1990
Massimiliano Perez—Mario Meloni—
Valter Marini—Andrea Capardi

1991
Andrea Pesce—GianPaolo Monaco—Massimiliano Cappuccini—
Daniele Marcolini

1995
Fabrizio Scelfo—Gianluca Longo—Leandro Bocchicchio

1996
Roberto Imperi

1997
Massimiliano Menei

2000
Francesco Barranco

2001
Alfred Koenen—Claudio Conti—Erika Lotti—Andrea Lombardi

2002
Luca Cammarano—Luca Pellegrino—Barbara Maltagliati—
Antonello Maiorano—Eric Bourbonnais

2003
Giuseppe Lippi—Paulo Neiva

2004
Edoardo Parodi

2007
Edoardo Cenci—*Danilo Vespa*—Giulia Cerini

2008
Giovanni Sciaccaluga—Andrea Cristofanini—*Maurizio Iorio*

2017
Daniel Dos Santos

Endorsements

Grand Master GEORGE BIERMAN

"There are tens of thousands of martial artists around the world. Only very few make a difference, however. Paolo combines passion, expertise, technique, speed and power into an energy that only a true master can deliver."

Grand Master MAURICE ELMALEM

"Paolo Cangelosi is a martial arts warrior and champion. His depth of knowledge and technique are outstanding, performed with great style and flair. With over forty years of practice under his belt, he is a world renowned, highly experienced and respected Grandmaster, a practitioner of several martial arts styles and producer of dozens of educational DVDs. I strongly recommend his biography to anyone interested in martial arts."

VINCENT LYN, *Actor*

"*Sifu* Paolo Cangelosi: there's so much to say about this martial arts warrior. And I don't use that term lightly. I have met countless martial artists all over the world, but there are two major qualities that he possesses that raise him far above the masses. Not only is his martial arts skill extraordinary and knowledge immense, but above all his warrior spirit embodies the true essence of the martial way. It was apparent the first moment I saw him teach, with flawless execution of technique and mastery of the art. I have only the greatest respect and admiration for this true martial arts warrior."

CYNTHIA ROTHROCK, Actress

"*Sifu* Paolo Cangelosi is the best in the world . My dream is to come to Italy for a month and train with him. I would only do this with the best."

General SANTIAGO SANCHIZ

"It is an honour for me to be considered a friend by *Sifu* Paolo Cangelosi, a great person and a great master who displays incredible courage, honour, dignity, chivalry and loyalty. In my 66 years in martial arts, I have encountered few like *Sifu* Paolo. He is a living legend."

Grand Master NIKOLAI SMIRNOV

"Paolo Cangolesi has blended Western pragmatism with Eastern mysticism and wisdom. The physical and mental skills of this amazing Master prove the value of his martial arts path. Results are always determined by the depth, the approach and determination of an individual, and all this can be observed in Paolo Cangelosi's life. From Russia with not only love, but great respect too."

SANNY TANG, Friend

"I met Paolo back in the days when I studied Kung Fu many years ago. He was friendly, hardworking and sincere. It was an honour to have met him. His passion for martial arts is amazing and admirable. He has devoted all his time and energy to the martial arts cause and made constant effort to make it shine. His achievements today are worthy of a great master."

ALFREDO TUCCI, Shidoshi, Director, Budo International

"*Sifu* Cangelosi is one of the best martial artists I know. And I have known many! We first met many years ago, well before the Italian edition of our magazine was released. We collaborated on many articles, books and DVDs, all of which were greatly successful. But well beyond work, Paolo is an incredible human being, honest, humble and who will leave behind an incredible martial arts legacy. I say this not because I consider him to be a true friend, but because he has demonstrated countless times his many virtues, in the many ups and downs of life. His biography is rife with exceptional experiences and events, which the reader will greatly enjoy."

A Small Big Thank You

Writing this book was not easy, but it was a special experience.

Working on this text meant diving into my past, unearthing old emotions—both good ones and bad—and reliving moments of joy as well as of sadness in my life.

I had tried to write something about my life on a few previous occasions, but nothing tangible had ever materialized.

One day, Nathalie Tocci, a student from our school in Rome who had come up to Genova for a private lesson, asked me with great simplicity and enthusiasm: "*Sifu*, why don't we write a book about your life?"

I had received similar requests in the past and I was not in the mood to waste time, but I knew that it wasn't just any person asking me this time around; it was Nathalie. Nathalie is the Director of the International Affairs Institute in Rome and a great expert in her field. Plus, she has been a student in my school for almost twenty years and has been passionate about martial arts since childhood. She has always demonstrated humility, commitment, and professionalism, and I have always liked this about her. We immediately clicked and her enthusiasm matched mine, since I have always lived with great love and passion for everything I do. We discussed the logistics and soon our adventure began. As time went by, my esteem for her grew, confirming my impressions about her professional and emotional character. Nathalie has all my respect and trust. My belief in her comes from the bottom of my heart.

This project has opened the door to a friendship, a special bond of trust and loyalty between us. It is the trust and affection between two people who, with total respect for one another, have learned to work together, sharing passion, emotion and, in our case, an Art.

By telling the story of my past, I managed to open up, unpack, and untie some of the knots that I still carried within me. I have freed myself from old anxieties and shed light on some of the old ghosts that were still haunting me.

All this is thanks to a person who, working hand in hand with me, managed to understand my strength as well as my fragility, translating both in the story of a life that is no doubt interesting, but also complex, and exists across different continents and cultures.

Thank you, Nathalie.

ACKNOWLEDGMENTS

Heartfelt thanks to all those who have accompanied us on this journey.

First and foremost to Marco Sciaccaluga, who left us only a few days before the publication of this book, but who followed us step by step in its writing and is no doubt still following us up there with a smile.

Thanks to Minou Risso, Enrique Alvarez, Angela Podeschi, Giovanni Sciaccaluga, mom Lidia and Elisabetta Grassia for their memories, ideas, suggestions, commitment, and care, which made this book richer and more vivid.

Thanks to all those cited in this book, without whom this story would not be what it is.

Our deepest gratitude goes to Sandro and Barbara Ferri for having believed in this project since our very first meeting.

Thank you to Claudio Ceciarelli and Gabriela D'Addario for their professionalism, enthusiasm, and passion in the revision of this text.

And last but certainly not least, thanks to the wonderful team at E/O and Europa Editions for this first wonderful journey together.